BOOKS BY HALFORD E. LUCCOCK

PREACHING VALUES IN NEW TRANSLATIONS
OF THE NEW TESTAMENT
PREACHING VALUES IN THE OLD TESTAMENT
IN THE MODERN TRANSLATIONS
JESUS AND THE AMERICAN MIND
THE STORY OF METHODISM
(WITH PAUL HUTCHINSON)
THE EAST WINDOW AND OTHER SERMONS
SKYLINES
THE HAUNTED HOUSE
STUDIES IN THE PARABLES OF JESUS
FARES, PLEASE!

Preaching Values

In New Translations of the New Testament

HALFORD E. LUCCOCK

ABINGDON-COKESBURY PRESS
NEW YORK • NASHVILLE

CONTENTS

FOREWORD

"Sure I am, that there commeth more knowlege and understandinge of the Scripture by their sondrie translacyons than by all the gloses of oure sophisticall doctours."

These are the words of Myles Coverdale in the Prologue to his translation of the Bible into English published in 1535.

This present volume is put forth in the hope that it may direct increased attention to the riches of "knowledge and understanding of the Scriptures," brought to light by "sondrie translacyons" of the New Testament made in our own time. In particular the aim of the book is to suggest, by presenting more than one hundred and fifty texts, the great values for preaching as well as private reading, to be found in three modern translations of the New Testament, those of Dr. James Moffatt, Dr. Richard Francis Weymouth, and Dr. Edgar J. Goodspeed.

The texts chosen are merely a few of the many renderings of these three notable translations which add a new, significant idea or a fresh insight, which does not so readily appear, if at all, in the more familiar language of the King James and Revised Versions.

With each text there are a few short paragraphs of comment. These comments are not sermons. Nor are they intended at all to serve as sermon outlines. They aim simply to afford, if possible, starting points for thought. They are indications of possible ways in which these fresh, gripping and vivid renderings of the words of the New Testament into the daily speech of our time may be put to the service of winning an eager hearing for New Testament truth.

Grateful acknowledgment is made to the publishers of the translations of the New Testament used in this volume.

To The Abingdon Press and to George H. Doran Company, New York, for permission to quote from *The New Testament—a New Translation*, by James Moffatt.

To James Clarke and Company, London, for permission to quote from *The New Testament in Modern Speech* (Fourth Edition), by Richard Francis Weymouth.

To The University of Chicago Press, Chicago, for permission to quote from *The New Testament, an American Translation*, by Edgar J. Goodspeed.

The italics, in the printing of selections from the foregoing translations, are in every case mine, and not the translators'.

HALFORD E. LUCCOCK.

PREACHING VALUES

THE INSIPID CHURCH

If salt becomes insipid, what can make it salt again?—
Matt. 5. 13 (Moffatt).

THIS word "insipid," which Doctor Moffatt uses
for salt which has lost its savor, is a new window
through which to view an old landscape. The
word speaks with great vividness to our time. It
represents the peculiar danger to a church. The
greatest danger which confronts the church is not
that it may die. The church will not die. The
ever-present danger which always lurks before a
church is that it may become *insipid*—that it may
stand for nothing in particular. Jesus was giving
expression to his fear that his truth and his cause
might be committed to those who would lose the
bitingly Christian flavor which characterized his
way of life.

When does a person become insipid? The dictionary tells us that an insipid thing is something
"without tang." That word "tang" is hard to
define, but what intensely real pictures, tastes,
feelings it suggests! The crisp air of a spring
morning, the blue smoke of burning wood, the
taste of a russet apple, what Browning calls "The
cool silver shock of a plunge in the pool's living
water"—all of these things have *tang*. You can
remember them thirty years without any effort.

In one of the most beautiful of all his poems Rupert Brooke has listed with vividness a few of the concrete things of earth which have this individual tang. The words take form and leap out of the printed page:

"These I have loved:
  White plates and cups clean-gleaming,
 Ringed with blue lines; and feathery, faery dust;
 Wet roofs, beneath the lamplight; the strong crust
 Of friendly bread; and many-tasting food;
 Rainbows; and the blue bitter smoke of wood,
 And radiant raindrops couching in cool flowers;
 Shining and free; blue-massing clouds; the keen
 Unpassioned beauty of a great machine;
 The benison of hot water; furs to touch.[1]

Jesus was looking for people with tang; for those who had a penetrating, peculiar flavor in act, in viewpoint and in spirit. Jesus' way of life was both a criticism of the life around him and a redeeming agency to lift it up. If we lose our tang, if we become insipid, what good are we, as far as Jesus' purpose in the world is concerned?

When the church's message loses its piercingly Christian flavor it becomes a thin broth. We have far more respect for a thing we hate than for a thing so insipid that we need not dignify it even by anger. A man was recently saying of another, "He's as insipid as"—and then he paused, hunting for an appropriate simile—"as insipid as the white of an egg," he concluded. The simile was well chosen. Most people would probably admit that there is nothing which excites them less than the

---

[1] *The Collected Poems of Rupert Brooke.* Copyright by Dodd, Mead & Company, Inc., publishers. Used by permission.

white of an egg. Yet the gospel of Jesus has frequently been denatured into such a neutral dish:

How many slippery ways there are of becoming
insipid! "We have bleached all the color out of
Jesus," declares Dr. W. R. Maltby, describing the
way in which the rugged concreteness of the Master
has been blurred. Jesus had a coat of many colors,
blazingly bright positives. What a tragedy when
they are toned down into thin pastels of platitude
or the dull gray of generalities, as vague as a New-
foundland fog! Surely we have not so learned
Christ. Philip Guedalla reports the French states-
man Thiers' conjecture that the morning prayer of
Napoleon III was, "Give us, this day, O Lord, our
daily platitude." Does it not seem sometimes also
to be the daily prayer of the preacher whose eloquence exhausts itself on bromidic generalities which
have long since lost their power to arrest or pierce?

We can sidestep live questions or delve into
antiquarian researches which are eminently safe.
We can, and frequently do, straddle controversial
issues and flee to the safety zone of the fervent
reiteration of obvious platitudes. Or we can occupy
ourselves with the mere cranking of ecclesiastical
machinery and shrink from the more dangerous
business of prophetic leadership. But, as Jesus
asked long since, "If we become insipid, what good
are we?"

John Kelman says: "It is not for the mere sake
of adventure that the preacher of to-day must
often go upon 'the dangerous edge of things.' It
is for the souls of men and the love of Christ."[1]

---

[1] From *The War and Preaching*, Yale University Press. Used by
permission.

The Church of Christ started in the world with a cutting edge to its truth. It came into the Roman life of the first century with a message so peculiarly different from the standards of life then current that it literally turned the world upside down. Then as it grew it became more reasonable, more sane, more strategic—in a word, insipid. The glory and the radiance had departed. So to-day if the church has nothing to give but a weak sevenfold "Amen" of blessing on the standards of the world, if it has no shrill reveille of alarm against the forces which prey on human life, it is a mere bankrupt. If it has nothing piercingly Christian to say about the issues of the day, if it merely echoes in resonant, pious tones the safe generalities to be heard everywhere throughout the land, what good is it?

"Insipid"—a good word to look at, with the question in our hearts, "Lord, is it I?"

⁂

THE VILLAGE AND THE PRINCE

From thee shall come a Prince.—*Matt. 2. 6* (Weymouth).

WHAT are the great cities of the world? Rome, Paris, London? Interesting, all of them. But in the very literal sense of the word, they are not *outlandish* enough to be in the first rank. "Princes," as a rule, come from the *out-lands*, the back districts, the despised small town, from the "sticks."

These words, spoken of Bethlehem, are the char-

ter of the small village, its crown of fame, its immeasurable service to the world. The really great
places of the world, in a vital sense, are its little
Cinderella towns, despised through all the ages by
the *intelligentsia* as the abode of "yokels" and
"peasantry," yet the givers of princes to humanity.

With high truth we may parallel these words
and say: "And thou, Hodgenville, art not least
among the cities of America, for out of thee shall
come a prince." Hodgenville, Kentucky—why, the
very name is grotesque, almost barbaric! Yet what
place could file a stronger claim as a Royal City?

"And thou, Epworth, art not least among the
cities of England, for out of thee shall come a
prince." Epworth? Why, you cannot even find
the place on a railway map! Stuck in the mud in
the northern moors! Outlandish! Exactly, from
the outlands again came a Prince.

"And thou, Eisleben, art not least among the
cities of Germany, for out of thee shall come a
prince"—"The monk that shook the world."

The encyclopedia will list the towns of the world
in the order of their importance this way: London,
New York, Tokyo, Chicago, Berlin. Encyclopedias
are useful but fallible.

Thousands of the world's children drew up a
different list a few months ago. Many thousands
of the school children of thirty countries partici-
pated in a voting contest to choose the twelve
greatest characters in history. In choosing the
twelve greatest servants of humanity the children
also unconsciously made up a new list of the great
towns of the world. And here is the list, the wierdest
collection of impossible towns ever put in a row:

Dole	Florence
Hodgenville	Domremy
Genoa	Athens
Bridges Creek	Mainz
Boston	Blantyre
Staunton	Wylam

Yet they are authentic Royal Cities. For in Dole, France, Louis Pasteur was born; Hodgenville, Kentucky, Abraham Lincoln; Genoa, Italy, Christopher Columbus; Bridges Creek, Virginia, George Washington; Boston, Massachusetts, Benjamin Franklin; Staunton, Virginia, Woodrow Wilson; Florence, Italy, Florence Nightingale; Domremy, France, Joan of Arc; Athens, Greece, Socrates; Mainz, Germany, Johann Gutenberg; Blantyre, Scotland, David Livingstone; Wylam, England, George Stephenson.

The only true measure of any locality is the quality of the manhood which it produces. Any other standard of greatness is impertinent. If we could only learn that in these days of frenzied efforts to swell the mass of cities, and slogans of "Greater This" and "Greater That"!

It is the princes, the servants of mankind, the lovers of humanity which justify a town's existence. And the final and searching question for every town is this: Are we furnishing the environment that can produce a prince—a servant of God and the world? Are the social forces at work which will train, inspire, empower true princes?

❧ ❧ ❧

THE ART OF MALIGNING

Whoever maligns his brother.—*Matt. 5. 22* (Moffatt).

WHAT subtle art it is—that of maligning! And what adepts men are in its practice! The Authorized Version translates the word "gets angry with his brother." But this word "malign" gives the deadly flavor of prussic acid to the boiling mixture of anger. Anger may clear itself like a running stream. When we malign we have venom.

Maligning is a branch of the art of murder. And it is here linked up with the punishment for murder. It murders reputation and influence, both of which are sacred, inseparable parts of personality. When men malign they may murder by *poison*, the most cowardly type of murder. Arsenic, before modern tests were discovered, used to be greatly favored by poisoners because its evidences passed away. We can malign by insinuations which are much like arsenic in that it is hard to establish positive guilt. This sort of murder has often been done by the mere lifting of the brow or a half-formed sneer. It is more often done in this manner than by direct assault and battery. The most deadly way of maligning is to misstate either carelessly or with malice another's position. He is rarely able to refute.

What a text this is for Christian controversialists! In contrast to this study in murder in the first degree set these principles of Christian controversy which come from the mind and heart of that rare Christian spirit, Dr. Henry T. Hodgkin:

I will always seek to discover the best and strongest points in my brother's position.

I will give him credit for sincerity.

I will try to avoid classifying him, and assuming that he has all the characteristics of the class to which he is supposed to belong.

I will emphasize our agreements.

When others criticize, I will try to bring out favorable points.

When there is misunderstanding, either I of him, or he of me, I will go to him direct.

I will seek opportunities to pray together.

I will try to remember that I may be mistaken and that God's truth is too big for any one mind.

I will never ridicule another's faith.

If I have been betrayed into criticizing another, I will seek the first opportunity of finding out if my criticism is just.

I will not listen to gossip and second-hand information.

I will pray for those from whom I differ.

❧ ❧ ❧

YES OR NO

Let what you say be simply "yes" or "no."—*Matt. 5. 37* (Moffatt).

THIS is a timely word for the twentieth century, for we have fallen heir to a bewildering variety of ways of saying both *Yes* and *No* at the same time. Jesus' rule of alternatives seems to make life too meager for a rich age like ours. Our powers of expression run beyond the choice of little monosyllables. Inclusiveness is more alluring.

Bishop Francis J. McConnell has recently satirized the eclectic skill of saying both Yes and No in one breath:

During the Boxer Rebellion, hundreds, yes, probably thousands, of Chinese Christians were martyred. There they knelt, with their heads on the blocks, and the knives trembling in the hands of the executioners. All they needed to do was to grunt out a Chinese word that meant "I recant" and their lives would be saved. Now, what should I have done under these circumstances? And I speak not simply personally, but in a representative capacity, for I think the rest of you are very much like myself. With my head on a block, I think I should have said, "Hold on! I think I can make a statement that will be satisfactory to all sides."

How well that fits so many noble resolutions adopted after prolonged laboring by ecclesiastical and other gatherings! How well it pictures the nimble compromises in personal life, the Yes-No disciples! Trying to locate them definitely on one side of a moral issue is like trying to tell time by the clock, with which the following directions were furnished: When the hour hand points to four and the minute hand to six, the thing strikes nine, and then you know it must be about seven o'clock.

One of the unforgettable characters in Bunyan's *Pilgrim's Progress* is Mr. Facing-Both-Ways. He had a most hospitable and catholic mind. The firm foundation of his philosophy was, "There is much to be said on both sides." And he always said it, charmingly, persuasively, *seriatim* and *in extenso*. He has left a large progeny. After all, there is something to be said for old Cyclops with his one eye. He had a definiteness of outlook that Argus with his thousand eyes missed. A little more of the Cyclops strain in our make-up and a little less

of the versatility of Argus would be a decided asset
to the kingdom of God.

For Mr. Facing-Both-Ways has the futility of a
long, complicated equation in algebra which cancels
out, one side against the other, till the net result
is beautifully simple, $X = O$. Current styles in the
Yes and No designs, now popular, are the Wet-
Dry, the militaristic devotee of peace, and the
theological chameleon whose doctrinal coloring re-
flects accurately and successively his immediate
environment.

      ❧ ❧ ❧

LIVING BY ROTE

Do not pray by idle rote like pagans.—*Matt. 6. 7*
(Moffatt).

DON'T live by it either!   For rote is the arch enemy
of the creative life as well as of creative prayer.
The abundant life which Jesus strives to open up
to men is essentially a creative life as opposed to
a mechanical or a petrified one. His warning
against idle rote becomes increasingly timely, it
seems, as the processes of regimenting and standardizing life go on in our age of mass production and
mass thinking. The forces making for conformity,
for making men march in the goose-step of thinking
and acting, are causing the minds of multitudes to
become as interchangeable as Ford parts. Our
industrial paradise, with its vast machines for
standardizing thinking, glorifies *rote* as never before
in history.

A Syrian and an American were sitting together in the salon of a Mediterranean steamship, when the ship's orchestra began to play that lively little march tune, "The Parade of the Wooden Soldiers." The Syrian gravely and courteously rose and stood at attention. The American, quite puzzled, asked him why he did it. The Syrian answered, inquiringly, "Why, I thought it was your national anthem!" He was not joking. He had merely mistaken the tune. He honestly thought that the "Parade of the Wooden Soldiers" was the American national anthem.

Perhaps it is worth while to ask the question seriously: "Is it the national anthem?" Are the forces flattening out individuality and independent personality, the characteristic activities of our national life? Are we becoming standardized into living by rote? That frustration of creative living is deadly to the purposes of Jesus.

❧ ❧ ❧

THE GENEROUS EYE

If your eye is generous.—*Matt. 6. 22* (Moffatt).

How penurious to have a stingy eye! Eyes are ungenerous when they refuse to *light up* and when they refuse to *see*. Miserly eyes that never glow, that never kindle with luster, fail to achieve one of the highest uses of the eye—that of being the outward and visible sign of a living soul. The human eye is an organ of sight but it is also an organ of speech, and it carries messages too deep, too high for the voice to utter. The life-giving power of a generous eye, flashing the quick movements of a sympathetic heart, is well expressed in Browning's words, "We lived in his mild and magnificent eye." Even the animals which have no equipment of distinctively human muscles—those we use to smile with—nevertheless have the gift of eyes which speak. The human whose inert and stingy eye, holding back like a miser its possible healing and cheering radiance, never speaking the warm glow of the spirit, descends even below the level of the dog and horse.

Ungenerous eyes are also those which see only a pitiful fraction of the human and divine scene. Such stingy eyes do not swing on a pivot like a searchlight; they are set solid like a lamppost. They see only a groove running in one direction. Edwin Arlington Robinson paints a memorable picture of Aaron Stark, a miser, in his line, "With eyes like little dollars in the dark." Little dollars in the dark—what an equipment with which to see God's world! And yet how many people have traded eyes for little dollars! Goodspeed translates it "if then your eye is sound"—if it can do all that eyes should do—if it is whole, not fractional. Sound eyes are generous eyes. Miserly eyes are diseased, self-blinded.

Generous eyes see the *inside* of life as well as the outside. We are told that man looketh on the outward appearance but God looketh on the heart. But the power to see into the heart is part of our inheritance from our Father. That inheritance may be increased and multiplied by use.

Generous eyes see the *top* as well as the bottom;

the sky as well as the earth; the high as well as the low; the Mount Everests of human nature and achievement as well as the Mammoth Caves of descent.

Generous eyes see the *light* as well as the dark. They see the *far* as well as the near.

But, "if your eye be selfish"—your portion is with the bats, in a night without a sunrise.

⚜ ⚜ ⚜

LIFE AMONG THE PAGANS

Pagans make all that their aim in life.—*Matt. 6. 32* (Moffatt).

HERE is Jesus' definition of paganism—it is the great preoccupation with *things*—with food, clothing, and drink. It is interesting to note that Jesus, at the very outset of his training of the disciples, threw up into their vision and warned chiefly against this toughest, deadliest, and everlasting enemy of his gospel and way of life. Paganism in a variety of forms flourished luxuriantly in the world in which Jesus moved. He did not bother about any of them except this, the essence of paganism, this practical denial of God by smothering the very thought of him with food and clothes. All the other first century paganisms have died; have been embalmed in a Dictionary of Classic Antiquities. We need to call in Bullfinch's Mythology for first aid when we are asked about them. But this Paganism still strides the earth like a Colossus, a hungry giant who leaps on men with a strangle hold.

What a commentary this sharply etched picture
of the pagan aim in life is on Christendom, on its
ruling motives, on what we call (with far less complacent pride than a generation ago) Western
civilization! "What shall we drink?" There is the
obsession of a host of Americans, frantically scurry-
ing after the bootlegger, as though it were life's
major question. "What shall we wear?" That
preoccupation calls forth the empire of Paris and
its gods of style and display; that paganism whose
first article of faith is that life is a show window.

The struggle against that fundamental atheism of
materialism seems to grow more intense—certainly
it grows more complex—as the number of things
to buy is multiplied by new industrial magic.
J. George Frederick has put this intensity in our
generation in a few sentences:

Statisticians have calculated that one hundred years
ago the average person had just about 72 wants, of which
16 were necessities; whereas, the average person to-day
has 484 wants, of which 94 are nowadays rated as necessities. Furthermore, one hundred years ago there were
not more than 200 items urged upon the average man by
the seller, whereas to-day there are something like 32,000.
A home containing all the modern inventions and im-
provements available to-day would have a grand total of
about 100 separate mechanisms. The total number of
items sold to-day, including different brands of one-type of
article, reaches the dizzy heights of approximately 365,000.

A state of civilization such as this gives very especial
point to the phrase of Emerson, "To be simple is to be
great," for, indeed, it requires a certain kind of greatness
to be simple in days when complexity spins about one
like a whirlpool drawing us toward a vortex of endless
wants and mechanisms.

Especially do young people need to be guided when they come upon this vast bazaar of brilliantly illuminated merchandise. They almost literally never spend a moment beyond the range of the electric signs, printed advertisements, and seductively arranged window displays of merchandise, of our 365,000 material things. They are plainly bewildered and put at a disadvantage, whatever may be the air of nonchalant sophistication which they wear. The great numbers of young criminals and the preponderance of economic crimes by the young plainly demonstrate the intensity of the money-pressure which the young who start in life feel.[1]

We would bitterly resent being called a pagan. But let us dare to lay Jesus' definition of paganism down beside our own life and test it.

There is only one preoccupation that defeats this essential paganism—"Seek God's realm and his goodness."

This was Lesson One in Jesus' curriculum with his disciples. Unless it were learned there was no need of further lessons. For unless, empowered with God's help, we shake life free from the strangling of materialism, we shall never know either peace or power.

❧ ❧ ❧

SPLINTERS AND PLANKS

Why do you note the splinter in your brother's eye and fail to see the plank in your own eye?—*Matt. 7. 3* (Moffatt).

THESE words, "splinter" and "plank," do not

---

[1] *The Christian Advocate*, March 31, 1926.

add anything to the meaning of the words "mote" and "beam" of the Authorized Version. But they make the meaning harder to get away from. We cannot duck it so readily. The question hits us right between the eyes. We know splinters; we run them into our fingers quite often enough. Sometimes we can hardly see them they are so small. And a plank is enough to stop a street car.

The contrast is so great that we think the parallel with our actions exaggerated. But if we stop to think of those actions, it does not seem half big enough.

A. D. 27 or A. D. 1927—how much fuss we make about minor infractions of laws that are or never were much more than customs, and complacently we ignore denials of the whole Christian ideal of life!

The splinters and planks of other days look grotesque to us. In colonial Virginia a man could be sent to jail for failing to attend church twice on Sunday. For a third offense he could be legally executed—while all the time the slave trade, "the sum of all human villanies," went on with the holy blessing of the church. That was a plank big enough to carve the Leviathan out of!

A century later in England many Victorian families were quite agitated over the monstrous impiety of playing the piano on Sunday. But many of these heads of families, noting the piano splinter, were drawing their income from the fat profits of child labor, during that orgy of child murder which the industrial revolution brought in England.

But why stay back in the last century? Has the splinter and plank scandal become history?

The irony of Jesus still comes to our own day with blistering truth. How many people fussed about the splinter of the omission of the name of God from the Peace Treaty of Versailles at the end of the Great War, and did not notice the violation of both Christian idealism and practical political wisdom by some of its harshness and blindness.

There has been great discussion over the correct keeping of the American cemeteries at Belleau Wood and other places in France. Rightly. But some concerned over that matter have given small care to the larger question of whether future wars shall be allowed to fill the earth with similar acres of white crosses.

Theological splinters have distressed many souls with a passion for regulating orthodoxy—while they have cared far less for the business of getting on with the task of making over the world after the mind of Christ.

Many parents who denounce the young people of to-day, including their own sons and daughters, are oblivious to the fact (as big as a California redwood tree in an open field) that they have failed to supply them an example of persuasive Christian living.

We all have enough planks to build an ark!

❧ ❧ ❧

THE ART OF NOTICING

On entering the house of Peter, Jesus *noticed* his mother-in-law was down with fever.— *Matt. 8. 14* (Moffatt).

Jesus *noticed:* It was a habit with him. That word "notice" gives a shade of meaning not found in the more general word "saw." It pictures the alert and sensitive sympathy of Jesus. You can almost see his eyes take in the whole situation with a keen, swift glance. No one had to shout it into his ear. He noticed it; "so he touched her hand." We have an instance of the play of that sympathetic eye, restlessly on the *qui vive*, in Luke 8. 47, where the woman who touched the hem of Jesus' garment "saw that she had not escaped *notice*" (Goodspeed).

It was a trait of Jesus, this art of noticing every detail that affected the lives about him, which was close to the very center of his personality and message. It cannot be left out if we are to understand him or imitate him. James Russell Lowell once gave this wise advice to James T. Fields, concerning writing: "Be sure and don't leave anything out because it is trifling; for it is out of the trifles only that it is possible to reconstruct character, sometimes, if not always." Jesus never missed "trifles" where a person was concerned.

Nothing human was foreign to his eye. He noticed the patched garments of children, the long lines of men out of work. In the midst of his loftiest discourse he noticed when people grew hungry. He noticed the flushed anxiety of a woman at that critical moment in a housekeeper's day of transferring a dinner from the fire to the table. When his disciples were intent on the architecture of the Temple he noticed a poor widow casting her mite into the alms box.

What a high art it is—just noticing! Some people

never really notice anything. A fact has to hit
them in the face or they miss it. It must be shouted
through a megaphone. And life's deepest things
never come through megaphones. The deepest
needs of men and women must be noticed, or we
miss them. If we stalk through life with a glazed
eye and a blunted heart, we are barred out from
life's finer adventures in human relationships, those
in which we discern of ourselves the unspoken
aspirations, hopes, needs, frustrations of people
about us.

A Christlike eye notices so many things the
world in general misses. "How are you?" we ask
one another and rarely stop to see for ourselves.
The question is merely a routine exclamation. It
is a sadly rare thing to notice what another person
really wants, even when we have known them for
years! In *The Cathedral*, Hugh Walpole has drawn
a powerful and painful picture of Archdeacon
Brandon, who lived for twenty years with his wife,
a sensitive, gentle woman, without coming within
a thousand miles of ever learning what she really
was, how life seemed to her, what she wanted of
life. It was the tragedy of the man who never
noticed.

This art is one in which science and religion
unite in a perfect harmony. Science is just organized noticing. Science began when men ceased to
guess, and theorize from guesses; when they threw
over superstition and began to notice facts. Christian love, like science, is the genius of noticing.

Contrast the things which Jesus noticed with
what the eagle eyes of the scribes pounced upon.
Mark 7. 2—the scribes noticed "unwashed hands."

Aha! They were on the outlook for picayunish infractions of tradition, prospecting for quibbles. What kind of things do *you* notice?

❧ ❧ ❧

FATHERS AND SONS

We have Abraham as our forefather.—*Matt. 3. 9* (Weymouth).

AND the answer was, What of it? God is not much interested in forefathers. He cares about *sons*.

❧ ❧ ❧

BIGGER AND BETTER SALUTES

If you salute only your near relatives, what praise is due to you?—*Matt. 5. 47* (Weymouth).

THAT'S our long suit—saluting our near or fancied relatives. To those within the sacred circle, gathered round the same totem pole of race or nation or class privilege and profit, we are adepts at saluting. We "snap into" attention, the heels click smartly, and the hand goes briskly up and down.

We need some new salutes, but our minds and muscles are awkward at new gestures. We do them stiffly or not at all. Salutes across the barbed wire barriers of race are new tricks for old dogs. Millions of us have been accustomed to read our Bible in this fashion: "God so loved the Nordics

that he gave his only begotten Son (also a Nordic)
that whosoever believed on him might not perish
but have everlasting life in a Nordic heaven."

Saluting the family only gets to be such tame
stuff. It is an eternal variation of the chant, "We
are it." We know it forward and backward and
there isn't a bit of thrill in a whole year of it. W.
S. Gilbert has put the whole rigmarole of such
mutual saluting societies into classic words:

> "I am right and you are right,
> And we are right as right can be."

Walt Whitman is a wonderful drill master for
leading bigger and better salutes. He does not
waste his time on measly little salutes of twenty-
one guns to ruling monarchs and other minor
character. He salutes the whole horizon. His
mind stretches the whole human octave:

"I see Africa and Asiatic towns,
  I see Algiers, Tripoli, Derne, Mogadore, Timbuctoo,
    Monrovia,
  I see the swarms of Pekin, Canton, Benares, Delhi, Cal-
    cutta, Tokyo;
  I see the Kruman in his hut, the Dahoman and
    Ashantee-man in their huts;
I see the Turm smoking opium in Aleppo,
I see the picturesque crowds at the fairs of Khiva and
    those of Herat;
I see Teheran, I see Muscat and Medina, and the inter-
    vening sands;
I see the caravans toiling onward.
  . . I mix,
I see ranks, colors, barbarisms, civilizations; I go among
    them, indiscriminately,
And I salute all the inhabitants of the earth."

Frequently our salutes are confined to one sub-division of our own little tribe, with some such deforming result as that pictured in the creed of the Pendyce family, given in Galsworthy's novel, *The Country House:*

I believe in my father and his father and his father's father, the makers and keepers of my estate, and I believe in myself and my son and my son's son. And I believe that we have made the country, and shall keep the country what it is. And I believe in the Public Schools, and especially the Public School that I was at. And I believe in my social equals and the country house, and in things as they are, for ever and ever. Amen.[1]

Yet that pathetic credo would serve for millions of people.

Bigger and Better Salutes are Needed:

1. THE SALUTE ACROSS RACE DIVISIONS. The form of this salute is with the uplifted hand. It is the hand lifted up to one Father and stretches out in the grasp of brotherhood.

2. THE INTERNATIONAL SALUTE. Nations are learning better salutes. The world cannot go on if nations are to form merely a mutual irritation society. But the salute of good will and trust across national boundary lines demands the over-powering of selfcentered, egoistic, aggressive nationalism. The signs found on buses in large cities should be posted conspicuously in the world's parliaments, "Courtesy will prevent accident."

3. THE RELIGIOUS SALUTE. Across the lines of different religions must come the recognition of

---

[1] Charles Scribner's Sons, publishers. Used by permission.

the common pilgrimage of all men in search of the one God.

4. The Salute across *the picket fences of caste and class*.

※ ※ ※

IN THE WIDER STREETS

You must not be like the hypocrites. They are fond of standing and praying . . . at the corners of the wider streets.—*Matt. 6. 5* (Weymouth).

THEY had an instinct for the Boulevard. There is a very fine touch in Weymouth's phrase, "the wider streets." The back alleys were no place for a splurge. Side streets and narrow lanes might do very well for simple souls but only the wider streets gave proper scope for leaders of public opinion.

So the spiritual descendants of these first-century publicity experts gravitate to Broadway and Fifth Avenue, to Michigan Avenue and State Street, Trafalgar Square, the Rue de Rivoli, but always to the wider streets, the traffic centers.

It is a word with a sharp thrust for an age and a nation in which publicity is one of the major industries. The desire for splurge bulks so largely in our national mood at the moment that the instinct for wide streets very easily gets into even our labors for good causes. Without any conscious hypocrisy we easily lose our sense of proportion. The bright lights blind us. We forget that the bulk of the world's business is done in side streets and country roads and that "the streams which turn the machinery of the world take their rise in solitary places."

Look down one or two of the wider streets which have a very seductive appeal to the mind of our time.

Certain kinds of *public meetings* hold a will-o'-the-wisp promise of magical effectiveness, to the discount of more routine gatherings. Banquets hold forth to many a pastor a throne from which to orate to fascinated and applauding audiences. Compared to such wider streets, the Sunday morning service or the bedraggled midweek meeting seems a back lane indeed. Or the meeting of the Association for the Improvement of Statistics beckons as a surpassing street corner on which to do really big business.

Social work of every sort, tackling the problems of society wholesale, is the characteristic wider street of our day. In the recognition of the indispensable need of the social expression of the gospel, and its application to all of life, there has come also to many people a tendency to onesidedness, a delusion that the world can be saved by organization and public crusade and agitation alone. They regret such retail employments as dealing with individuals because that street does not seem wide enough.

A wide street of perennial appeal is that of *dealing with evils by public meetings and resolutions*. The native hue of resolution may be "sicklied over" with the pale cast of thought, but the crop of resolutions never fails in these days. They are turned out of meetings in quantity production like Ford machines from the factory. They give a fine thrill especially to the mover and seconder and the committee which has labored to bring them forth. They create the illusion of doing business in big waters. The snare is in the fact that they so easily become a substitute for real work.

What gloriously wide streets *railroad tracks are!* The joy of getting into such avenues of prominence was denied to the Pharisees of Jesus' day. And how they would have reveled in them! There is no more subtle way in which a man gets the delusion that he is doing a tremendously influential work than in the fact that he is always hopping a train to go somewhere. Now, of course, some of the most influential people living are continual travelers. But travel is no proof of influence. It is frequently an escape, a refuge from the hard, grinding work of concentration.

We read in the book of Acts the assertion of Peter, speaking of the crucifixion and resurrection of Jesus, that "this thing was not done in a corner." True. But nine tenths of Jesus' days were passed in obscure corners of earth. The Lord's Prayer was taught in a corner. The impact of his life on his disciples, those men who were to be the main channel of his influence on the world, was made in side lanes. It could not be made anywhere else. He spent much of his life in a steady effort to keep away from the wider streets, so that he could do his supreme work of shaping and training men in personal contact. And we suffer an irreparable loss if the current frenzy for publicity blinds us to the truth that the widest opportunity in the world is the quiet spot where one soul comes into contact with another with lasting influence.

WEAR AND TEAR

Where . . . wear-and-tear destroy.—*Matt. 6. 19* (Weymouth).

WEAR and tear are the chief destroyers of things, beyond all other calamities. It is a more inclusive phrase than the word "rust." The depreciation of property and possessions is usually a story of wear and tear. And the depreciation of spirit, of soul, is usually the same prosaic, but tragic story.

The deadliest war is always a war of attrition. It is not the thundering charge of temptation, not the onslaught of opposition or trial, which is most fatal to the life of the spirit. It is the incessant rubbing of the daily entanglements of life. Life is a war of attrition. It is the standing in the trenches, the fatigue duties, the route marches, which wear down the spirit as well as its clothing, the body. When the fine promise of a life becomes overcast, when the eager sensitiveness to moral values and achievement drops out, when the spiritual glow dwindles to a black ember, and we ask, What happened? the answer is not usually to be found in anything special. It is a case of not standing the wear and tear.

The morale of the spirit is broken by wearing down.

> "To-morrow and to-morrow and to-morrow,
> Creeps in this petty pace from day to day."

The sharpness of vision is lost in a dull mist. The need of repeated effort finds a lessening response. Bishop Francis J. McConnell, in *The Christlike God*, has put this deterioration from wear and tear very realistically:

The wear and tear of daily living is such that men tire out in the pursuit of the good life. With the best intentions men get discouraged by repeated failures. They do not definitely give up, it may be, but they loosen hold of the higher principles and cease to care. The chief tragedies of the moral life come of the moral weariness. The most deadening question one can ask as to the moral life is, "What is the use?" When life is young there is a tingle about the moral battle on its own account; but the years come on without fail. All sorts of compromises have to be made as practical adjustments to the world in which we live. Legitimate hopes are thwarted, griefs settle down upon us, power begins to slacken. The mockery of death is on every hand. Then comes the question, "What is the use?" This does not mean that a man who has fought a noble battle all his life is about to cease fighting. It does not mean that he will give himself up to selfish indulgence. It does mean that he has lost the zest of the moral struggle. He may hang on grimly to the end, but with the inner fire burning low.[1]

Hopeless, is it? Is life then necessarily a tragedy of degeneration?

The answer is furnished by the human body. When we realize what science has to tell us of the appalling tearing down that goes on in the body in the course of a day, we wonder how anyone can live a week. We die daily. Wear and tear are ceaselessly destroying at a rate that threatens every vital organ every day. The only reason we live five minutes is that a rebuilding process is going on as incessantly and relentlessly as destruction.

[1] The Abingdon Press, publishers. Used by permission.

Every breath is a new life, a rebuilding of worn tissue. We could live only a few days without constant rebuilding by food, air, water, exercise of the tissues worn out by the mere process of existence.

The soul must be restored by replenished strength to offset wear and tear, just as the body must be. Just as the body can be kept in abundant energy and vigor, by constant restoring, so the process may be as sure with the spirit.

❧ ❧ ❧

JESUS AND THE ADVERTISING PAGES

Do not worry and say, "What shall we have to eat?" —*Matt. 6. 31* (Goodspeed).

WITH these words in mind and the verses which follow them, run through the advertising pages of any large popular magazine. You will come to the conclusion that one of the major obstructions to the Christian way of life in our day is the steady impact of the advertisements on our minds and hearts. With the cumulative force of endless repetition, with the persuasive power which an increasing employment of science, especially that of psychology, gives, there is an insistent bombardment of our eyes and ears with the gospel that life *does* consist in the abundance of things. Buy! Buy! Buy! We have it screamed at us from the newspaper, magazine, billboard, electric sign, street car. And even the sky is being annexed as advertising space.

The "sales resistance," even of the strongest, tends to weaken under the hypnotic suggestion.

But that is not all. Read the advertisements with care, particularly that large class of advertisements of luxuries, and you will find many aimed deliberately and with diabolical seductiveness at some of the most ignoble human traits, such as, for example, pride, envy, acquisitiveness, covetousness, the desire for ostentation, snobbery. "Do you want your neighbors to envy you?" inquires a recent automobile advertisement. The answer implied is, "Of course." The result of such appeals is not merely to sell goods. It is also to stir up in multitudes who react to the suggestions, attitudes and moods and qualities which are utterly unchristian. Right here is one of the often unnoticed but tremendously strong forces working against the establishment of the Christian way of life.

A correspondence school offers to teach a course for sales managers on "How to break down sales resistance." Stuart Chase comments that one of America's greatest needs at present is someone who can teach effectively "How to *build up* sales resistance!"

Jesus has the power to redeem life from the dominance of things. There is no other name given in heaven or earth which can save life from degenerating into a sordid scramble of covetousness and acquisitiveness.

❧ ❧ ❧

THE BEWILDERED CROWD

As he saw the crowds he was moved with pity for them; they were *harassed* and *dejected.*—*Matt. 9. 36* (Moffatt).

They were *bewildered.*—(Goodspeed.)

No one else saw it but Jesus. His followers saw the people, of course. But they were used to crowds. Crowds were frequently a nuisance. They did not see the soul of the crowd. Only Jesus saw that. For him alone did the curtain of appearances lift so that he had an overwhelming sense of the pathos of the lives and hearts of men and women. His imagination and sympathy both were stirred with the vision of the human pilgrimage—harassed, exploited, defrauded; dejected, with the gilt knocked off of life, with empty places in the heart which hope, now dead, had once filled; bewildered, wondering what it was all about.

That is just what the great portion of the human parade has been and is to-day as well as in all the yesterdays. Outwardly that crowd in Galilee is centuries away from the crowd of the rush hour in our great cities to-day. But disregarding the minor accidents of clothes and setting, inwardly it is the same heart beating, the same baffled aspiration, the same burdened trudge, the same fumbling bewilderment.

Many have looked at that crowd through the centuries, that lost battalion of the human host. Some have looked, like Thomas Hardy, with irony and pity; some, as is the current fashion to-day, with cynicism; some with dull, unseeing indifference, and some with the eyes of Jesus, sharing in his sympathy and dedication. John Masefield has caught marvelously this spirit of Jesus, looking out on the human scene, in one of his finest poems, "Consecration." He dedicates his song to "the slave with the pack on his shoulders," "the sailor," "the stoker of steamers." "Let others sing of princes," he cries, "but mine be the dirt and the dross, the dust and the scum." And of these, too, was Jesus' tale told.

These words hold a penetrating picture of our time. It is a *harassed* generation. Life has been smashed up for so many millions. Who can visualize the harassing of the hounds of war? See what modern war does to humanity: in round numbers, 10,000,000 known dead soldiers; 3,000,000 presumed dead soldiers; 13,000,000 dead civilians; 20,000,000 wounded; 3,000,000 prisoners; 9,000,000 war orphans; 5,000,000 war widows; 10,000,000 refugees.

It is a *confused* generation. Many are like sailors making for a port of which the very lighthouses seem themselves to move and blink unsteadily at times and the channel buoys float out to sea. An older simplicity has given way to a baffling complexity. In Baker Brownell's words: "Intellectually the modern world is a corral of wild horses. Each specialty kicks and bites at every other."

It is an age of *disillusion* to multitudes. Sometimes the disillusion is from the collapse of false gods, sometimes from the decay of a true faith.

Yet, now as then, the bewildered crowd is a wistful one, reaching out beyond the panorama of sense, "crying after lost desire;" and Rupert Brooke speaks for the hearts of many, an authentic voice of our generation.

> "O Thou
> God of all long desirous roaming,
> Our hearts are sick of fruitless homing,
> And crying after lost desire.
> Hearten us onward! as with fire
> Consuming dreams of other bliss.
> The best thou givest, giving this
> Sufficient thing—to travel still
> Over the plain, beyond the hill,
> Unhesitating through the shade,
> Amid the silence unafraid,
> Till, at some sudden turn, one sees
> Against the black and muttering trees
> Thine altar, wonderfully white
> Among the Forests of the Night."[2]

Jesus facing a bewildered world was never helpless. "He had for weary feet, the gift of rest;" for strayed minds a goal and a way.

❧ ❧ ❧

IMPIOUS!

"Such language is *impious*," said some of the scribes among themselves.—*Matt. 9. 3* (Weymouth).

HORRORS! A new vocabulary! No wonder the scribes sputtered. The fear of a new word, a new idea, is the most terrifying fear a literalist and traditionalist can ever know. And the unfailing reception which every true word of prophecy has met through the centuries has been—"Such lan-

---

[2] *The Collected Poems of Rupert Brooke.* Dodd, Mead & Company, Inc., publishers. Used by permission.

guage is impious." "He does not speak the same shibboleths; we don't hear the metallic click of the worn counters of speech. He uses strange words and we have to think. It is a nuisance to think. It isn't pious."

Emerson pictures this hatred of a fresh vocabulary:

As soon as we hear a new vocabulary from our own, at once we exaggerate the alarming differences, account the man suspicious, a thief and a pagan and set no bounds to our disgust or hatred, and late in life, perhaps too late, we find he was loving, doing and thinking the same *things* as we under his own vocabulary.

Jesus cared about *things;* the scribes cared about *words*. We search the New Testament in vain for any instance that they ever once made an effort to understand what Jesus meant, what spirit was his. They asked him scores of questions. Evidently, it was one of the popular sports of their day to try to trip or snare Jesus in a verbal net. But never did they ask Jesus a question for the elementary and obvious purpose of finding out something. Robert Lynd, in a very charming, and thoughtful essay on *The Pleasures of Ignorance*, points out that one of the finest delights of life is that of asking questions. "The man who has exchanged that pleasure," he says, "for the pleasure of dogma, which is the pleasure of answering, has already begun to stiffen."[1]

The scribes knew no "pleasure of ignorance." They had long since stiffened. They cared only for the sound of their stereotyped phrases. When Jesus came, caring more for truth than for "bab-

---

[1] Charles Scribner's Sons, publishers. Used by permission.

bling repetitions," more for God than for phrase books, more for man than for traditions, he was "impious."

Which do we care most about, God's universe or dictionaries? Things or words?

❧ ❧ ❧

NEWS; NOT ADVICE

Proclaiming the *Good News* of the Kingdom.—*Matt. 9. 35* (Weymouth).

"CHRISTIANITY is good news, not good advice." It was first preached as news. Wherever it has been preached with power it has been preached as news. Christianity is first and foremost a historical religion. Something happened: The Word became flesh and dwelt among us, full of grace and truth. When the Christian evangel ceases to be good news and dwindles down into mere advice it has ceased to be itself and loses its power.

❧ ❧ ❧

MAKE YOURSELF AT HOME!

While Jesus was *at home* at table, a number of tax collectors and irreligious people came in.—*Matt. 9. 10* (Goodspeed).

JESUS was at home everywhere. These words from our daily life, "at home," give a touch which illuminates Jesus' whole life, all his contacts with

men, women, and children. He set people at their
ease in circumstances which to another would have
been painful with embarrassment. He inspired
utter confidence in the most unlikely folks.

Try to imagine one of the Pharisees sitting down
at a hastily gathered dinner party of Matthew's
cronies—tax-collectors, ward politicians, and irreligious people. His very entrance would have
brought a December chill that would freeze the
genial current of the feast. He would have suffered himself and induced in all the rest a paralyzing
self-consciousness. A provocative sense of superiority would have charged the air with electric
antagonism and resentment.

But Jesus was *at home*. Without either compromise or patronage, with ease and naturalness,
he created the climate of home wherever he went.

It was no trick of manner. It was nothing put
on. It was an inevitable result of his conception
of God and man.

1. The world was his Father's House, all of it.
So he was literally and profoundly at home everywhere. How could it be otherwise? There is a
beautiful old proverb which says, "To him to whom
God is a Father every land is a fatherland." There
was no nook or corner of earth which was not
fatherland to Jesus.

2. To Jesus, everyone belonged to his Father's
family. The intensity of that truth literally made
every company a home circle for him. All folks
were "home folks," brothers and sisters. That
truth was the very air in which he moved. Go
through the gospel records carefully and you will
discover that he never met a stranger in his life.

He met only brothers. He was at home in his Father's family.

That was Jesus' secret. That may be the priceless faculty of anyone who really shares that tremendous faith of Jesus. The Christian religion says to man, "Make yourself at home." This world is not a battle ground of blind forces. It is not a machine shop. It is not an orphan asylum. It is your Father's house. At its center is

> "Immortal love, forever full,
> Forever flowing free."

This phrase "at home" raises an inescapable personal question: Where do we feel most at home? It was said of Henry Drummond, "He was more at home with Jesus Christ than with anyone else."

❧ ❧ ❧

JESUS' APPEAL TO THE IRRELIGIOUS

I did not come to invite the pious but the irreligious.— *Matt. 9. 13* (Goodspeed).

THESE words bring a new shade of meaning to the Authorized Version—"I am not come to call the righteous, but sinners." For the contrasted types of people, "the pious" and "the irreligious" represented not merely, or even chiefly, differences in ethical conduct but in temperament and disposition.

It is well worth pondering deeply that Jesus had a strong appeal for a class of people who are conspicuously absent from our churches to-day—the irreligious. They are people of whom we cannot say that the religious instinct is lacking in their make up. We cannot say that of any individual, and much less of any group. They are people who are much less susceptible to the moods and feelings of piety than others. Religious ceremonies and observances do not appeal to them or yield them the satisfaction which they do to the group Jesus called "the pious." Frequently they have little of the mystical temperament with which many seem to be endowed. Usually they are not by disposition either docile or credulous. Institutional religion has at all times found "the irreligious" a hard class to win, a hard class to hold. Perhaps part of the reason is that many within the church have found them a hard class to like.

Church people have often taken two lines of least resistance in dealing with the irreligious. They have tagged them with the label "sinners" and here left them alone. And in doing this they have been treacherous to the example of Jesus.

There is an unfailing attraction in men who possess large endowments of human energy and force. Their power may be undisciplined and misdirected, but the power attracts. No one can study Jesus' life without feeling that he would be attracted to that kind of men too. His fellowship with the irreligious was one of the major scandals of his life.

Marguerite Wilkinson, in her poem, "Black Sheep," has pictured with striking force these two contrasted groups, the pious and irreligious, and suggests the eager quest of Jesus for those whose temperaments make them hard to shepherd.

"The white sheep are placid
    And feed in quiet places;
Their fleeces are like silver
    That the moon has known.
But the black sheep have vigor
    In their ugly faces.
The Best of all the shepherds
    Wants them for his own.

"The white sheep are humble,
    And they will always follow
The soft call of leaders
    To the dear home fold.
But the black sheep are wayward
    In many a wintry hollow.
The Best of all the shepherds
    Would save them from the cold.

"The white sheep are gentle,
    And bend their necks together;
They crop in God's pasture
    Grasses sweet and mild.
But the black sheep are starving
    Alone in heavy weather.
Oh, Best of all the shepherds,
    Feed them in the wild!"[1]

Think of that phrase in the first verse—"But
the black sheep have vigor." No wonder Jesus
loved them! How he loved energy! Run through
his parables and note how many of them extol
energy—the talents, the importunate widow, the lost
coin and the lost sheep. Look at the men he chose to
be his disciples many were entirely outside of the
inner circles of the professionally religious. Men of

---

[1] From The Ladies' Home Journal. Used by permission.

prodigious energy, whose chief virtues did not rank high, if at all, on the regulation religious score cards of the day.

Where have we lost this appeal of Jesus to the irreligious, to those not pious in the conventional sense? For, in losing it, the church has suffered an immeasurable loss. This particular class of people is growing in numbers to-day and seemingly destined to increase in the future.

Some elements in this appeal of Jesus to the irreligious, to be recovered in our time, may be merely suggested.

1. Jesus had a tremendous liking for men—all kinds of men, for the whole Noah's ark of the human race. Let us use the word "liked" in this connection. The more adequate word, "love," has theological associations which are not stressed here. We are thinking not in theological terms but in terms of the personality of Jesus. He did not have a pigeonhole mind or a synagogue-mind, which classified men by types. He never thought, what we so often think of a person, "He is not our type." All men were his type because they were God's children.

2. Jesus never underrated or disregarded any fine human quality or virtue in the way his followers so frequently have. Magnificent human virtues have even been discounted as pagan virtues because they did not fit into a neat preconceived schedule of ecclesiastical goodness. As Dr. W. R. Maltby so well says:

Our theological coat was cut for the figure of total depravity, but when it was tried on it was found not to fit any kind of human nature. Accordingly, we let out a

seam in the back, and the margin thus gained, with the
stitches still showing, we called prevenient grace. Still
the coat does not fit, for it is not by any afterthought
that we can do justice to that boundless patience and holi-
ness of God which loves goodness everywhere, labors for
it, and delights in it everywhere. . . . These vast tracts
of the unbaptized human life we make over to poets and
novelists and dramatists, who explore them with inexhaustible interest and sympathy. Yet that interest and
sympathy come from God, who loves this human life of
ours, not only as a novelist, approving where it is good,
and disapproving where it is bad, but as a poet or an
artist loves it because he cannot help loving a thing so
strange, piteous, and enthralling as the story of every
human soul must be. For the most part the church has
only taken account of the baptized virtues. The other
kind she did not deny, but she has often acknowledged
them with uneasiness—much as the vicar allows the
saintliness of a Dissenter within his faithful parish, or a
squire concedes that there is a very savory smell in the
poacher's kitchen.[1]

3. There is an immense appeal to the "irreligious," an appeal not used in anything like its
full power, in Jesus' disregard of petty legalisms and
formalisms of every sort.

4. We have held off men who might have been
won, as Jesus' first disciples were won, because
we have emphasized intricacies of opinion, and
raised barbed wire entanglements in God's open
lanes of invitation.

5. Jesus had a lasting appeal to people largely
occupied with practical affairs in his emphasis
on the expression of faith in practical conduct.

---

[1] From The Methodist Recorder, London.

CAN YOU DISMISS A CROWD?

When he had driven the people out.—*Matt. 9. 25* (Goodspeed).

THESE words occur in the story of the healing of a little girl. They bring to mind Jesus' attitude toward crowds and furnish a fine theme for meditation in an age of crowds, such as ours is to-day.

Jesus lived amid crowds. Any moments of privacy—and he made many—were deliberate achievements. From Capernaum to Jerusalem he was rarely outside of the hearing of tramping feet. Yet the crowd never trampled him down. He never seeks it. He is never dependent upon it. Further, whenever he wants to do anything of first importance, as a rule he dismisses the crowd. With us, on the other hand, whenever we feel that any prospect really big is on foot, the first question usually is, "How shall the publicity be handled?"

Jesus' concern was to dismiss the crowd; ours is to gather one.

Is it not probable that the reason we are able to do so little with the crowd is that we do so little apart from it? Does not a man's final and lasting influence with a crowd depend on what he does away from the crowd—alone?

That is a truth so easily forgotten in an age of publicity. The glare of the crowd has the same effect on a man and his message as the glare of the desert. The streams dry up. There is often deep irony in the phrase, "a public man." For the man who revels in the crowd depends upon it. He becomes more and more the public figure and less and less the *man*. Many a preacher has allowed

his message to become a thin trickle of soothing
syrup, because he could not dismiss the crowd and
replenish life from deep inner springs. Without
those springs the rôle of prophet is impossible; one
must perforce become a showman.

Can you dismiss a crowd? It seems the last
thing a modern man can do. The heady wine of
publicity, the intoxication of print, the glare of the
spotlight—all these rush upon our generation as
upon no other that has preceded it. Without
eternal vigilance they become meat and drink to us.

It is a strong verb used here. Jesus had to *drive*
out the crowd. So do we, if we are not to be trampled down. Can you get along without the crowd,
more eager for inner realities than market place
notice, measuring life's significance by the eternal
standards of God rather than by inches of newspaper
space? What we can do in the crowd depends on
what we become away from it. If we cannot dismiss a crowd, we will never be able to do much
else with it.

❧ ❧ ❧

CONTROLLED POWER

Wise like serpents and *guileless* like doves.—*Matt. 10.
16* (Goodspeed).

THE familiar phrase "harmless as doves" has a
somewhat unfortunate sound in that it seems to
suggest weakness. Who wants to be called "harmless"? As ordinarily used, the word has a contemptuous ring. "He could not do any harm if

he wanted to," it seems to say. The phrase "harmless lunatic" is a frequent one, almost a technical expression to describe a person out of his right mind but of a mild disposition and so not dangerous.

Unfortunately, that phrase "harmless lunatic" describes exactly a common idea of Christian character. The Christian is thought of as a weakling, a gentle, sisterly, ineffectual type of being, perfectly harmless and, by so much, perfectly useless.

Doctor Goodspeed's word "guileless" corrects this distortion. It suggests not the absence of power but *controlled* power; not impotence but might in leash; not the absence of force but the domination of hatred and guile by the positive power of good will.

❦ ❦ ❦

THE GREAT BETRAYAL

The father will *betray* his child.—*Matt. 10. 21* (Weymouth).

THESE words sketch a detail of the testing times which it is predicted that the disciples of Jesus will see. It is a crowning touch. The inference is that there could be nothing worse than to betray a child.

All will agree to that. Yet is not that a fairly common occurrence about us? Not in the literal sense the words contemplate—yet not in any remote metaphorical sense either. The child is not betrayed intentionally or even consciously, very often. But it is done continuously and effectively.

Of course the risks of such a preposterous adventure as parenthood are enormous. No insurance company, not even Lloyds, has ever issued a policy against the possibility of being a bad parent. The risks would be too great. Emerson has well expressed the seat of the trouble when he says: "Children are all foreigners. We treat them as such. We cannot understand their speech or mode of life and so our education is remote and accidental and not closely applied to the facts."

Yet the word "betrayal" is too strong to apply to the fumbling all parents do in trying to penetrate the mysteries of that baffling foreigner, their child. Betrayal implies "handing one over to the enemy," and that is exactly what sometimes happens—the child is handed over to the enemy.

How many children, for instance, have been betrayed into the hands of *fear*—to remain captives for life. Bondage to fear is not a natural state— the child is betrayed into it by the timidities, hesitations, and terrors of the parents, and the possibility of a victorious stride through life, buoyant and confident, is lost. What a wonderful parent Jesus was in his training of the disciples! "Fear not!" "Trust!" That was an early lesson. Unless it were mastered there was no use of going on to any other lesson.

Betrayed into *conventionality*—is the fate of others. That does not sound like a base betrayal perhaps. Look closer. No doubt a parent who deliberately set out to train his children to be rebels would be looked upon as a madman. Yet

he would come much nearer to saving their souls
alive than the parent who deliberately trains them
for "success," in the common vulgar meaning of
that term. For conventionality is an ogre which
transforms children into wax statues, fashion plates
and machines. It strips them of individuality, of
God-given spontaneity, robs them of the priceless
gifts of independence of thought and spirit of adventure, which are the world's chief hope of redemption from the tyranny of tradition and sanctified
stupidities.

A common betrayal of a child is to *keep him out
of a great inheritance.* A guardian who would de-
fraud a child from sharing in a large money inheritance would be sent to jail. A parent who defrauds
a child from sharing in his great religious heritage
is so common that he is not noticed. Yet the
betrayal in the first case is slight compared with
the other. A large company of parents subscribe
to the program of Charles Lamb, who once said
jokingly, "I am determined that my children shall
be brought up in their father's religion, *if they can
find out what it is.*" What Lamb proposed face-
tiously is acted upon seriously and the children,
being unable to discover what the father's religion
is, naturally adopt the same religion for themselves.

Miriam Van Waters, of the Los Angeles Juvenile
Court, has written entertainingly and effectively on
"Nineteen Ways of Being a Bad Parent." Probably to cite nineteen distinct yawning pitfalls would
be discouraging to the average amateur parent.
But the theme is one that greatly needs discussion
and is an admirable theme for timely and direct
preaching in these days.

Here are some ways of betrayal common enough ways of being a bad parent that are to be met with on nearly every block.

Half-Time parents are bad ones: parents who act as such only spasmodically and then frequently at the wrong time.

A Bad Parent is one who never lets a child grow up, who does all his thinking for him; the "mother-knows-best" type of parent.

A parent betrays a child who builds up in him a feeling of inferiority. He has crippled the child for life.

Many a parent, in demanding rigid obedience, succeeds only in arousing rebellion.

A parent betrays his child if he fails to distinguish between major and minor values. In a home where "manners" rank higher than moral values it is hard to expect any development in genuine Christian character.

❦ ❦ ❦

THE REPELLENT CHRIST

Blessed is the man who finds nothing that *repels* him in me.—*Matt. 11. 6* (Goodspeed).

THERE is a shock in the very words—the repelling Christ. Christ repel men? We prefer to think of him as the universal magnet. And rightly. Yet we know only very superficially the life and spirit of our time if we do not realize that there is real meaning in the words—the repellent Christ. There are elements in Jesus distinctly repulsive to the spirit and ruling ideas of large numbers of people in our day. It was true in Jesus' day, as even the most cursory reading of the Gospels shows. It has always been true. It is true in many peculiar ways to-day.

1. The spirit of acquisition, so dominant a force in such wide areas of life, the love of power, the motive of profit, the measurement of life in material terms, the worship of success—these find much in Christ that repels them. Jesus' demand for humility and repentance, seems a strange language to-day. "How," asks Reinold Niebuhr, "can we get a gasoline-propelled, fur-coated congregation of prosperous Americans to share that uneasy sense over possessions that is so characteristic a note of the New Testament?" The feeling that there is anything fundamentally wrong with our whole way of life is repulsive to a materially successful industrial civilization.

2. The modern love of comfort, nursed by a thousand modern labor-saving and luxury-producing inventions, is repelled by the whole sacrificial character of Jesus' teaching and life. Consequently, Jesus is, as Dr. Bernard I. Bell declares, "an enigma to the mood of the moment." He thus describes the spirit that is reflected by Jesus.

As for comfort, we twentieth-century people are soothingly immersed in it. Ours is a steam-heated, well-lighted, cunningly upholstered, warm-bathed era. With almost incredible ingenuity we ward off the pumps, plane the sharp corners, "escalate" the heights. From twilight sleep birth to narcotized death we insist on ease. It is that without which all else is intolerable. Only to ex-

ceptional people has it yet occurred that the whole cult
is petty, ignoble, unworthy of human nature.[1]

"Let him take up his cross"—that repels children of comfort whose only contact with rough
roads is on balloon tires.

3. There is a moral austerity in Christ which
cannot be fitted into the spirit of multitudes of
pleasure-loving people with wavering moral standards. With all appreciation of Jesus as the bringer
of joy—yet there is a severity of personal discipline
in his demands which cannot be blinked even by
the loosest thinking. To the current mood of
many—that of obsession with sex—Jesus is a disturbing, a rebuking figure. Frankly—though it is
not often expressed frankly—he is repulsive.

4. To the cult of self-assertive nationalism Jesus
is repulsive. Here the repulsion is more outspoken.
It does not take the form of open reviling so often
as that of distortion. Militarism tries to twist
Christ into its own likeness. Blustering and aggressive nationalism substitutes itself for Christianity as
a religion. Jesus' disregard for boundaries of race
and tribe, his universal mission, his repudiation of
force all make him a dangerous enemy to that competitive nationalistic spirit which generates war.

❧ ❧ ❧

WISE FOOLS

Hiding all this from the . . . *intelligent.*—*Matt.* 11. 25
(Goodspeed).

[1] *The Atlantic Monthly*, 1927. Used by permission.

THAT word *intelligent* sort of "clicks" in our mind. It calls up that unlovely modern word—with such a deadly aroma of snobbishness—*intelligentsia*. And it would be rather hard to find a word which describes more exactly the kind of people Jesus had in mind—so grievously learned that they miss what is best worth learning. The *intelligentsia* are the consciously, the self-admittedly, intelligent. They are the "highbrows." They are so intent on complexities that they have forgotten the simplicities; so eager on the quest of the whims and the crazes that they have lost the "ancient, beautiful things."

The picture of some of these wise fools has perhaps never been sketched with more telling irony than by James M. Barrie in his play, "The Admirable Crichton." The characters are a family of society people and their butler wrecked on a desert island. They are possessed of an impressive variety of sophisticated learning and skill. They know Burke's Peerage by heart. They have a complete mastery of the technique of auction bridge. In the knowledge of good form for all occasions from a court reception to a hunt they are letter perfect. Yet they would have speedily starved to death had it not been for the butler. He alone had any knowledge of the common, elementary processes of sustaining life. Their crazy jumble of artificial learning had about as much connection with elementary human needs as if they had lived on the moon.

This titled family on their desert island were a fair picture of "the intelligent" Jesus had in mind, ignorant of life's most vital primary truth.

What a boisterous crew our self-styled *intelligentsia* are to-day! From the heights of sophistication they look down with Olympian contempt on the poor "morons" who make up the average run of the human race. They are the "civilized minority." Whatever the majority has valued and admired must necessarily be passé, outworn drivel, fit only for "yokels." To such emancipated minds Dickens is impossible, George Eliot hopelessly mid-Victorian—mere pygmies compared to James Joyce and Dreiser. Tennyson is food for babes, not to be mentioned in the same breath with Ezra Pound.

The suggestion that anything of worth could be hidden from the wise and learned would be intolerable. A study of what such intelligent minds miss is vastly rewarding.

"I thank thee, Father, Lord of heaven and earth, for hiding all *this* from the learned and intelligent"—

All *what?*

For one thing, any conception of the reality of *religious experience*. There has been a progressive emancipation of humanity from superstition in recent years. And many in throwing over superstition have thrown out all the precious and tested religious experience of millions of men and women throughout the centuries. They have been so painfully clever that this deepest, most vital of human quests and achievements has been hidden from them. One modern wise man—and a rare wisdom he has in many ways—George Santayana, grows positively gay over the prospect of unloading what he calls the "burden" of faith.

"Farewell, my burden! No more will I have
The foolish load of my fond faith's despair,
But try the idle race with careless feet.
The crown of olive let another wear;
It is my crown to mock the runner's heat
With gentle wonder and with laughter sweet."[1]

The learned and *intelligent*, in Jesus' use of the word, frequently miss the deep wisdom distilled from the experience of the race. The lasting, immemorial joys of family life, won and tested by the experience of the ages, are too naïve, and simple and "stuffy" for many of these learned. Traditional sex morality is too intolerable a repression for many of the truly emancipated. Listen to Bertrand Russell. Speaking of the sex education of his own children he declares, "I shall not teach that faithfulness to one partner through life is in any way desirable or that a permanent marriage should be regarded as excluding temporary episodes."

The *intelligentsia* frequently miss the wisdom of *sympathy*. "A loving heart," says Carlyle, "is the beginning of all knowledge." For a feeling of kinship with common humanity, a sympathetic understanding of and identification with the life and aspirations of all kinds and conditions of men, many have substituted the delights of a superior contempt and cynicism. And the price they always pay is blindness.

---

[1] Charles Scribner's Sons, publishers. Used by permission.

✄ ✄ ✄

THE KINDLY YOKE

My yoke is *kindly.—Matt. 11. 30* (Moffatt).

A MUCH better word than "easy." Jesus' yoke is not always easy. It *is* always kindly. Just as a father's discipline of a child is not always easy— sometimes it is very grievous. Yet it may be kindly even when it rests heavily.

Some people find Jesus' way of life easy only because they have followed it very superficially. A congregation can sing lightly and absent-mindedly,

> "His yoke is easy;
> His burden is light.
> I've found it so—"

who have never felt the fellowship of his sufferings at all. No wonder they've found it easy! They've never tried it! The yoke of Jesus is *kindly.* He asks much. But he asks it from love, so that by bearing it our joy may be full and our life abundant.

✤ ✤ ✤

THE WRANGLERS

He will not *wrangle* or *shout.—Matt. 12. 19* (Moffatt).

YET how much of it his disciples have done! These words occur in an Old Testament description of the Messiah. They are characteristics which Jesus supremely fulfilled. They should be outstanding marks of Jesus' disciples. Yet how little would an outsider in most any century have ever guessed that the Christians were the followers of One whose distinguishing mark was that he would not wrangle! They have been the senior wranglers of all history! Frequently they have been too busy wrangling to do much of anything else. The different things they have wrangled over would fill pages in the dictionary with a catalogue of "isms" all the way from gnosticism down to the "isms" of our own day.

And many of the wrangles have been a fresh crucifixion of Jesus. The greatest obstacles to the establishment of the kingdom of God have not been the outside oppositions but the inside wrangles. Again and again the curtain has been rolled back to disclose new opportunities of world winning, only to find the forces of Christianity largely divided into preoccupied debating societies. The call from over the seas, "Come over and help us," has been drowned out by the hoarse cries of debaters shrieking rebuttals and invective.

Of course it should not be forgotten that Christianity has necessarily had to make its way against competitive religions and intellectual opposition. Argument has not only been a necessity; it has been an indispensable means of evangelization in many instances. Again and again has it been necessary to state the Christian evangel in adequate terms in the presence of very real dangers of movements toward fatal distortion or compromise.

But such argument is high above the level of mere "wrangling and shouting." A wrangle is an acrimonious, wordy warfare over secondary or incidental aspects of religious opinion or ecclesiastical tradition. There is a fine insight in this matter in

Emerson's statement that "truth has already ceased to be truth when it is polemically said."

What a future would open out for the Christian forces of the world if it should ever become a major characteristic of them, as it was of their Master, that they shall not "wrangle"! Even so, come, Lord Jesus!

❧ ❧ ❧

THE CARELESS WORD

For every *careless* word that men utter they will have to answer on the Day of Judgment.—*Matt. 12. 36* (Goodspeed).

THE meaning of "idle words" of the Authorized Version is much the same—but the word "careless" adds arresting suggestions. For careless words may be very busy words: in fact the busier our words the more careless they are liable to be.

One large class of careless words are those that run like the driftings of a leaky spigot. The person who is not "gifted with flashes of silence," or who does not acquire the gift by dint of self-control is bound to have most of his words careless words. Don Marquis has put into brisk, humorous verses this insidious process by which words just run on endlessly with hardly any oversight from the mind. He describes his task as being merely that of taking the words which Noah Webster has collected and arranging them in a row till a column has been filled. "It's so easy, it's a cinch," he cries. Niagara Falls seems to be the ideal which many have set up, con-

sciously or unconsciously, as a model for conversation.
It runs on with an endless continuance, with all the
resources of four great lakes and the clouds of an
infinite heaven behind it. It is one of the natural
wonders of the world. The Niagara Falls type of
conversationalist, however, is one of the *unnatural*
wonders of the world, an endless flow with negligible
supply.

This kind of mass production lays up an enormous liability for every Judgment Day. And Judgment Day is to-day, to-morrow—not merely off in
some remote future. For we are all in the same
position as the person under arrest—"everything
we say will be used against us"—in the determining
of the weight and quality of our influence.

Another class of careless words are all those that
do not have a bit of our real selves wrapped up
inside of them—just words, conventional rubber
stamps, that do not carry any flavor of our own
personality. No matter how pompously we intone
them, words which are not really parts of our
selves are perniciously careless words.

❧ ❧ ❧

THE DULLED MIND

This nation's *mind has grown dull.—Matt. 13. 15*
(Goodspeed).

THESE words, first spoken by Isaiah of his own
nation, Judah, make a penetrating text for America

to-day. By that we do not imply that any blanket charge of dullness or slow-wittedness, uttered in a querulous spirit, should be made against the United States. But it is a very timely and rewarding inquiry to ask in what sense and over what areas of our life this judgment of Isaiah, quoted by Jesus and searchingly applied to his own nation, might be true of our nation to-day.

At the outset of every such inquiry it is well to bear in mind the weighty word of Henry James, "Most forms of contempt are unwise but one of them seems to us particularly ridiculous: contempt for the age one lives in." There is a vociferous brood of critics of America to-day whose chief stock in trade is contempt. Their only gesture is a leer, their only vocal utterance raucous laughter. Contempt is always sterile. It yields no desirable fruit. Any valuation of a nation's life and trends, if it is to have any valid worth, must issue from love and understanding of its virtues and strength as well as its liabilities.

On the face of it to say of America that "this nation's mind has grown dull" seems the height of the ridiculous. Nowhere has education been diffused over so large a proportion of the populace as here to-day. In every field there is the keenest competition of sharpened wits.

Yet the text has a deep meaning even for a nation living on its wits. For sharpened wits may easily go with a dull mind. Dullness has to do with perception of values; and a nation may gain a whole world of technical and intellectual agility and yet remain dull in the discernment of other and deeper life values.

It is in that sense that this text is a searchlight. We cannot look deeply into many characteristics of large areas of life without feeling the presence of a disconcerting dullness in the estimate of relative values.

A nation's mind is dull when it is dominated by *things*. Alcohol befuddles the judgment of a mind; proportions and perspectives are lost in an opaque haze. In just the same disastrous manner, materialism, the lust of acquisition, the measurement of life and definition of success in terms of outward possessions, clouds and dulls the mind. Disraeli diagnosed many years ago the malady that infects and threatens a large section of Western civilization to-day when he said: "The European talks of progress because by the aid of a few scientific discoveries he has established a society which has mistaken comfort for civilization." Oswald Spengler in *The Decline of the West* has put the results of this same dullness of mind which elevates material things over the life and achievements of the spirit in striking form:

The ossification and death of ancient civilizations occurred when they concentrated in great cities, as the classical civilization did in Rome and Alexandria, and the Arabic civilization did in Damascus and Bagdad; and when their creative and vital principle, which expressed itself in a living religion, true art, and the higher spiritual manifestations of the mind and soul, had spent its force and was replaced by absorption in material progress. That is the present stage of our Western civilization, which has now spread over the whole world.[1]

[1] Copyright, 1926, by Alfred A. Knopf, Inc., publishers. Used by permission.

Trial by market is the final test of a large multitude of people. An American traveled all over
France recently using only one French word,
"Combien?"—"How much?" He got along perfectly. That was all he wanted to know. He had
only one measure of values. The tragedy of the
man was not that he knew only one word of French
but that he knew only one word of any language.
He knew only one word of English. His mind had
grown dull. His was not a unique case. His one
word is a symbol for a large number of people.
To be fair to them, it is not so often money they
idolize but money as a symbol of success. Gamaliel
Bradford has pointed out that the American has
not the miser's passion for accumulating, as such.
"He is just as ready to spend as he is to gain, to
fling away dollars for amusement or benevolence as
fast almost as they come in, unless retaining them
is clearly necessary to get more." Success in money-
making is the crude, obvious form that appeals
to a nation which has not yet wholly grasped, or lost
to some extent, the finer issues and interests of life.

Edwin Arlington Robinson has some searching
verses, words which he puts into the mouth of a
modern "Cassandra."

> "I heard one who said: 'Verily,
>   What word have I for children here?
> Your Dollar is your only Word,
>   The wrath of it your only fear.
>
> "'You build it altars tall enough
>   To make you see, but you are blind;
> You cannot leave it long enough
>   To look before you or behind.

"'Are you to pay for what you have
  With all you are?' No other word
We caught, but with a laughing crowd
  Moved on. None heeded, and few heard."[1]

"Are you to pay for what you have with all you are?"—that question probes to the heart of a prosperous industrial civilization.

Clinging to the outworn sophistries of militarism, wallowing in a rising tide of vulgarity, are not such things also symptoms of a nation's mind grown dull?

❦ ❦ ❦

THE MAN WHO SHOCKED PEOPLE

Do you know that the Pharisees were *shocked* to hear you say that?—*Matt. 15. 12* (Goodspeed).

The Pharisees were *greatly shocked.*—(Weymouth.)

JESUS never *tried* to shock people.

He was never *afraid* of shocking people.

In both characteristics he is well worthy of study and emulation.

Jesus never went out of his way to say shocking things. That was a juvenile kind of thrill in which he had no interest. Indeed, all through his ministry we can discern the care which he took to prepare a pathway for his truth to the mind of the people he was speaking to. He eagerly seized whatever he could build on in their minds. All his words were at the service of a positive, con-

---

[1] From "Cassandra," in *The Man Against the Sky*. The Macmillan Company, publishers. Used by permission.

structive purpose, "I am not come to destroy, but to fulfill."

Compared with this patient strategy of Jesus the sensationalism of people who find delight in shocking folks is not only pathetically childish but vicious. Such tactics on the part of those, whether in the pulpit or out of it, whose ostensible desire is to inculcate truth have aroused wholly avoidable opposition and resistance and have caused a world of futile bickering and unnecessary pain.

Sometimes this effort to shock people comes from a mere desire for notice. The English poet, Rogers, was once asked why he said so many malicious and scandalous things. "I have a weak voice," he confessed candidly, "and unless I say something shocking no one ever listens to me." His tribe is legion.

Sometimes this habit is from the domination of a mind by one idea. That becomes the universe, shutting out everything else. Such a state is always a form of fanaticism, which rides gayly and unconcernedly over the feelings and ideas of other people. Samuel McChord Crothers says very keenly, "When a new idea gets into an unfurnished mind it has the time of its life. There is nothing to oppose its autocratic rule."

Sometimes the effort to be shocking is merely the gratification of egotism. "I'll show these old fogies a thing or two" is the mood. Fortunately, this crass conceit is frequently only a disease of youth, like the measles, and is outgrown. But when it hangs on it is malignant.

The kingdom of God has suffered unmeasurable harm from such "shock troops."

The second truth which emerges from a study

of Jesus' teaching and preaching—that he was never afraid to shock people—may seem at first glance to be contradictory to what has just been said, but only on a superficial view.

Jesus never allowed his strategy in persuasion to cloud or tone down his message. When the truth would shock—let it shock. "To this end . . . come I into the world, that I should bear witness unto the truth." Nothing else mattered. He put his message in a way that it would be heard. His words stuck like burrs to the mind. If they shocked and stung like burrs, let them sting! He was never deterred from his witness to God by asking, "What will people think about it?" or "How will it affect my safety or popularity?" These two questions trip us up again and again. When either becomes dominant in our thinking truth is muffled so that it is never effectively heard.

Imagine how a cautious adviser might have spoken words of prudence to Jesus in this instance. "Now, Master, of course your ideas of the importance of ceremonial cleansing are all right, but don't just say them out bluntly. There is a way of putting it so as not to offend the Pharisees. They are very excellent and influential people and you can't afford to shock them. Put it this way: 'You are greatly to be honored, dear friends, for your devotion to your tradition. May I suggest that there are other things also that will perhaps bear looking into?' "

If Jesus had spoken in that strain, he would have shocked nobody, and nobody either then or since would have remembered what he said. It would all have ended in an incoherent mumble. Jesus

never mumbled. He spoke so clearly and forcibly
that he shocked the world into a new way of life.
He came to make "a new and living way unto the
Father." It was a task of building a new road,
and road building requires blasting.

The church which never shocks anybody will
never save anybody. When his disciples told Jesus
he had shocked the Pharisees, it never occurred
to him to apologize. He merely said, "Let them
alone." His example and counsel always was to
get on with their message, to preach the kingdom
of God. The test of a message is frequently the
same as the test of an electric wire—its capacity
to shock is an indication of life. When nothing
happens, it is dead!

❧ ❧ ❧

JESUS AND THE AVERAGE MAN

Are you *totally* ignorant?—*Matt. 15. 16* (Moffatt).

"Don't you know *anything?*" There is a clear
note of exasperation in this question voiced by
Jesus. And it is very easy to understand. He
had just been stating a principle that seems to us
utterly elementary and axiomatic—that it is not
the things which go into a man's mouth which
defile him, but the things which come out of the
heart; evil thoughts, murders, adulteries, lies, theft.
He had stated it in words as clear as sunlight. And
yet here comes Peter and asks, as though Jesus had
been speaking in Greek, "Please explain it to us."

Small wonder that Jesus exclaims, "Haven't you got any sense at all?" It is a mood that we all know. And such a momentary exasperation with dull, heavy, slow-wittedness does not detract from Jesus. It, rather, furnishes a new insight into the greatness of his patience.

For notice, there was no scorn in his question. Jesus on rare occasions expressed scorn. He could make devastating use of it. Some of the Pharisees who had felt its blazing heat could not soon forget it. But he never treated minds of common men with scorn, no matter how slow to understand they might be. He was never betrayed into any form of contempt for average humanity. Scorn is one of the most dangerous emotions anyone can allow himself to feel. It has high uses; but they are rare. No one can make light or frequent use of scorn without having it spoil his whole spirit. Scorn rapidly corrodes the spirit with egotistical superiority, cynicism, and loveless contempt.

The passage furnishes a fine starting-point for a study of Jesus' attitude to the average man, a study which has timely practical values in this day when contempt and derision are current popular poses.

These words of Jesus, "Don't you know anything?" are a common question to-day, in reference to the common mass of people. And the answer is frequently given in a much overworked modern word, "moron." It is quite fashionable to regard common humanity from an infinite height of superiority and call them "boobs," "morons." Moron is a particularly popular word. It has a pseudo-scientific flavor which flatters the self-conceit of the user. The contemptuous attitude of the average mind is helped on by the flood of intelligence tests which have burst loose upon our time. We are told that the "public" has the mind of a twelve-year-old child, and we feel greatly flattered and complacent.

No one ever arrived at a true estimate of men or influence on them by way of contempt. Jesus' attitude furnishes a sharp contrast to this current one of disdain for humanity in the mass. He was aware, painfully aware, of how slow the minds of average men could be, how heavily they got into motion. Yet he had a profound respect for that mind and went patiently to work, over and over again, to share his truth and experience with it. We can learn from him much to warm and hearten us. He never judged men by such superficial standards as knowledge or cleverness. He had a deep penetration into the larger values of common, human stuff. Even though for an instant he wonders whether his disciples were not "totally ignorant," yet always he purposes to bring the kingdom of God in the world through the agency of such average human material. His reverence for the common man, his patience with the common mind, form one great reason why Christianity has survived. It did not depend on experts or geniuses. It never became a self-satisfied little group viewing the common herd with patronage. Whenever any body of Christians have taken on those characteristics—and it has happened often—they have become sterile. Such is always the danger of a progressive group, that it becomes self-conscious and conscious of a superior enlightenment. And the final stage of uselessness is reached when sympathy

and patience with average humanity give way to
contempt and disdain.

Such a course always spells ruin to any hope of
making a better world. It is a measureless distance
from the spirit and method of Jesus.

* * *

"DISCUSSING SOMETHING"

But they were *discussing something* with one another.
—*Matt. 16. 7* (Goodspeed).

AND, of course, they missed the point which
Jesus was making. They did not hear him at all.
Jesus had just given the disciples a solemn warning
against becoming like the Pharisees. It was a
truth he wished desperately to get into their minds.
But they were discussing something and missed it.
They were arguing about the lunch.

How often in all the long centuries since that
day have Jesus' disciples been discussing something
as trivial as the contents of a lunch basket, and
missed the message he had for them!

Only a few hundred years later, before the Christian Church in North Africa there unrolled the
opportunity to win a whole continent for Christ.
Not often in history, before or since, had conditions seemed to conspire so as to make possible the
swift extension of Christianity over so vast an area.
But they were "discussing something." All their
energies were being spent in acrimonious doctrinal
controversies. They were so busy slaughtering each
other's arguments, and finally each other, that they

had no strength or desire to unite against the paganism. Jesus was saying to them—"Go ye into all of Africa," and "Lo, I am with you alway." But they were too busy with their epithets and arguments.

Again in a later century the high road to China was thrown open in a manner which has never happened since and never can happen again.

H. G. Wells, in his *Outline of History*, tells how the Mongol Emperor, Kublai Khan, who ruled over China and large portions of western and central Asia and Russia, in 1269, despatched envoys to the Pope at Rome to ask that one hundred missionaries be sent to his capital in order that his people might be taught the things of Christ and a better understanding be brought about between the East and the West. This story is told in detail by Marco Polo, from personal knowledge of what transpired, and we quote his words rather than the brief summary by Mr. Wells. Says Marco Polo: "He [the emperor] begged that the Pope would send as many as an hundred persons of our Christian faith, intelligent men, acquainted with the seven arts, well qualified to enter into controversy, and able clearly to prove by force of argument, to idolaters and other kind of folks, that the law of Christ was best, and that all other religions were false and naught, and that if they could prove this, he and all under him would become Christians and the church's liegemen. Finally he charged his envoys to bring back to him some oil of the lamp which burns on the sepulcher of our Lord at Jerusalem."

This remarkable message reached Rome at a time when there was a vacancy in the papacy, because rival factions in the college of cardinals could not agree on the new Pope, and it was two years before Gregory X despatched two Dominican friars to convert the greatest power in Asia to the rule of Christ. The emperor asked for one hundred, and the church answered with two. And those two, appalled by the length and perils of the journey, turned ignominiously back after they had reached Armenia. Most pertinently does Mr. Wells remark, "All Asia was white unto harvest, but there was no effort to reap it."[1]

They were too busy discussing something!

We to-day can wonder, "How can the stupid disciples have been fussing over whether there was any lunch or not, or who was to blame for neglecting it, when Jesus was right there trying to tell them something! Oh, if we had only been there, we would have heard him!"

Perhaps.

Look at our own time. Think of the momentous issues of this post-war world—a broken world, a world with so much disillusion, with old hatreds not put out but only banked, a world still armed to the teeth, with industrial and race conflicts present or impending—yet with a wistful searching for a better way of life. What a time for bringing to all these great human needs Christ's message of life! Yet how many have been in these years "discussing something"—and, like the disciples of old, have missed what Jesus has been saying! Not discussing lunch exactly but things as far removed from the world's needs—competitive ecclesiastical rivalries, denominational peculiarities, fratricidal warfare over details of science, all making such a frenzied clamor that the still small voice of God was drowned.

---

[1] *The Business of Missions*, by C. H. Patton. The Macmillan Company, publishers. Used by permission.

How tragically easy for some comparatively trivial discussion to preoccupy the attention of Christian people and churches—so that they miss Christ's message.

One of the great educational leaders of America has put vividly the same blundering absorption in incidentals to the exclusion of vital needs in the educational world:

Secondary education is asleep. She is dreaming of "I. Q's," of "administration vs. supervision," of dancing and cigarettes, of conformity to the requirements of colleges, of methodologies, of pedagogies, and the isnesses of many inconsequential whys, each in a degree good or bad; but for questions as big as the world and as enduring as eternity she has neither eye nor ear. World courts, leagues of nations, the waxing and waning of dynasties, the crash of nations as they crumble to dust, the struggle of peoples to arise from the horrors of war into the semblance of a decent status, the economic chaos of the world, the moral dilapidation of mankind; hate between nations and races and religions; the disintegration of the fireside; the apparent triumph of material over spirit; starvation among great groups of people; the hectic, post-war tenseness of the world's nervous system; the destruction of ideals and idealism—all of these receive but a passing glance.

Much contained in these words could easily be transferred to the church.

This picture points out the insidious danger to the disciples of Jesus.

We read that, when they were discussing the menu, Jesus "noticed it." "Why did you doubt?" he cried.

Shall we make him continue to ask?

YOU HINDER ME

You *hinder me*, for you do not side with God, but with men!—*Matt. 16. 23* (Goodspeed).

No wonder Peter was surprised at this vigorous outburst of rebuke from Jesus. Hindering was the last thing in Peter's mind. He was merely smoothing out the way, making things easy.

The answer of Jesus makes clear that the most formidable hindrances which can shackle any life are the hindrances of love. They are the forces which crowd a person or an organization of persons into the easiest way; which pull them down from the heights of achievement by well-meaning fears. It was a deeply seeing man who cried, "I can take care of my enemies; save me from my friends." The hindrances of friends are more powerful because more insidious. The direct onslaught of opposition only stiffens the high purpose; the loving remonstrance of friends acts as an opiate.

Friends often hinder each other, till a mistaken love's harping on safety and comfort becomes just what Jesus called it, the very voice of the devil. This easy slide into degeneracy, in the most intimate of relationships, has never been more realistically pictured than by Frances Power Cobbe. She pictures how a wife may play the part of a devastating wrecker to the one she loves:

The higher *moral* good of the husband occupies most wives comparatively little; and often a man who starts with a great many lofty and disinterested aspirations deteriorates, year by year, in a deplorable manner under the influence of a sufficiently well-meaning and personally conscientious wife. If you ask, "How can this be?" the answer is that, the wife's affections being of a poor and short-sighted kind, she constantly urges her husband to think of himself and his own interests rather than of the persons and objects for which he was ready to sacrifice himself. "Do not go on that charitable errand to-day: you have caught a cold. It will answer as well to-morrow." "Do not invite that dull old friend." "Do not join that tiresome committee." "Pray take a long holiday." "By all means, buy yourself a new hunter." "Do refrain from confessing your unorthodox opinions." This kind of thing, dropped every day like the lump of sugar into the breakfast cup of tea, in the end produces a real constitutional change in the man's mind. He begins to think himself, first, somewhat of a hero when he goes against such sweet counsel, and then a Quixote, and then a fool. And a curious reciprocity is also established. The husband cannot do less than return the wife's kindness by begging *her* not to distress and tire herself by performing any duty which costs a little self-sacrifice; and she again returns the compliment, and so on and so on, till they nurse each other into complete selfishness.

A memorable phrase that is—"this kind of thing, dropped every day like a lump of sugar into the breakfast cup of tea." We read a good deal about "poisoned liquor." Here is the real thing!

The blind, smothering care of parents sends children into the world maimed, as far as the possible powers of their spirits are concerned. We shudder at the story of the slaughter of the innocents in the Gospel of Matthew. But a slaughter of innocents goes on in our comfort-loving day, when the main drive of parents is so often to prepare children for conformity and the material success to which it leads. Every precious individual difference, giving promise of individuality, every spontaneous emotion which might lead to original independent personality is carefully snipped off, as a Japanese gardener binds back and cuts off branches in the training of a stunted tree. Thus they are hindered from ever achieving that self-forgetful enthusiasm which is the very core of Christianity. Soul binding is a far deeper hurt than foot binding.

Does it take much of a stretch of imagination to hear Jesus saying to his disciples and to his church to-day, "You hinder me"? He still sets his face toward Jerusalem. "On to Calvary" is still his watchword. He would lead on to the building of the kingdom of God, or righteousness, joy, and peace in this broken world. Yet many of his disciples take their stand with Peter and answer that call: "Not that, Master. Take the easier way. Don't be an extremist. We live in a practical world. Let's stay in Galilee. It is far pleasanter. There are crosses in Jerusalem." By our easy accommodations to the world as it is, by our premature satisfaction with unchristian conditions, we hinder him.

Jesus leads on to a world of peace. Peace means Calvary. George A. Dorsey, in *Why We Behave Like Human Beings*, says with a simpering superficiality, "we have discovered how to transmute imps into angels with miles of smiles."[1] We are long miles from a transformed humanity, but it is emphatically *not* "miles of smiles" which intervene. They are long weary miles up the dark hill of Calvary. Peace comes as Jesus brought it by costly sacrifice and self-dedication. Only as we cease

---

[1] Harper & Brothers, publishers. Used by permission.

hindering Jesus, by our clinging to the easier gods of force and aggressive nationalism, will we make a world of secure peace.

We lay hindrances before Jesus' determined onward push to real brotherhood. An air of patronage and condescension to other races is a far more subtle hindrance to fellowship than crude hatred, but it is just as real.

We hinder Jesus' passionate yearning for a church filled with his spirit and utterly at his service by choosing the easier way of a conventional attachment which answers the demands of correct form, without violently revolutionizing our life.

❧ ❧ ❧

GOD'S OUTLOOK

Your outlook is not God's, but man's.—*Matt. 16. 23* (Moffatt.)

A PICTURESQUE phrase—God's *outlook!* An amazing suggestion, when we think of its implications—that we should have God's outlook. The word suggests rather accurately the one thing we can have in common with God—a point of view, a standpoint from which to look at the world, a common purpose. We cannot have the mind of God—"His thoughts are above our thoughts." But having the mind, the purpose of Christ, we can have God's outlook. It was a more intangible and far-reaching thing than the actual suggestion of Peter which Jesus rebuked; it was the direction in which Peter's mind looked—the limited arc through which his thoughts swung.

Any outlook has four dimensions, depth, height, length, and breadth. And those dimensions may be clues to the inexhaustible meaning of these words—God's outlook.

Jesus revealed a new *depth* to life. He plumbed beneath all outward observances to the heart; beneath all outward acts to the motive. He added a new dimension to righteousness. He uncovered values in the inner life beside which the surface of life shrank in proportion. H. G. Wells, in his novel, *The World of William Clissold*, records a sort of waking-dream experience which symbolizes the new outlook on the world which Jesus brings to men.

I am reminded as I write of this of a queer little thing that happened to me at times, most frequently in my adolescence and when I was a young man. I do not think that it has occurred at all during the last ten or fifteen years. It was this: The visible world, remaining just as bright and clear as ever it had been, would suddenly appear to be minute. People became midgets, the houses and the furniture, dolls' houses and furniture, the trees, mere moss-fronds. I myself did not seem to shrink to scale; it was only the universe about me that shrank.[1]

With the experience of a new depth to life which Jesus brings, material things, while still remaining in the picture, shrink in relative magnitude.

Jesus' revelation of God puts new *height* into man's outlook. Without God we have a worm's-eye view of the world.

The inclusive love of Jesus gives a new *breadth*

---

[1] Copyright, 1926. George H. Doran Company, publishers. Used by permission.

to our vision and concern. We are so adept at building fences, which shut out other races, nations, classes. On his release from a long prison term, a prisoner looked out across a valley and remarked, "I haven't looked more than two hundred yards in front of me in twenty years." Many men are prisoners in a self-made jail. They have erected walls of exclusion about their minds. Jesus had no use for fences. Paul adduces the fact that Jesus broke down walls of partition as one of the surest evidences of his divinity. Our outlook is not God's when we take in any less circle of humanity in our interest than Jesus did.

Length to our thinking is a mark of God's outlook. "God does not pay every Saturday night." We chop time into convenient blocks, of sevens, thirties, and three sixty-fives. The middle of next week is the usual outpost of our thinking. With God's outlook the present moment partakes of eternity.

❧ ❧ ❧

DON'T UPSET THE APPLE CART!

He *upset* the tables of the money-changers.—*Matt. 21. 12* (Moffatt).

A VERY modern outlook to this word "upset." The money-changers had no objection to Jesus until he upset the cash drawer. And in that sensitive spot they represent a powerful section of the business world to-day. The worst crime a prophet can commit is to upset a cash register. Business has nothing but praise for the Christian religion—as

long as it does not really upset anything. But let
it dislocate even so slightly the flow of cash into
the till—and the modern prophet, and the church
which stands by him (if it does) will be in the
midst of the same hubbub which swarmed about
Jesus when he disturbed the profits of the Temple
Merchants' Mutual Protective Association.

One of the great liabilities of the church to-day
is that unintentionally and almost unconsciously it
may allow the injunction not to upset any of the
sacred tables of profit to shape its policies and
throttle its life. A new first commandment might
be written thus:

> A new commandment I give unto thee:
> Thou shalt not upset the apple cart.

These words fairly express the unconscious fears
and timidities of many a congregation. They express
the sense of a never-forgotten obligation to refrain
from collision with current economic traditions and
practices and with financial powers behind those
practices.

Sometimes the elevation of this commandment to
a place of first importance is due merely to an
affinity on the part of many in the church for the
good, the true, the beautiful (and the prosperous!).

Sometimes, however, the bonds which unite the
church to the powers that be in the economic world
are of a firmer nature. The church must go on.
Its overhead runs twenty-four hours a day and
each year seems to see an increase in the amount
of overhead that must be kept running. The under-
lying philosophy is not very different from that

piece of distilled prudence, "Don't bite the hand that feeds you." There is nothing so crude or simple as a deliberate betrayal of the gospel or cowardice in its presentation. The situation is far more complex and subtle and complicated than that.

But like the pressure of the atmosphere of fifteen pounds to the square inch on all of us, there is the ever-present pressure of the ruling ideas of the masters of the economic and business world and the situation of the church itself. That situation is complicated in thousands of instances by the fact that the church has given large hostages to the business world to further a building program. Millions of dollars of mortgages are held over churches. There are unpaid pledges of other millions of dollars. It is for the temporal interest of the church to avoid any disturbance in the placid calm of business prosperity. It is not to be wondered at that the first concern of a large number of trustees and other officials is for carrying through their venture successfully.

Hence there is a very strong feeling to this effect: "There is no use of us or our minister being quixotic. We can very well postpone playing on some notes of the Christian gospel until a more convenient season. Prudence is the better part of valor. *Don't upset the apple cart.*"

With the full organ of the great redemptive message of Christianity to sound in the world to-day, it is tragic if a church harps only on one monotonous string—"Play it safe." The gospel of Jesus is more than a counsel of prudent caution. It is a great message of redemption for the whole of life, redemption from every force that exploits or maims human life.

How can we be real disciples of a Master who upset the world, if we don't upset anything in such a world as ours?

❧ ❧ ❧

"THAT'S YOUR AFFAIR"

I am innocent of this good man's blood. It is *your affair!*—Matt. 27. 24 (Moffatt).

Four times in the trial of Jesus he was "handed over" to someone else on the plea that he was their affair. The high priests handed him over to Pilate. Pilate handed him over to Herod. Herod handed him back to Pilate. Pilate finally handed him over to the soldiers to be crucified, with a theatrical gesture of innocence and a weak whimper: "It is not my fault. That's *your* affair."

Twice the very words "your affair" are used— once by the high priests and elders to Judas when he brings back the thirty pieces of silver; once by Pilate to the Jews in this passage.

Anything to get Jesus off their hands was the motive. He was a thorny problem. Let someone else handle it. "Here, he is your affair"—each one said as he gave Jesus a push on to someone else. "You do something—anything." This passing of Jesus from one to another is the supreme instance of that circular game of side-stepping responsibility which is so painfully familiar and to which is given the slang name of "passing the buck." There is

no need to describe it; it is part of the daily picture
of life. Nearly every large organization can exhibit
it developed to the point of genius. The matter
at issue is found to belong to "some other department." The other department discovers that it
is really in the province of still another department.
And the game is on. Trying to locate responsibility and getting action becomes a life career.

Every time the words, "That's *your* affair," were
said they were a lie. Jesus was Pilate's affair. He
was the high priest's affair. He was Herod's affair.
Jesus is every man's affair. He cannot be side-
stepped. Men try to hand him over to the church
and evade any personal responsibility by saying,
"He is your affair." He cannot be made an organization matter. He is *your* affair.

The whole trial of Jesus is a looking glass for
humanity. In the play of motives that conspired
to bring Jesus to the cross, in the X-ray light which
the drama throws on human character, we see ourselves and our actions vividly portrayed.

Jesus presented to all these officials a situation
about which they would actually have to do something. And that was bothersome. They preferred
to stand from under any responsibility for so terrifying a thing as a decision. It is easy to judge
these struggling cowards, desperately searching for
an alibi—until we pause to think how often we do
the same thing. When moral responsibility comes
home to us, it is very common and comforting to
shove it on to someone else.

Take the appalling crime record in the United
States. You cannot get into that matter without
hearing on every hand echoes of this claim of

Pilate's, "That's your affair." The blame for
crime is put on the home, on the school, on the
laws, on the police, on the newspapers, on the
movies, on prohibition. Each group or institution
points a finger in some other direction and says:
"That's your affair. It is not my fault." With
the multiplication of accusations and evasions, there
seems less disposition to say: "It's *my* affair. It's
our affair. What can we do to redeem it?"

We do the same with war. We pass on the
responsibility around the circle with a vigorous
shove away from ourselves. That relieves us from
really doing anything about it. Men blame human
nature. They lament it but call for Pilate's wash
bowl and repeat his formula, "That's your affair."
They blame the diplomats; they blame the soldiers; they blame race; they blame trade. Then,
like the high priests, they hand Jesus over to the
government. They allow governments to decide
questions which cannot rightly be delegated to
government officials—the validity of the gospel of
Jesus. And Calvary goes on.

We play this sorry game of "round the circle"
with our personal failings and responsibilities. We
say to heredity: "I'm your affair. I'm not to blame
for my sins, you know. In fact, they are not sins
any more in this day of light. They are psychological tendencies. It's heredity." Or it's environment, an ever-ready scapegoat. Or it's the social
order. Someone has well said that in the face of
an obvious personal call or duty we make the prayer,
"What wilt thou have the social order to do?"
instead of Paul's unevasive response, "What wilt
thou have *me* to do?"

Two warnings among many from this bit of history may be singled out: 1. The whole spectacle is an exhibition of what happens when a man's mind can deal only with routine matters, but shrinks and sidesteps when a genuine moral problem which cannot be avoided comes up. 2. How different it would have been if someone had broken through this vicious circle of evasion and said: "Here, this is *my* affair. I'll stop this murder myself"! Pilate, Herod, Caiaphas, any one of them could have done it. How different our neighborhood, our world would be, if more breaks in the same sort of a vicious circle might happen; if we stopped passing on to others duties and tasks that we might do; if we were as intent on the building of the Kingdom as we are on the building of alibis! For the crucifixion of Jesus shows with a tragic light where this sort of thing leads. It always happens when no one says: "I'll take this upon myself. It's my affair."

❧ ❧ ❧

A STUDY OF MILITARISM

All the *regiment* round him.—*Matt. 27. 27* (Moffatt).

THE conduct of the Roman military force during the trial and crucifixion furnishes a good basis for a study of many characteristics of militarism in general. This is all the more valuable for an unbiased study, because, throughout the New Testament, soldiers, as a rule, appear in the most favorable light possible. The conduct specified here is not to be taken as characteristic of individual soldiers. The great body of military forces, being just a cross-section of the human race, varies as the race itself varies. It includes multitudes of the noblest men who have ever lived.

But there are characteristics of the strictly militaristic mind, of the system of militarism in government, which are revealed truly and clearly in the historical events of the crucifixion.

1. For one thing the military force never understood what the trial and crucifixion were all about. They did not get to the bottom of the issue at all. They did not bother. Theirs not to reason why, theirs but to jump in and settle it by force. Here was something bothersome to the established order. Suppress it! After it was all over there was a belated recognition on the part of one of the most intelligent of the officers that a tragic blunder had been committed. "Surely," he exclaimed, "this was the Son of God." Now, of course, it is not within the province of the soldier to pass upon the justice of the cause in which he fights. But it *is* a responsibility of militarism in control of the state—or as a predominant influence. And it is a characteristic that it does not bother to get to the bottom of issues. It is not concerned primarily with justice or human values. Above these it sets prestige— nationalistic self-assertion. The crucifixion shows with a white light what happens when justice and human values are forgotten in the determination of action.

2. The treatment of Jesus was marked by unnecessary cruelty and contempt—an abiding accompaniment of war and militarism everywhere.

3. We see the familiar "smoke screen" at work—the falsification of facts, so characteristic of waging war and inciting peoples to war. "We will *screen* you from punishment, if this is reported to the Governor" (Weymouth, Matt. 28. 14), the soldiers are told after the resurrection.

4. Then the military crowd lied about the whole thing—another familiar earmark of the technique of militarism. They noised about a story explaining the resurrection that was a barefaced lie. But that did not bother them so long as it contributed to the security of their caste and order. The "die-hard" militarist will not scorn any weapon that will discredit sincere workers for peace—lies, slander, invective, ridicule.

5. "They took the money" (Matt. 28. 15)—a symbol of the historic relation of the war system and the greed for profits.

It is the persistence of these characteristics in the militaristic mind which makes it such an unrivaled obstacle to loosening the grip of the war system on civilization and the establishment of the kingdom of God.

❧ ❧ ❧

CROWDING CHRIST INTO A UNIFORM

They put on Him a general's short crimson cloak.—*Matt. 27. 28* (Weymouth, 1st Edit.).

THESE words are symbolic of much that has happened in Christian history. In those tragic hours immediately preceding the crucifixion there

were many cruel indignities heaped upon Jesus.
But one of the crowning indignities was dressing
him up in the cloak of a Roman general. What a
piece of irony it was, to dress the Prince of Peace
in the trappings of a war lord! This indignity was
committed by the enemies of Jesus—if those who
had no understanding of him at all could be called
his enemies. But the same indignity has been
often forced upon Jesus by his friends and adherents,
and that wrong is still being done him.

All through the centuries Christ has been crowded
into a *general's uniform*. Each age has made violent wrenchings and distortions of Jesus to make
him fit the war lust of men and the interests of
militarism. In Pilate's day Jesus was put into the
scarlet cloak of a Roman general. Men no longer
use scarlet for war. To-day the color is khaki,
and Christ has been crowded into a khaki uniform
again and again. During the Great War there was
much loud talk about "Christ in khaki," and he
has been made the supporter and inciter of war.
Christ cannot be put into khaki. We may dress
up a mechanical figure and put the sentiments of
angry men into his mouth, but it is not Jesus.
Dean Inge in very vivid words has described how
this process has hidden the real Christ:

Institutional religion does not represent the gospel of
Christ, but the opinions of a mass of nominal Christians.
It cannot be expected to do more than look after its own
interests and reflect the ideas of its supporters. The real
gospel, if it were accepted, would pull up by the roots,
not only militarism, but its analogue in civil life, the
desire to exploit other people for private gain. But it
is not accepted.

But that is not the only uniform which has been fitted upon Christ. He has been dressed up in *ecclesiastical regalia*, smothered with vestments of church officialism. The living Jesus, the Divine Christ, has been lost again and again in the uniform of the ecclesiastical prince, the priest, the monk, the bishop, or any other conventional figure of religion. He has been interpreted as the spokesman for the interests of an intrenched system. By a crowning irony he has been so distorted that he has been made to stand for the very evils of loveless, petrified officialism, against which he contended all his life and which finally did him to death.

We are witnessing in our own day the curious process of dressing up Jesus in a new uniform. Naturally, it is the characteristic uniform of our time—*the business suit*. Jesus has been dressed up in a sack suit and interpreted as the founder of much that the business mind glorifies in our time. He has been pictured as the "go-getter," the "high-powered executive"—a fine man for president of the Chamber of Commerce. This outfitting of Jesus in a new uniform has been done with unconscious perfection by Bruce Barton in his chapters on Jesus, the world's greatest executive and the founder of modern business. But all such interpretations, even though intended as honor, are only another indignity to the real Jesus.

There is no need in the world greater than to strip away from the regal figure of Jesus everything that is foreign and let him stand out unhindered and undisguised!

❦ ❦ ❦

THE RESURRECTION AT THE CRUCIFIXION

Many of the saints who had fallen asleep *rose.*—*Matt. 27. 52* (Goodspeed).

CONSIDERED as a symbolic picture, the truth of this miracle has been attested through all the centuries. We have here the statement that, at the supreme moment of the sacrifice of Jesus on Calvary, the dead arose. It is profoundly true that whenever the spirit which Jesus manifested on Calvary finds expression in life—it shocks men into life. "Saints who have fallen asleep" arise. There is nothing which has proved so powerful an awakener as Jesus' spirit of sacrificial love incarnate in a personality. It plays havoc with cemeteries, whether in the church or out of it!

When God's springtime has seemed to come again to the church, and new tides of abounding spiritual life are set running, the miracle which has awakened the new life is the old, old miracle of Calvary. When Francis of Assisi took to the road and showed men the love of Christ in its genuineness and simplicity, there was startling awakening of life. It was so with the pioneer souls who began the modern missionary movement, Henry Martyn, William Carey, David Livingstone. "God's trumpet wakes the slumbering world," sings Samuel Longfellow in a stirring modern hymn. God's most effective trumpet is a sacrificial life which brings that love of Calvary freshly into view. Tertullian in the early days of the church expressed the miracle for all time, "The blood of the martyrs is the seed of the church."

How delicately the little verse entitled "Miracle" pictures this awakening of "sleeping saints"!

> "Ten thousand musics never could
>   Stir an image out of wood,
> But let love knock at the church door
> And saints in niches, gray with lore,
> Step from their halos to the floor,
> And laugh, and are alive once more."

There is a world of suggestiveness in the phrase, "saints who had fallen asleep." In depressed moments we feel there are an undue proportion of such sleepy saints in the church. How we long for a General Resurrection—a quickening into life—a new flood of energy!

Resurrection will always follow crucifixion. When anyone takes Jesus seriously, when the sacrificial love of Jesus, instead of being an airy nothing, becomes a local habitation and a name in a human life, that miracle always brings life to the dead. It was simply but effectively expressed in the remark of one student to another, quoted by Bertha Condé, "I've always known what the Bible says about it, but I never saw anyone before who had the nerve to live it. You've given my thinking a jolt."

That is the final hope, and the only hope of the kingdom of God; when that passionate, sacrificial love finds expression in a whole church the resulting miracle will be a quickened world.

✳ ✳ ✳

GOOD MORNING!

"Good morning!"—*Matt. 28. 9* (Goodspeed).

THERE is a touch of genius to Goodspeed's translation of the word "Hail," the first word of the risen Jesus, by the words "Good morning!" The word "hail" has passed out of our common speech as a spoken word. It is now a literary word, relegated to odes and elegies and national anthems. But the words "Good morning" are almost the most familiar words of daily life. To find them used on this highest peak of all history seems to relate Easter a bit closer to common life.

These words are Jesus' victorious greeting to humanity—"Good morning!" It was morning forever, *the* good morning, first among all the days that ever dawned or ever will dawn. Indeed, it was the first full dawn that ever rose on human life. The salutation embodies the truth of Harnack's words—"This grave was the birth place of the indestructible belief that death is vanquished and there is a life eternal."

It was "Good morning" for high and low—the same lifting hope for the furthest extremes of the race in estate and education. Place two instances of the foregoing statement side by side. Sir James Simpson was one of Great Britain's greatest scientists and surgeons. When his heart was broken over the death of his dearly loved little daughter, he had carved on her gravestone the text—"Nevertheless I live." At the other extreme of education the same radiant hope finds striking expression in one of the less known of the Negro spirituals. There is a thrilling and unexpected climax to the verses.   The song puts the question: "Who will be a-living when I am dead?" and proceeds to answer it in this fashion:

> "Trees will be a-living and a-waving
> When I am dead.
> Birds will be a-living and a-singing
> When I am dead."

And so it goes on until the listener feels utterly diminished—less than the grass, less than the dust. Then suddenly the song restores his spirit with a triumphant shout:

> "Who will be a-living when I am dead?
> *I will!   I will!*"

That jubilant "I will! I will!" is the response to the salute of Jesus to the world—"Good morning!"

The Easter "Good morning" of Jesus is the one great exclamation point of human life on which the height and depth of every joy depend.

> "Joy, shipmate, joy!
> Pleased to my soul at death I cry,
> One life is closed, one life begun,
> The long, long anchorage we leave,
> The ship is clear, at last, she leaps,
> Joy, shipmate, joy!"

Because of that one "Good morning" uttered nineteen hundred years ago every day may partake of its spirit. In Old Russia, on Easter day, after church service the exalted nobleman would without hesitation kiss his coachman three times on the lips, exclaiming, "Christ is risen." This was only a gesture, too soon forgotten, in most cases. But there was a true instinct behind it. The resurrection "Good morning" should be reflected in a new spirit of fellowship which transforms every day and every relationship.

❊ ❊ ❊

LET'S GO SOMEWHERE ELSE!

"Let us go *somewhere else*."—*Mark 1. 38* (Moffatt).

AT the very outset of the ministry of Jesus, as recorded by Mark, he evades two deadly dangers which have beset his cause ever since: he refuses to become *localized;* he refuses to become *institutionalized*. The future of Christ's church depends to a large degree on the measure to which the paralysis of those same two calamities can be avoided.

It was natural that the townspeople of Capernaum should say, "Stay here!" Jesus' healing had been a blessing to the town. His presence would become a permanent asset. He was among friends. What would be better than just to stay? To Jesus there was one thing better—the road to the world. He came not to be a town doctor but a world's Redeemer.

The play of those two same opposing forces in all life is artistically expressed in the verses of Josephine Preston Peabody,

"The little Road says, 'Go';
The little House says, 'Stay':
And Oh, it's bonny here at home,
But I must go away."[1]

Threatened, for the moment, by loving but mistaken hands which would have imprisoned him in a local provincialism, Jesus said, "Let's go somewhere else." In those words and in that spirit there was the universal destiny of Christianity, its unresting outthrust into all the world. It broke through the bounds of Judaism, broke out of the wider bonds of the Roman Empire, burst the bonds of Europe, across the Pacific. Christianity has lived because as each new frontier came into view, men with a spirit akin to their Master's have cried, "Let's go!" Always that preservation of Christianity as a world force has been won only by overcoming the seductive voices, which demanded, as on that first day at Capernaum, "Let's *stay*." How many snug little homes have had to be left behind! The little house has cried "Stay"—threatening to make of Christianity merely a local tradition. The whole history of the rebirth of the missionary passion in the nineteenth century is the struggle between Go and Stay. The Christianity which degenerates into provincialism and forgets the call of the road speedily becomes a mummy.

Jesus' departure from Capernaum, on the road that led eventually to Jerusalem, Calvary, and all the world, was a refusal to become *institutionalized*. The Prophet, the Teacher, the Redeemer, would

---

[1] From *The House and the Road*. Houghton Mifflin Company, publishers. Used by permission.

have been transformed into a kind of impersonal clinic, a hospital and dispensary. Another institution, a blessed one of course, but still an institution, in the town's life. That subtle danger is never completely escaped and has strangled the spiritual life and power of Christ's church again and again. Whenever Christianity has been expressed in a statement of doctrine, in a form of organization, and men say in satisfaction, "This just fits. Let's keep it this way forever," the institution begins to set like a plaster cast, throttling the spirit within. It is inevitably so. The Christian gospel is *yeast*, not concrete. It should ferment, upheave, grow, not solidify. The hope of the Kingdom depends on the persistence of the Spirit of Jesus, "Let's go somewhere else." When Christianity is identified with any form of organization, the organization is soon substituted for the inner life. Then the church becomes like the man who said to his soul: "Now we're all set. We have goods laid up for many years. We don't need to think, or to plan or to work or to worry." When he reached that stopping-place, of course, he stopped. His soul, his life was gone.

❧ ❧ ❧

DON'T GET PONDEROUS!

There were some scribes sitting there *pondering.—* Mark 2. 6 (Goodspeed).
Argued in their hearts (Moffatt).

JUST like owls blinking in strong sunlight! Here was something they couldn't quite grasp. Jesus had just healed a paralytic. That was bad enough from their standpoint—a breach of ecclesiastical etiquette. But he had done more—a shocking thing. He had said, "My son, your sins are forgiven." That set them pondering in a heavy, confused manner. The simile, "like owls," is more than fanciful. They were exactly that—wise owls—blinded by the fresh light which Jesus threw on life. They could find their way around in the dim region of legal distinctions; in the daylight of clear moral issues and spiritual values they were lost. They could only blink and ponder.

Jesus did not fit into any of the familiar pigeonholes in the scribes' minds. That was what bothered them. They had no ready ticket or label for him. They did not possess the power or the inclination to think about him, to grasp his meaning, to look at him as a human being, to discover him as a divine revelation. That achievement could not be done by pigeonholing and all their thinking was of the pigeonholing character.

It is a pernicious substitute for thinking. The mental operations in a great many minds are like the process in a railway mail car in which envelopes are tossed, with a marvelous mechanical dexterity due to long practice, into different sacks. New ideas and personalities are tossed into preconceived notions and prejudices, regardless of whether or not they fit. That was what the scribes did. They had a large, roomy pigeon-hole labeled "Blasphemy" and they immediately tossed Jesus into it. He was speaking a new language. Therefore it must be blasphemy.

That type of "thinking" unfortunately did not

pass from earth with the scribes of Jesus' day. It is the favorite and often the only exercise of lazy and narrow minds. It is responsible for the persistence of malignant prejudice of all sorts— race, class, and religious; and for the stagnation which keeps the world in ruts.

The pondering of the scribes never got beyond the business of rearranging legalistic precedents and traditions. When they "argued in their hearts" they never reached the realm of vital human need or spiritual realities. They did not live there. They pondered over quibbles. The deep need of the body and soul of this poor paralytic, which so moved the heart of Jesus, never touched them at all. They were fussing about some impertinent technicality. They missed the human values. Their estimate of life is as impertinent as the estimate of the Lincoln Memorial in Washington, which might be given by a statistical pedant. He could sum it up in a catalogue of the materials which went into it, so many tons of such and such kind of marble, arranged in such and such architectural patterns. It would all be true and utterly meaningless as an interpretation of the building. It would miss two things, both spiritual realities, the beauty of the structure and the moral values symbolized. Nor would it convey the "still small music of humanity" which sounded out over the world through Lincoln's great soul.

Philip Guedalla in his book, *The Second Empire*, has a memorable description of a latter-day scribe, one of the ministers of Napoleon III of France:

. . . He remained, as he had begun, a successful law-yer with a professional aptitude for detail and a forensic profusion of second-rate reasoning. Never at a loss for an argument and untroubled by the doubts which oppress finer, if less professional, intelligences, his burly figure dominated the Chamber and in the steady boom of his uninspired, his inexhaustible eloquence the later empire had found its accompaniment.[1]

Those words fit closely these scribes in the presence of Jesus—"A professional aptitude for detail and a forensic profusion of second-rate reasoning!"

Alas, how closely they fit the multitude who have, like the scribes, "nullified the law of God through their tradition"! Do they fit us? The whole scene whispers to us: "Don't get ponderous. Look what it leads to."

* * *

JESUS' VALUATION OF OBSTINACY

Hurt by their obstinacy.—Mark 3. 5 (Goodspeed).
In anger and vexation at their *obstinacy* (Moffatt).

THE word "obstinacy" does not occur in the authorized translation of the Gospels. But it has played an extensive and tragic part in Christian history. It did not find a place on the mediæval list of the seven deadly sins, but it deserves one on any list.

Goodspeed and Moffatt both substitute the word "obstinacy" for the words "hardness of heart" in

---

[1] Courtesy of G. P. Putnam's Sons, publishers, New York and London. Used by permission.

PREACHING VALUES 105

the King James version of this passage. The
meaning, of course, is much the same, but the word
"obstinacy" comes much closer home to us. It
is not so easy for us to escape with the plea, "Not
guilty."

The Century Dictionary makes a good prose-
cuting attorney in the case. Obstinate is "not
yielding to argument, persuasion or entreaty; a
strong and vicious or disobedient refusal to yield;
an unmanageable standing upon one's will." An
obstinate man will try to "carry out his intention
in spite of advice, appeals, remonstrance, or force."

Do you recognize any traces of a portrait of
yourself?

Obstinacy is a deadly sin for three reasons, at
least.

1. *It so easily passes for a virtue.* Who ever admitted he was obstinate? The trait has so many
disguises. It takes on virtuous airs as firmness,
perseverance, strength of will, loyalty, integrity.
The only sin which has so great a repertoire of
plausible disguises is covetousness. Montaigne
paints it in its true colors. "Obstinacy," he says,
"is one of the surest proofs of stupidity. Is there
anything so assured, resolved, disdainful, contem-
plative, solemn and serious as the ass?" Yet this
mental trait, which we share so generously, with
that typical "die hard," the donkey, passes itself
off on us as a virtue worthy at least of the *Croix
de guerre* or the martyr's crown.

2. *Obstinacy is a deadly sin because one rarely
gets over it.* It fastens on the vital centers of personality. It sinks deep. Its grip increases with
expression. Once in a while some rare soul grows

more reasonable, open-minded, and pliant with age, but the spectacle is so rare that we mark it with a double star. The usual process is to get more and more "set in his ways."

3. *It blocks such a wide variety of traffic.* There is not a project for the betterment of life, for an advance on any sector of the kingdom of God, which cannot be obstructed by plain, old-fashioned obstinacy. It has raised barricades on every avenue of human progress.

❧ ❧ ❧

JESUS CRUSHED BY THE CROWD

So he told his disciples to have a small boat ready; it was to prevent him being *crushed by the crowd.*—*Mark 3. 9* (Moffatt).

How often Jesus has been crushed by the crowd! He has been pushed out of a place of commanding influence, in a life or a community or a nation, by the sheer weight of multitudinous competing interests. He has been flattened out, in the minds of multitudes, till his teaching and purposes have only a shadowy, ghostlike existence.

It is a danger with peculiar intensity in our time, for the simple reason that never before were there so many different things to crowd into the mind like the contents of a ten-story department store. Mass production, both of material things and of ideas, lays upon the mind the necessity of a conscious and stalwart resisting power, if Jesus' interpretation of life and his estimate of values are to be preserved.

1. *The overcrowded mind* is a menace to Jesus'
formative influence on our personality and life.
The diversity of things tends to scatter the attention
and interest until life becomes helter-skelter and
hodge-podge through sheer lack of emphasis.   Just
through such a process, often quite unintentional
and sometimes unconscious, has Jesus been crushed
in many lives.   Big and little, vital and trivial, get
the same amount of attention.   By the overcrowded
mind is not meant a mind richly stored with knowledge.   No mind is ever overcrowded in that sense.
The more real knowledge a mind has, the stronger
its powers become.   The evil of an overcrowded
mind occurs when there is no selective power to
cast aside the trivial and focus on major issues,
just as a threshing machine tosses chaff to one side
and grain to the other.

2. *Mass thinking* is a cause of Jesus being crushed,
in that his distinctive way of life is lost.   The
modern demand for conformity, helped on by a
bewildering increase in the agencies for making
thinking standardized, results in flattening out
individuality.   The result of this process in America
is already seen in great multitudes of people whose
minds are about as alike as Ford parts.   Standardizing the thinking of the nation usually means
flattening it to a low level.   And as a result Jesus
is crushed.   Jesus is a mountain.   When he is leveled
until nothing is left of his ideals that rise above
the plane of "things as they are," he is lost.

His disciples, on that day when the crowd threatened to crush Jesus, took him away from the throng,
to a place where he could be seen and dominate
the crowd.   Only such a care on the part of Jesus'

disciples to-day to preserve and live his peculiar and uncompromising gospel will save it as a redemptive force in an age of mass thinking.

❦ ❦ ❦

THE ART OF SAYING GOOD-BY

After saying good-by to them he went up the hill to pray.—*Mark 6. 46* (Moffatt).

CAN you say "Good-by"? Jesus here illustrates it as one of the highest of the fine arts. When we say good-by it is so often wrung from us by compulsion. We have no other choice. So it is said grudgingly, reluctantly. Jesus said good-by to the crowd, to his public work, to the world, for a period, voluntarily and positively, in the interest of personal replenishment through prayer for larger service.

Unless we can learn to say good-by to things we must inevitably say good-by to the possibilities of largest power and influence. There used to be an old gospel song which had for its refrain, "We'll never say good-by in heaven." The weakness of many lives is that they never say good-by on earth; never get away from the milling of a throng of people or things, never get away to a solitude in which the deep springs that reinvigorate strength and clear the vision are opened up. Without that retirement, the mind becomes like the public waiting room of a railway station—a scene of bustling movement and confusion, not unified in any one object or purpose.

There is a quaint and beautiful custom in Russia for people who are starting on a journey and are leaving the house, to sit down and spend half a minute in silence. Life is just a series of journeys, short, sudden raids into the bustle of events and long marches. If it is to have either poise or carrying momentum, the only effective approach is from what corresponds to "half a minute's silence," when in communion with ourselves and God we can see it steadily and whole.

Our need of this art of saying good-by increases with the complexity and confusion of life. The very noise in which we pass our days disintegrates poise and power. Walter Lippman, in his book, *Public Opinion*, draws a realistic but not exaggerated picture:

Can anything be heard in the hubbub that does not shriek, or be seen in the general glare that does not flash like an electric sign? The life of the city dweller lacks solitude, silence, ease. The nights are noisy and ablaze. The people of a big city are assaulted by incessant sound, now violent and jagged, now falling into unfinished rythms, but endless and remorseless. Under modern industrialism thought goes on in a bath of noise. If its discriminations are often flat and foolish, here at least is some small part of the reason.[1]

The multiplying "shriek and glare" emphasizes as nothing else could the wisdom of Amiel's classic plea for the recreative powers of solitude and prayer:

We are too busy, too encumbered, too much occupied, too active! In an inaction which is meditative and attentive the wrinkles of the soul are smoothed away, and the

---

[1] The Macmillan Company, publishers. Used by permission.

soul itself spreads, unfolds and springs afresh, and, like the trodden grass of the roadside or the bruised leaf of a plant, repairs its injuries, becomes new, spontaneous, true and original.

Reverie, like the rain of night, restores color and force to thoughts which have been blanched and wearied by the heat of the day. With gentle fertilizing power it awakens within us a thousand sleeping forms, and, as though in play, gathers round us materials for the future.

Trader Horn, in that amazing story of a lifetime spent in tramping over savage Africa, called Trader Horn, says in commenting on the savage's utter dependence on his family and kin, "The savage when separated from his kind pines like a dog. The first thing education teaches you is to walk alone. Aye, you can sure stand on your own spear when *you've learned the word good-by and say it clear.*"

An imperious "good-by" is the only word which will save the soul alive. On our busy calendars of appointments there must be wedged in an appointment with ourselves, an appointment with God, against the conspiracy of modern civilization against our privacy. There must be a conspiracy with God, as Jesus conspired, ascending the hills of solitude that we may come down into the thronged plain of life with something to give. Without that approach to life, we become like the futile, flustered busybody of Colton's picture, quoted by Glenn Frank:

Like a turnstile, he is in everybody's way, but stops nobody; he talks a great deal, but says little; looks into everything, but sees nothing; and has a hundred irons in the fire, but very few of them are hot, and with these few that are he burns his fingers.

Jesus said good-by to friends, that in the reinvigorated powers of soul he might be a stronger friend; good-by to work, that he might return to do it better; good-by to the world, that he might overcome it and redeem it.

* * *

ARGUING WITH A TRAGEDY

When they reached the disciples they saw a large crowd round them, and some scribes *arguing with them.—Mark 9. 14* (Moffatt).

THAT was all the scribes could think of doing in the presence of heartbreaking suffering—argue about it! Coming down from the mount of transfiguration, Jesus finds the epileptic boy in the midst of a distressing seizure. The scribes are waging hot arguments with Jesus' disciples. The disciples, helplessly enough, were at least trying to do something to relieve him. The scribes were merely disputing with them, rushing eagerly from secondly to thirdly and fourthly.

That heartless argument of the scribes represents a permanent liability of humanity confronted by acute need—the danger of approaching it from the angle of a theory, of being lost in arid speculation when the demand is for sympathy and help. Emerson records a biting picture of a professional mind, more interested in analysis and speculation than in cure. "How is the patient to-day?" he once asked the village physician of Concord, concerning the minister, Doctor Ripley, lying at death's door. "It's the most correct apoplexy I ever saw," replied the physician. "Face and hands livid; breathing sonorous, and all the symptoms perfect." And he rubbed his hands with delight!

Correct apoplexy! Fine comfort for the patient and his family!

Argument has been a persistent reaction to tragedy. In the presence of some monstrous social evil decades of argument and fiery rebuttal have been engaged in as to whether the State or federal government should regulate it. What matter that the tragedy went on unchecked as long as the argument was engrossing? It has been the same with war. Men have even gone out to non-Christian lands and, in the very presence of appalling miseries, have allowed much of their energies to be dissipated in theological and ecclesiastical pitched battles.

There is only one Christian response to suffering —well expressed by Shakespeare's heroine Miranda, "Oh! I have suffered with those that I saw suffer." When that Christlike identification with need is made, there is no heart, mind or breath left for disputation. The cure for heartless argument has been perfectly pictured, strangely enough, by the author of the most terribly pessimistic poems in the English language, James Thomson, author of *The City of Dreadful Night*. Thus he describes a walk in London:

And I wandered about the city, the vast metropolis, which was become a vast necropolis. . . . Desolate indeed I was, although ever and anon, here and there, in wan, haggard faces, in wrinkled brows, in thin compressed lips, in drooping frames, in tremulous gestures, in glassy, hopeless eyes, I detected tokens of brotherhood, I recognized *my brethren in the great Freemasonry of Sorrow*.

Jesus was the Founder of that greatest of all fraternal orders, the Freemasonry of Sorrow.

Have you ever joined it?

✤   ✤   ✤

CONSECRATION BY DISCIPLINE

Every one has to be *consecrated by the fire of the discipline.—Mark 9. 49* (Moffatt).

CONSECRATION by *discipline!* It is a great word for an undisciplined age. No doubt it is a slander to call the present age undisciplined. But the description fits a large and very vocal element i-. the life of to-day. The cult of freedom has been exalted as the final wisdom of the ages. "Emancipation" is the watchword of the new salvation. "Discipline" is not a popular word. All the jargon of the truly "advanced thinkers" heaps scorn upon it—"Freedom to experiment," "I must live my own life," "escape from stuffy conventions." To the devotees of the cult of freedom life's only tragedy seems to be the suppression of instincts. Lady Mary Wortley Montagu reported in the eighteenth century a plan on foot for taking the "not" out of the Commandments and putting it in the Creed. That is a flash of feminine satire; but it represents the theory on which whole multitudes lived then and live now.

From another angle, the very idea of discipline is under fire. We live in the age of the short-cut. Mastery of an art, a science, a skill is long, toilsome, dull work. Cut across lots! Our magazines are full of screaming proclamations in the advertising pages that almost anything can be acquired in a few painless doses. "French in six lessons," so that we can astonish our friends by talking to the head waiter, and ordering salad dressing in its native language; fifteen minutes a day spent in the immediate vicinity of a set of leather bound books (bought on easy installments) makes hard study unnecessary; and to many the acquirement of a superficial line of chatter, composed largely of what are known as "wisecracks," is an acceptable substitute for culture.

Short-cuts to wealth are alluring for the same reason, as an escape from the discipline of toil, sacrifice, self-control.

The cult of comfort—the product of labor-saving mechanical genius—works against discipline as an ideal. Pushing electric buttons is so much easier than extending either muscles or minds. "Button, button, who's got the button?" has become our national game. A recent book on camping has the alluring title, Roughing it Smoothly. It promises to eliminate all the hardship and discomforts of life in the open. "Roughing it smoothly" well expresses a current national mood.

For such a day comes this word of Jesus, "Every one has to be consecrated by the fires of the discipline." The real mastery of self and the world can come only by the pathway of discipline. That great conception of life's highest significance, bound up in the word, "consecration," devoting it to a great purpose, depends on discipline for its fulfillment. Kipling has expressed this need in a noble prayer:

"Teach us to rule ourselves alway
Controlled and cleanly, night and day,
That we may bring, if need arise,
No maimed or worthless sacrifice."[1]

The discipline of Christ, however, is not some compulsion laid on from without, but a growth of mastery from within.

❧ ❧ ❧

JESUS MAKES A CHURCH SURVEY

And he came . . . into the Temple and *looked it all over.*—*Mark 11. 11* (Goodspeed).

HERE Jesus is engaged in an occupation very familiar to the church life of our day. He is making a church survey. Some twenty years or so ago someone hit upon the world survey as a name for appraisal and evaluation of conditions and the work of a social organization. Since that time it has been one of the hardest worked words in the language in America. Especially since the Great War have churches been beset before and behind

[1] "The Children's Song," from *Puck of Pook's Hill.* Copyright, 1905, 1906, by Rudyard Kipling. Doubleday, Page & Co., publishers. Used by permission.

with surveys. The familiar lines of the hymn, "Awake, My Soul," might well fit the modern church,

> "A cloud of witnesses around
> Hold thee in full survey."

Here Jesus walks through the Temple giving that religious agency an appraisal. What did he think of it? How did he estimate it, as a fulfillment of its purpose? How interesting it would have been to have walked with him. From what happened that day we may discern how deep his criticism went. He laid the actual conditions alongside of the original purpose. That was judgment enough. The original purpose he stated: "My house shall be a house of prayer." The drop from that use was literally immeasurable—"You have made it a den of robbers." When Jesus made a survey of how God's church was working—it went deep.

The trustees of the church had allowed two things to be done with it, which have been endlessly repeated in Christian history. They had allowed it to be *commercialized;* they had allowed it to be used as a *convenience*.

It stirs the imagination to picture Jesus making a survey of the church to-day. Not the church in general so much as any local church. It is so easy for us to escape general conclusions. No theme could be worth more clear honest thinking about, on the part of a congregation. How would Jesus go through our church life and work? What would he think about it? We cannot escape the probing question, "Would he recognize it as his own?"

One thing is sure, he would not be the sour, prowling critic who overhauls the church with raking fire every few days. Jesus loved the church. He loved the Temple. The depth of his judgment comes from the depth of his love. The most vital criticism of any institution always comes from a lover of it. It is inevitably so. Only love can see deeply enough and care strongly enough. Only love can know what the institution ought to be.

How would Jesus evaluate our church on the point of retaining his own emphasis? Are the things which were supremely great to him as supremely great to us? Or have we lost his proportions and pushed to the front things which he passed over? It takes honesty and humility to press that question home to ourselves. Our danger was well put by a candid European. "When you Americans get an idea," said he, "at once you make an organization. By the time you have the office organized and the secretaries working you begin to wonder what the original idea was."

Have we lost the "original idea" of Jesus, through the very machinery designed to promote it? An art critic has made a very pointed observation on the over elaboration of detail by Velasquez. He says that it is not easy, in looking at an Infanta by Velasquez, to focus attention on the face, so absorbed is one in the "cascade of crinolined embroidery." Have we ever made it hard for men to "focus" on the face of Jesus Christ by an emphasized "cascade of crinolined embroidery" of ecclesiasticism? The classic story of the artist Whistler points the same searching question. Looking at the work of a pupil drawing a portrait of an old woman holding a candle he said, enigmatically, "How beautifully you have painted the *candle!*"

How would Jesus appraise the church on the score of daring, on the score of breadth of love?

❧ ❧ ❧

THE SOPHISTICATION OF JESUS

He *saw their trick.—Mark 12. 15* (Moffatt).

AN interesting Rogues' Gallery could be made up of the men who tried to fool Jesus! The inventive genius demonstrated in the intricate snares prepared for him commands high intellectual respect. Yet something always went wrong. He saw their trick! This Galilæan peasant, this simple-minded innocent, as they thought, somehow turns out too sophisticated to be trapped.

One of the eternal fascinations of Jesus is in his uniting characteristics and qualities usually violently opposed or mutually exclusive. Jesus had faith in men, but he was never "taken in." He had a keen eye for the worth of men. He believed in the possibilities of certain men when no one else did. But he had the keenest eye for "tricks" that ever looked into the souls of men.

Many people fail either on one side or the other. They are like the leaning tower of Pisa, out of plumb in some direction. They are either gullible or else cynical. Jesus was neither.

He presents a fine picture, in a day when we badly need such a picture, of a noble *sophistication*. He "knew his way around" both in the obscure recesses of human nature and the tangled lanes of logic. The word "sophistication" has an enormous vogue in our time. The adjective "sophisticated" is worn as though it were a medal of honor. The chest is thrown out like that of a pouter pigeon. But when closely examined, this ideal of "sophistication" is composed of very tawdry stuff. It is usually made up of an intensive knowledge of a small slice of life (and a trivial slice at that), an ignorant contempt for all of life outside of that slice, and a strange mixture of conceit and an affectation, at least, of cynicism for humanity in general.

Such sophistication regards itself as cosmopolitan; as a matter of fact, as Booth Tarkington has dexterously shown, it is always provincial. In his novel, *The Plutocrat*, Mr. Tarkington thus lets the air out of the balloon:

Sophistication is always provincial, because nobody can know intimately a great deal about the whole world. The greatest cosmopolitan knows a little about a great many parts of it and can adapt himself to many kinds of people; but in his one lifetime he can't become a sophisticate among the Kabyles and among the Esquimaux and the Patagonians and Samoans and Javanese and Japanese and Russians and Portuguese and Chinese and Sicilians and Spanish and the French and Germans and Italians and English and Americans. A lifetime isn't long enough, my friend. Cosmopolitanism is a little knowledge about many places and kinds of people; sophistication is a great deal of knowledge about one place and one kind of people.[1]

As opposed to this kind of affected sophistication contrast the wisdom of Jesus. He truly united the

[1] Doubleday, Page & Co., publishers. Used by permission.

wisdom of the serpent with the guilelessness of the dove. He was never imposed upon by pretentious frauds or led astray by verbal tricks, as we so often are. Consider some of the commonest "tricks" of specious reasoning which befuddle so many.

1. Take that old, old trick called the "fallacy of the false alternative." What confusion it has led to in Christian history!

Thus we are called upon to choose between two alternatives when both are false and we should take neither, or when both are true and we should take both. We are told by doctrinaires that we must choose either faith or reason, either God or law, either Christianity or evolution, either individual or social gospel. It is not a question of "either or" but of "both . . . and." To imagine that we must choose either one or the other exclusively is to be fooled by a trick.

2. *The delusion of the explanation.* Many in this age of expanding knowledge imagine that when they have explained how a thing works they have explained the thing itself.

3. Many people to-day are helpless before the trick of substituting an epithet or an adjective for an argument. Tell them that religion is "old-fashioned," or "traditional," or a "fairy tale for naïve minds," and they become so paralyzed that their mind resigns. They throw over their faith, for "one must be modern" at all costs!

4. *The fallacy of the majority* acts on the minds of many like chloroform. What "everybody" thinks must be right. At least, it is fashionable, and that is the only meaning the adjective "right" has in many quarters. To have a conviction that

cuts across the grain of current customs and clamors, would make one seem "queer." And as Dr. Henry Sloane Coffin has said, the one commandment which many people really obey in these days is: *Thou shalt not be queer.*

Should not the imitation of Jesus include his detection of tricks?

❧ ❧ ❧

AN ANSWER TO THE POINT

Then one of the Scribes . . . knew that Jesus had given them *an answer to the point, and a forcible one.*— *Mark 12. 28* (Weymouth).

HERE is a new approach to the appeal of Jesus to men—the force of his sheer common sense. Here was a man evidently indifferent to Jesus until he listened to the Sadducees trying to bait him. All the scribes were not pedants and bigots. Here was one with an open mind. Before the clear, forcible reasoning with which Jesus answered the malicious quibbling of the Sadducees every possible bar against Jesus in this man's mind goes down. Pursuing his study of Jesus further, his mind and that of Jesus meet in agreement, and Jesus returns the scribe's tribute with the praise, "Thou art not far from the kingdom of God."

This scribe's response to Jesus' conduct of an argument indicates an effective way of presenting Jesus to a large number of people. The compelling approach to people of this class, thoughtful, open-minded, but entirely outside the circle of Jesus' disciples, is not through emotion, sentimentalism, or fear or authority. It is in the demonstration of the truth that *Jesus brings pointed and forcible answers to great questions* which cannot be evaded, such as the existence and nature of God, the meaning and destiny of life and the goal of human effort.

⚜ ⚜ ⚜

JUMBOISM

"Look, teacher, *what a size* these stones and buildings are!"—*Mark 13. 1* (Moffatt).

THIS exclamation of the disciples, awed by the bigness of the Temple, sounds both very human and remarkably modern. They reflect our awe and reverence for bigness of whatever sort. Perhaps it may not be amiss to call this a peculiarly American text!

Jesus was never overawed by size or bulk. No doubt that is one thing which makes him a baffling personality to many people. Our most delirious enthusiasms are often reserved for the biggest. "Bigger and Better" is assuming the proportions of a gospel. Jesus was unimpressed by the mere size of anything, whether buildings, money, crowds. He had a deeper interest—quality. He weighed the Temple and found it wanting, in spite of its size. Size was no substitute for poor quality of vision or service.

Our obsession with size might be considered either as a national disease or a religion or both. "Jumboism" is a good name for it. One of the most famous animals which ever lived was P. T. Barnum's elephant, Jumbo. His fame rested on one thing. He was the biggest elephant in captivity. He may have had other endearing and noble qualities. If so, they were never widely known. He was the biggest. That was enough.

That is enough for many of us. The city with the biggest population, the man with the biggest fortune, the actor with the biggest salary, the store with the biggest sales, the preacher with the biggest crowd—these are the ones to which popular interest and acclaim run. They are the Jumbos before which the crowd bows.

Booth Tarkington puts this worship into realistic form, in this imagined prayer of a growing industrial city:

"Give me of thyself, O Bigness,
  Power to get more Power;
  Riches to get more riches;
  Give me of thy sweat to get more sweat;
  Give me of thy bigness to get more Bigness for myself.
  O Bigness, for thine is the Power and the Glory
  And there is no end but Bigness for ever and ever.
  Amen."[1]

This awe of size may be well symbolized in a characteristic modern machine—the adding machine. It typifies an attitude toward life which is destructive to the life of the spirit. It is a marvelous invention. The principal trouble with it is that so many people try to make it do things it cannot do. It can add up dollars and things. It can never

---

[1] From *The Turmoil*, by Booth Tarkington. Doubleday, Page & Co., publishers. Used by permission.

add up life or express its meaning, because it deals only with quantity. The worship of the adding machine is the enemy of personality when it results in a person's substitution of quantity for quality. Such a confusion is a pernicious danger to the church in the insidious temptation it brings to measure success in columns of things to be added. For then the church uses precisely the words of the disciples of Jesus—"Look, Master, what a size!"

The church is in continual danger of measuring achievement in terms of size, of crowds, for instance. Whenever it does so, it always parts company with Jesus' valuations. Jesus was never impressed with the cry, "Look, what a size!"

One Sunday in September more than six hundred thousand people paraded up and down the boardwalks of Coney Island.

What a stupendous crowd! That is a larger number of people than engaged in all the crusades of Europe in the Middle Ages. It is a larger number of people than have gone out as missionaries of the Christian faith since the resurrection morning.

What did such an enormous crowd mean? The answer can be given pretty largely in one word— *peanuts*. It meant nothing! That massive crowd walked up and down the thoroughfare eating peanuts and popcorn and went home again. It was not a crowd with any natural unity. It was not a crowd with any purpose. It was just a crowd.

That crowd of over half a million is well worth thinking of in an age beset with the fundamental vulgarity of confusing the size of a thing with its significance. A crowd, taken just as a crowd, with not much regard for its purpose, its quality, or its influence, usually means as little as a Coney Island crowd means.

One of the greatest dangers which the church faces is the continual danger of becoming merely a Coney Island crowd instead of a company of twelve disciples. It is instructive to recall that Jesus feared few things as much as he feared crowds. He knew that the five thousand who got a free dinner made a trivial gathering when compared in influence with the twelve people on whom he so lavishly expended himself.

*   *   *

THE APPALLING HORROR

The appalling Horror standing where he had no right to stand.—*Mark 13. 14* (Moffatt).
The dreadful desecration (Goodspeed).

WHATEVER may have been the exact meaning of the phrase translated in the King James and Revised Versions of the New Testament as "the abomination of desolation," there can be no question of what the supreme abomination is in the world to-day. Goodspeed translates it "the dreadful desecration"; Moffatt calls it "the appalling Horror." Both are vivid and yet restrained descriptions of *war*. War is the appalling horror "standing where it has no right to stand," in the very center of civilization, a devastating explosive force.

Can we think of the four years' nightmare, 1914–1918, and not yield to war this crowning distinction of being the appalling horror? One vast conflagration, four and a half years long, spreading over three continents; one half of the accumulated wealth of the world destroyed; ten million soldiers killed, more hate concentrated than in any previous period in human history.

That is merely a tithe of the cost. War used to be an affair of armies and navies; now it is a slaughter of whole peoples.

We may give it the worst name we can think of. (That was literally what this term was—the most odious and terrible name the prophet's imagination could devise.) Yet when we are through we must realize that all previous war has been merely practice, bungling and amateurish, compared to what can be done in the slaughter of the future. The chemical warfare service of the United States government has opened the veil of the future to cheer us up with this glimpse. It has developed a liquid approximately three drops of which when applied to any part of the skin will cause a man's death. One plane carrying two tons of the liquid could deposit material enough to kill every man in a large area by action of the skin.

In one of Joseph Conrad's powerful stories, *The End of the Tether*, the central figure is an old man crouching at the wheel of the vessel whose command he will not relinquish although he has gone blind. It is a true picture of the war system clinging to its grip on the world.

That grip can be broken only by moral and spiritual force. The old notion that to build ship against ship and gun against gun and fort against fort was the way to secure peace has been discredited. The world knows now that men cannot make peace while they have war in their hearts.

To offset this perversion of science men and nations must set their hearts, their minds, and their wills toward lasting peace. Skeptics will meet the believer at every step of his way and tell him that his is a useless mission. But so might any proud Roman, with his cynical culture behind him, have spoken to the twelve humble men in Judæa two thousand years ago. Yet the "pale Galilæan" conquered the material empire. What the friends of peace need to-day is the faith and the spirit of those simple men who made that conquest possible.

        * * *

DIED OF HEARTBREAK

Jesus uttered *a loud cry* and yielded up his spirit.— *Mark 15. 37* (Weymouth).

DR. ERNEST F. SCOTT thus comments on the actual death of Jesus on the cross:[1]

Jesus died long before the time which was usual in crucifixion, and perhaps his death was not wholly due to the effects of the torture following the terrible strain of the preceding days. The loud cry with which he died seems to betoken a sudden spasm, and the fourth evangelist tells us that when a spear was thrust into his side after death there issued what appeared to be mingled blood and water. It has been conjectured, on medical grounds, that the *immediate cause of his death was a rupture of the heart.*

---

[1] *The First Age of Christianity*. The Macmillan Company, publishers. Used by permission.

The italics are ours. The conjecture is so striking
to the imagination that it is well worth the emphasis
of italics. We speak, in reference to the deep significance of the death of Jesus, of "the heartbreak
on Calvary." It is very suggestive to find the
medical conjecture that Jesus died of actual, physical heartbreak. That heartbreak is a vivid physical
symbol of the spiritual reality of the atonement.

❧ ❧ ❧

LIVING ON TIPTOE

She . . . gave thanks to God and spoke about the
child to all who were *living in expectation* of the liberation of Jerusalem—*Luke 2. 38* (Goodspeed).

A FINE way to live—in expectation of liberation!

There existed a definite class of people in the
Israel of Jesus' day consisting of sentinal souls who
lived in the expectation that something was going
to happen. And the very expectation that God
would do something helped immeasurably to make
it happen. For that group of people were the seed
plot in which Jesus' message first took root. They
received him because they were looking for him.

It is such sentinel souls who make possible the
liberation of mankind from the grip of ancient
wrong. Nothing really great ever happened without a great many lives being lived "in expectation."
Arthur J. Gossip says finely:

They are the kind of folks by whom the world moves
forward: who live in a *qui vive* of expectancy, always
standing on tiptoe, always sure that something big may

happen at any time. Hush! Is not this it coming now?
With people like that God can do anything. But you
and I keep thwarting him by sheer dullness of spirit.
We are listless, apathetic, blasé, bored; our hopes are
small and thin. There is no audacity in our expectation.[1]

Lorne Pierce traces the same truth back to the
Old Testament:

A. B. Davidson once called the prophets "always terribly one-sided people." That single idea was that "God
is going to do something." "God is surely coming!"
cries Isaiah. "He is here, at our very door!" answers
Zephaniah. And so each and every one by their faith
made it possible, yea, certain, for some great spiritual
surprise to take place. It is upon this that the rest is
builded: "And when the time was fulfilled—Jesus came."
Did it ever happen otherwise? Truth is an emperor that
only comes to visit his subjects along the highway of
great longing. Science advances to its kingdom along
the avenues of expectancy. Religion comes into its own
along the road of loving hearts, that great-hearted clan
of intrepid believers.[2]

But not all of Christ's followers feel this quickened
pulse beat of expectant faith.

Some are *asleep*.

Some are *satisfied*. Their eyes never wistfully scan
the horizon. Their hearts are never hungry.

Some are looking but they are *looking back*.
The golden age for them is in the past. For some
reason yesterday belonged to God but not to-
morrow. They say good-by to sunsets but never
welcome a dawn.

---

[1] *The Galilean Accent*. Charles Scribner's Sons, publishers. Used
by permission.
[2] From *In Conference with the Best Minds*. Cokesbury Press,
publishers. Used by permission.

There is an even deeper meaning in the words "living in expectation" than appears on the surface. It is this: only as we live in expectation do we truly live at all.

Are our spirits on tiptoe or stretched on a couch? There is one easy way to learn the answer. What is our habitual attitude to the world's "impossibles," to the great dreams of men—the abolition of war, the coming of brotherhood, the curbing of greed, the exploitation of the unprivileged? Do we live, and work, in eager expectation of these things?

❧ ❧ ❧

A GOOD TIME TO PRAY

It was *in these days* that he went off to the hillside to pray. He spent the whole night in prayer.—*Luke 6. 12* (Moffatt).

WHAT days?

The words immediately preceding these are: "This filled them [the Pharisees and scribes] with fury, and they discussed what they could do to Jesus."

Jesus had just healed a paralyzed man on the Sabbath day and had met the hard, inflexible, closed mind of the scribes and Pharisees. It was a turning point in his ministry. The opposition to him becomes a conspiracy to kill him. It was definitely established that he could not win them by any means. Their hearts were as hard as their heads.

Then it was that he spent the whole night in

prayer. No doubt we should not press too hard the significance of the night in prayer following after this conflict with the Pharisees. Immediately following the night he chooses his twelve disciples. That great step surely had its relation to a night of prayer. Yet the two events in the record, the stubborn and vindictive opposition and the whole night of prayer, have an important relation—and a warning. When this attitude of the Pharisees appeared, Jesus recognized one of the deadliest and most formidable enemies of the Kingdom. Whenever we feel in ourselves or see at work in others anything akin to the attitude and mood and mentality of these scribes and Pharisees, we too ought to recognize it for the malign and terrifying thing it is, one of the chief obstacles to the Kingdom. It was something Jesus could do absolutely nothing with in the Pharisees. He can do absolutely nothing with it in us.

For that mentality of the Pharisees is not a thing very far away from plain, everyday stubbornness that we know so well. Jesus' action was opposed to their tradition. That settled it. Jesus was a new fact in their experience. They had no eyes for new facts. They loved their tradition, their habitual ways of thinking, better than facts. They loved it better than men. Their hearts had not a single twinge of sympathy for the cripple. There was not a trace of common, elementary, human emotion rejoicing over a cured man.

Two characteristics of this mental condition which was Jesus' supreme obstacle stand out glaringly.

1. They had no *flexibility*. Their minds were like

Babylonian tombs, rooms hewn out of rock on which were carved cuneiform inscriptions. Nothing could grow there. Oliver Cromwell once cried out to the Parliamentarians, "For the love of Christ, gentlemen, I beseech you to think that it is possible that you may be mistaken." These Pharisees and their many spiritual descendants could not do any thinking of that type. Edward Carpenter in his autobiography, *My Days and Dreams*, describes a man as "having swallowed a principle like a poker, he would remain absolutely unbending and unyielding." These opponents of Jesus had swallowed their tradition exactly like a poker.

2. There was no warm fire of sympathy, or identification with humanity in their minds. They had catalogued life rather than experienced it— an error unfortunately rather common. Instead of warm, pulsing hearts they had legal storerooms. H. G. Wells has described exactly the mental furnishing of the Pharisees, in writing of a character in *The World of William Clissold*.

His mind was like some great furniture depository, safe from fire, corruption, or admixture; nothing seemed to happen in it, and nothing ever got lost in it, and he could, with every appearance of pleasure, reproduce the most commonplace facts at any time at the fullest length and in the completest detail.[1]

Whenever we feel any symptoms like these—it is a good time to pray.

[1] Copyright, 1926. George H. Doran Company, publishers. Used by permission.

❧ ❧ ❧

GETTING INTO THE PAST TENSE

Alas for you who are rich, for you *have had* your comfort!—*Luke 6. 24* (Goodspeed).

THE worst accident which can happen to a person is to get into the past-perfect tense. "Have had"—there is a crack of doom about the words. It's all over. There is nothing more.

The most charmed words in human speech are those which frequently irritate us in reading a serial story: *"Continued in our next."* For the glory of life *is* that it is a serial story. When it ceases to be a serial it ceases to be life. When there is no expectancy, when there is no "next" to look forward to and prepare for, when we have majored on the things which end with the consuming, we have wandered into that "never, never land"—and a desert land it is—the Past Tense.

Getting into the past tense—as Jesus uses the tense here—is not to be confused with old age. Jesus was not talking about old age. Age does not lose the future. The tragedy of the past tense goes far deeper than that. It is not anything so superficial as the number of years. It is the tragedy of absorption in things that wind up completely— that have no mysterious remainders. Wealth is one of the most obvious of such dead ends. A person devoted to material accumulation plays a part in life like those characters who get killed in the first act. They fall into the past tense before the real plot unweaves.

One of the reasons for the great hold of the drama of *Faust* on the imagination of men is that it is so true a transcription of human experience.

We have the terrible choice of either grasping things that can be completely encompassed, and so inevitably land us in the past tense, or of pursuing things which move on to ever new horizons.

Robert S. Hillyer has a little poem, terrible in its bleakness, describing an abandoned farm in New England, which accurately pictures the devastation in any life which has gotten into the past tense!

"Shutters bang in the wind outside;
   Cobwebs hang from the mildewed walls;
Stale, damp mould in the lifeless cold;
   Doors flung wide to the darkened halls.

"Love and strength of the new keen race
   Lie full-length where the weeds grow high,
All things swept to the past, except
   This ruined place the wind roars by.

"Blank disaster of empty windows;
   Broken plaster strewn on the floor;
Darkness spills from the wild, bleak hills
   And the winter wind blows under the door."[1]

The glory of life is in its expectancy. Marmont said of Napoleon, "There is so much future in his mind." It has been characteristic of great souls, such as Paul, who have had a far nobler future than Napoleon's in their minds.

It is not merely in materialistic choices that we run the danger of getting into the past tense. There is the same danger in a cosy dogmatism, that leaves no room for the additions of experience; in a finished

---

[1] From *The Hills Give Promise*. B. J. Brimmer Company, publishers. Used by permission.

aim in life; a "fixed" character, or in a religious experience which has petrified.

There is a very common noun which describes getting into the past tense—*death*.

❧ ❧ ❧

EXPERTS

The . . . *experts* in the Law thwarted God's purpose for themselves.—*Luke 7. 30* (Goodspeed).

AND for everybody else! *Expert* is a favorite modern word. But the expert is not a modern invention. Here he is, face to face with Jesus, a man with voluminous technical information and the slenderest stock of broad human wisdom; able to delve into prodigious researches into the traditions of Jewish ecclesiasticism, unable to grasp elementary spiritual realities, or the significance of a personality like Jesus.

The expert is abroad in the land. And of many of to-day's "experts" the comment of Jesus on some experts of his time is true—"they thwart God's purpose for themselves." We may add— "and for others also."

These words of Jesus are not to be twisted into a disparagement of genuine knowledge or science. Jesus was not disparaging knowledge. The "expert" of his scornful description was the man whose legalistic refinements nullified God's law. There are many experts in our own day who thwart God's purpose for humanity. There is the expert who has mastered the details of one branch of learning and mistaken it for an explanation of the whole universe. He conforms exactly to the classic comment on the English scientist Whewell—"His forte was science; his folly omniscience." There is the expert who builds an imposing theory on insufficient data or wrongly interpreted data. There is the expert who blithely leaves out of view a whole body of facts which do not fit in with the theory he is constructing.

Carlyle gave a picturesque description of one of this class of experts. "He is a slightly impertinent man with several dictionaries about him but with small knowledge of God's universe."

There is the *psychological* expert (not to be confused with all psychologists, by any means) who expounds a materialistic "behaviorism." He bows the soul out of the universe and by counting and describing nerve cells, molecules, atoms, and electrons imagines—or pretends—that he has explained the mind and soul of man.

Albert E. Wiggam's conclusion is fairly representative of the tribe: "The universe stands revealed at last in all its gaunt nakedness, as a mere machine without sympathy or purpose."[1] Anyone who by prestige or the pressure of intellectual fashion imposes that conception of the world on others is "thwarting God's purpose" as revealed in Jesus.

Take a few examples at random:

Dr. Irwin Edman, of Columbia, teaches that "man is a mere accident." George Santayana, the author, makes man "a little luminous meteor in an infinite abyss of

---

[1] From *The New Decalogue of Science.* Copyright, 1922–1923. Used by special permission of the publishers, The Bobbs-Merrill Company.

nothingness; a rocket fired on a dark night." Everett Dean Martin maintains that "religion is primarily a defensive mechanism," while Professor John Watson, of Johns Hopkins, asserts that the soul, consciousness, God, and immortality are merely mistakes of the older psychology. Bertrand Russell, the high priest of mechanism, wails "that man is the product of causes which had no prevision of the end they were achieving; that his origin, his growth, his hopes and fears, his love and his belief, are but the outcome of accidental collocation of atoms; that only on the firm foundation of unyielding despair can the soul's habitation be safely built."[1]

Then there is a vastly different type of expert—of the same variety that Jesus was speaking of—the ecclesiastical expert. He is the leader so intent and fussy over ecclesiastical procedure, manipulations of church machinery, animated over superficial issues, and with what Carlyle calls "explosions of all the upholsteries," that the great matters of the law such as mercy and justice in human relations receive but scant attention. He too grievously thwarts God's purpose.

Their name is legion—the *anthropological* "expert," whose labored arguments for the inherent superiority of the so-called Nordic races over all others of God's creatures thwarts God's purpose of human brotherhood; the *military* expert, whose technical impossibles block the movement of the human race toward peace.

A little learning is a dangerous thing.

---

[1] From *The New Decalogue of Science*, Copyright, 1922-23. Used by special permission of the publishers, Bobbs-Merrill Company.

❧ ❧ ❧

A TRINITY OF SUFFOCATION

The message is stifled by the *anxieties, wealth, and gayeties* of time.—*Luke 8. 14* (Weymouth).

HERE is the only Trinity of which many people have any real experience: a trinity of suffocation; anxieties; wealth and gayeties. These are three very different things—anxieties and gayeties seem at the very opposite poles of human emotion and experience. But they are strangely alike in their effect—they suffocate the spirit. In that respect their effect is much like the frequent effect of the application of ice or fire to the skin—they both feel the same. They give the same shock to the nerves in spite of a difference of one hundred degrees of temperature. So these three enemies of the spirit —as different as human experiences can be—"stifle the message," as these words of Jesus declare. They suffocate the soul.

Anxieties do it for more of us than either of the other two. Most of us do not have wealth. With most of us, our "gayeties" are a rather slight and pathetic array. But anxieties are the very atmosphere we breathe. In a very real respect they are an essential to sensitive life. They need not asphyxiate the spirit. They do so only when we have not acquired the art of selective attention, when we allow a flood of concerns to assume the same magnitude. The person suffocated by anxiety cannot take out of the central place in his mind any fears, irritations, worries. He is like a radio set without any selective power in which six or eight jazz bands destroy any melody, any harmony that might be won through concentration. Jesus brought the

great secret of preventing suffocation through concentration—"Seek ye *first* the kingdom of God."

Wealth, or the vain pursuit of it, can stifle the
message of life. It need not necessarily do it, but
the process by which it does is one of the commonest spectacles of our time. That process is
pictured strikingly in Frank Norris' novel, *The Pit*,
in which a grain speculator is trapped in a wheat
elevator and buried in an avalance of wheat. Here
was the means of supporting life, the wheat, becoming the agency of destroying it. The high purpose
of life is obscured with the clutter of its material
accessories. Emerson put it in a single sentence,
"The worst thing about money is that it so often
costs so much." So life loses its deep significance;
its spiritual flame is snuffed out.

When gayety becomes a conscious pursuit it becomes chloroform.

There is only one preventive against this trinity. Jesus described it in this very passage. "But
as for that in good ground, it means those who,
having listened to the message with open minds
and in a right spirit, hold it fast and patiently yield
a return" (Weymouth).

❧ ❧ ❧

"GET OUT!"

Then all the people of the neighborhood of Gerasa
asked him to go away from them, for they were terribly
frightened.—*Luke 8. 37* (Goodspeed).

IT would be very instructive to make a list of the

people who said to Jesus, "Get out!" It would provide not merely a study in New Testament history but likewise a picture of many forces in present-day life. For the burden of the world's attitude to Jesus in many areas of life to-day is exactly the same as in many towns of Galilee and Judæa. It can be expressed in two words—"Get out!"

1. The people of Capernaum threw Jesus out of town (Luke 4. 29). He had healed a man and challenged their traditions.

2. The people of Gerasa cried feverishly, "Get out!" They were afraid for their property and the placid order of their town. His coming had been the occasion of the loss of property. They preferred pigs to a miracle-worker.

3. Herod told Jesus to "get out." His ideas did not suit the purposes of the government, Herod being the government.

4. A Samaritan village kept him out. They had a violent, ineradicable prejudice against his race.

Here were four instances of people who threw Jesus out of their town, and as far as possible out of their life and affairs.

The same four antagonisms to Jesus operate powerfully to-day. Jesus is told to get out because his teachings run counter to sacred traditions and practices; because they would reduce business profits, if applied; because they challenge some purposes of governments; because they condemn cherished race and class and nationalistic prejudices.

❧ ❧ ❧

THE BLUNDERING CHURCH

How long must I . . . *bear with you?—Luke 9. 41*
(Moffatt).
How long must I . . . *put up with you?* (Goodspeed.)

THE ninth chapter of Luke is a wonderful portrait panorama of the problems which Jesus had
with his disciples, the blunders, the dullness and
the failings with which they continually confronted
him. It is also a panoramic picture of church history and of present-day church life. For the problems which the disciples presented to Jesus are the
same ones which the church at one time and another
and in one way or another presents. If Jesus was
driven to the point of asking them, "How long
must I put up with you?" must he not ask the
same question over us?

In the short space of this one chapter there are
nine separate occasions where the disciples exhibited
an attitude or engaged in an action which illustrated
a failure to share his spirit or his purpose. Each
of these nine situations is paralleled in the common
everyday life of the church to-day.

1. *"Send the crowd away."* This was the only
solution which the disciples had for the need of a
hungry crowd. Get rid of them somehow. Why
should we worry? It isn't our affair. It is exactly
the spirit of many of Jesus' disciples to big human
need to-day—"Send them away."

2. *"Who am I?"* Jesus asks them. And some of
his disciples make replies indicating a failure to
grasp the real significance of Jesus in the world.
To-day, in deeds, if not in the words, we often deny
the lordship of Jesus over life.

3. *"Let's stay on this mountain."* The conception of Christianity as a selfish emotionalism unrelated to human need.

4. *Failing to heal the paralytic at the foot of the mountain.* An instance of failing to supply the resources of God for the world's evils.

5. *Failing to understand the approaching suffering and death of Jesus.* How common it is for Jesus' disciples to overlook the demand for sacrificial living! The twelve shrank from the hard way. So do we.

6. *The dispute about who should be greatest.* What a glorious history Christianity would have had if this had been the last as well as the first dispute among Jesus' disciples on this subject! What a future it would have if there should never be another!

7. *Wishing to stop another disciple* of Jesus who did not belong to their circle. Comment is unnecessary!

8. *Calling down fire* on an inhospitable village. Here is the familiar experiment of attempting to use the weapons of hell in the service of the kingdom of heaven.

9. *Delayed discipleship*, in the case of the man who wished to follow Jesus, but only after something more pressing had been attended to.

What a mirror for us to look into!

Yet, lest this picture be one of unrelieved pessimism, there is the sublime truth to be recorded that it was from this same strangely mixed human stuff that Jesus formed the force that launched his gospel and his church in the world!

✣   ✣   ✣

THE BEST DISH AT THE BANQUET

"Mary has *chosen the best dish*, and she is not to be dragged away from it."—*Luke 10. 41* (Moffatt).

LIFE is not a *table d'hôte* affair. It is an *à la carte* menu. You can't have everything, though many are trying, with an impossible eclecticism, to take everything in the world in an indiscriminate gorge. Life's business is a terrible choice.

Moffatt translates Mary's action in listening to Jesus' conversation as the choice of "the best dish" at the banquet. He says in one of his rare footnotes: "I translate 'merida' by 'dish,' to bring out the point and play of the saying." The best dish at life's banquet is fellowship with God—the nourishment of the teaching of Jesus.

It is a timely figure of speech for our day, when so many forces of social compulsion are reducing life to a severely standardized *table d'hôte*, where people take what is laid down for them and go through life without any real exercise of sovereign choice. The lives of many people are characterized not so much by wrong choices as by the failure to make any deliberate choice of the "best dish" on life's bewildering menu.

And choice there must be, if life is to have any coherent meaning. What shall it be—the upholstery of a house or the spirit of a home; fashion or the fine and mellow graciousness of spirit which can ennoble the routine of everyday living however simple; a shifting vaudeville or the concentrated purpose of the New Testament?

Henry James, in a letter to a friend, advises a choice of the best dish, in a word of counsel, that might very well have come from this tenth chapter of Luke—"Let your soul live; it is the only life that isn't, on the whole, a sell."

Have you placed your order on life? Is it just a conventional demand for everything with no graduation of values—or is it the dish that satisfies life's deepest hunger?

There is a quaint story from the life of the English poet Coventry Patmore which throws a bright light on the business of living.

He always refused to marry any one (he was three times wed) until he had lent the lady a clean copy of his favorite book. He would then ask her to mark the passages that seemed to her important. If they were what he considered the right bits, the matter went forward.

The Book of Life is opened up before each of us with the injunction—"Mark the best."

❧　❧　❧

"DON'T PESTER ME!"

"Do not pester me."—*Luke 11. 7* (Weymouth).

THIS word "pester" is almost audible. We can hear the irritated snarl of this man wakened up out of the first moments of sleep; hear his loud protest over the vast injustice of his being called on to move and get some food for belated guests. He could not possibly do anything, he cried. He had balanced his books for the day. There couldn't be any new entries. "Everything is set. I'm all fixed for the night. I can't make any changes now."

That phrase, "Do not pester me," is the perfect expression of a mind that is completely set, that cannot readjust itself to any new set of facts or a new situation. Such a mind is a static thing, like a trunk neatly arranged, tightly packed, all locked and strapped. It's too much trouble to open it, and nothing will go in anyhow.

It represents vividly a risk that life has for all of us—of becoming so set and finished in our ideas and views of life that anything new, which demands an opening of the mind or a revision of opinion or an unexpected action, is a mere "pestering." We come to look at a new idea, not on its merits but simply as a disturbance of our snug nap.

It is the voice of reaction against any change or new demand—"Don't pester me." Stephen A. Douglas once cried out in a speech during the political conflict over slavery, "Why can't they let our country remain as our fathers left it?" That is the chief response of many persons to the experiences of life. They are "pestered" by anything that requires movement. It is partly due to an inborn inertia in human nature which resists change. Bergson stresses the tendency of animal life to relapse into the vegetable kingdom. "Torpor and unconsciousness," he says in *Creative Evolution*, "are always lying in wait for animal activity." Torpor and unconsciousness are always lying in wait for mental life and frequently "get" it. Habituated to some use or tradition, men prefer to leave well enough alone. They prefer to stay in bed to risking an adventure into the unknown. Richard Roberts has described the process:

Every class and caste, every community and country, has built for itself a house of life, has elaborated for itself a code of orthodoxies and habits, of familiar ideas and customs, within the pale of which the individual is at home. But let any new idea enter into this circle; immediately the community scents danger, feels its security imperiled, closes its ranks and is up in arms against the intruder. It will have nothing to do with it; it hurls hard and ugly names at it; it charges it with criminal intention and as often as not it kills the individual who imported it.[1]

This was precisely the attitude of the static minds of the religious authorities of Judaism to Jesus. "Don't pester us!" they shrieked. Early Christianity met the same irritated crowd. In Jerusalem Christianity was treated as an outrage upon religion; at Philippi as an outrage upon patriotism (Acts 16. 21).

It was the attitude of the Established Church toward Luther, toward Wesley. Later—by a strange repetition of history—that same Methodism, which had a century earlier been accused of "pestering" religion with wild, new demands, said to William Booth: "Don't pester me about your poor and outcasts. I'm all set and can't change my ways."

The early pioneers and prophets of the modern missionary movement met the same closed door, in the early days, and the accusation of being a pestering nuisance. It took half a century for the churches to begin to get up and provide the bread of life for the hungry.

And how often it has been the attitude of business

---

[1] From *The New Man and the Divine Society*. The Macmillan Company, publishers. Used by permission.

and industrial interests to any new insight of Christian social ethics. "Don't bother me," is the reaction. "Business is business. We're all fixed for good."

There are many large meanings to this story of Jesus. One which comes close home, with its challenge to self-examination, is this: "Don't get all set. Don't snuggle down into such a deep sleep that the call of human need for action and change strikes you merely as a nuisance."

✳ ✳ ✳

"CONGRATULATE ME!"

Congratulate me.—Luke 15. 6 (Weymouth-Goodspeed).

How often we use these words! And frequently in what trivial connections!—over a new dress, an automobile, a choice bit of flattery, a new decoration of some kind, an increase in salary; graduation from school. At other times the words, or the unspoken emotion, at least, mark a real red-letter day in life—the coming of life's great gifts and trusts, marriage, the birth of a child, or some significant toil and achievement.

The words here as Jesus uses them picture life's deepest and most lasting cause for congratulation —*that somehow we have become part of the redemptive forces of the world*. Beside that, congratulations on other scores are like the chatter of a child's tea party. Here is a real graduation—life's true Commencement Exercise!

Twice in Weymouth's and Goodspeed's translation of the fifteenth chapter of Luke these words occur—over the finding of the lost sheep and the lost coin. They are both works of redemption; a force out of use and circulation is restored; a life wandering in aimless and baffled circles has been saved from waste.

There is pictured here a double cause for rejoicing. For one thing, life was organized into a *search*. Anyone has reached the place for supreme congratulation when his life has in the furtherance of a great purpose, an exploration, focused on a high quest. For another thing—any life is blessed, no matter what toil or pain it struggles through, which has become a restorative, reclaiming, building force in other lives. In this fellowship of redemption are the great spirits of humanity, names like Pasteur in medicine; Froebel, Pestalozzi, and Horace Mann in education; servants of men like John Howard and Florence Nightingale; and such indefatigable "finders" as William Booth, and that innumerable company who have shared their spirit and purpose.

What is true for an individual is, of course, true for a nation. "Congratulate me" may be the selfish, boastful, complacent expression of national wealth and egotism. The only final and valid basis for national congratulation is the basis of Jesus, that it has graduated from childish assertion into a redemptive force. National greatness is not to be measured by efficiency in *production* but by wisdom in *use*.

Many people, if their inward heart should speak, would frame their national anthem after this fashion:

"O beautiful for dividends
  Of twenty-five per cent
On oil and steel and real estate,
  On money freely lent.
America! America!
  May riches be our fate;

"Increase our wealth
And guard our health,
  America, the great!"

Katharine Lee Bates wrote the original anthem with a deeper insight into the only cause for real congratulation:

"O beautiful for pilgrim feet,
  Whose stern, impassioned stress
A thoroughfare for freedom beat
  Across the wilderness!
America! America!
  God mend thine every flaw,
Confirm thy soul in self-control,
  Thy liberty in law."[1]

❧ ❧ ❧

SLAVING

"All these years," replied the son, "I have been slaving for you."—*Luke 15. 29* (Weymouth).

THE perfect word for the spirit and attitude of the Elder Brother—*slaving*. That was just what was the matter with him—he slaved. The word

---

[1] From "America the Beautiful." Used by permission of author.

"serve" has such high uses in common speech that it cannot convey accurately the quality of the Elder Brother's relation to the father and to his work. That relationship never reached the height of a joyful partnership; it was conscript toil. It was labor without love; without the energizing force of a great affection either for the father or for his brother. The father calls him, "My dear son" (Luke 15. 31). The son never says, "Father." He gives an unconscious picture of himself in his persistent refusal to use the word "brother." He substitutes the contemptuous expression, "This son of yours."

There were no wings to his service. It was dull, heavy, unloving, plodding. And that kind of slaving ends up with a snarl. The return of his brother brought no explosion of emotion to him.

This last act of the drama of the Prodigal Son— the drama of the Two Lost Sons as it should be called—is an eternal warning, always needed, of the tragedy and futility of trying to do God's service without the spirit of sonship and love. There are multitudes of Christians in the position of the elder brother, not to the extent that they share his harsh, bitter feeling, but in that they are plodding along at the tasks of the church and Kingdom, without the lifting, propelling force of a real experience of fellowship with the father. Their lives are not replenished and sustained by the joy of communion. They know no ecstasy.

There is none of that liberating force in the soul which Emerson calls "latent joy." His words are a valid description of the fruit of sustained Christian experience:

Latent joy performs a great office in nature, so does latent joy in life. You may have your stock of well-being condensed into ecstasies, trances of good fortune and delight preceded and followed by blank or painful weeks and months; or you may have your joy spread over all the days in a blank, vague, uniform sense of power and hope.

One of General Foch's military maxims is this: "Every soldier must see his General—must feel himself in communication with him, and never be allowed to consider himself merely a poor pawn maneuvered by an unknown power." The conditions of modern warfare have rendered that maxim well-nigh impracticable. But it is a maxim of Christian warfare that can never be outdated. "Every soldier must see his Leader." Without that vision and communion service becomes slavery.

The propelling force of the Christian enterprise is emotion, it is love. It must get forward in the world as an automobile gets forward by *a series of explosions*.

The danger is that a fussy preoccupation over the technicalities of services of one sort or another may displace the replaceable power of an energizing outburst of love. Emerson has drawn the classic picture of the tragedy of substituting meticulous care over incidental details for the great experience of fellowship of soul.

I pray you, O excellent wife, not to cumber yourself and me to get a rich dinner for this man or this woman who has alighted at our gate, nor a bedchamber made ready at too great a cost. These things, if they are curious in, they can get for a dollar at any village. But let this stranger, if he will, in your looks, in your accent and behavior, read your heart and earnestness, your thought and will, which he cannot buy at any price in any village or city, and which he may well travel fifty miles and dine sparely and sleep hard in order to behold.

We merely slave when there is no renewed experience of joy in God. Samuel Rutherford, from his Scottish prison, wrote, "Jesus Christ came into my room last night and every stone flashed like a ruby." That is exalted language, but millions of Christians could testify from their own experience that it is not the language of madness but the word of truth and soberness.

We slave when there is no spontaneous exuberance of our own personality or no active sharing of the father's love for our own brothers.

❧ ❧ ❧

THE SNEER

The Pharisees, who were fond of money, . . . *sneered.*
Luke 16. 14 (Moffatt).

JESUS had just proclaimed, "You cannot serve God and mammon." And in doing so, of course, he had described one of the cornerstones of the philosophy of some of the Pharisees. No wonder they sneered. They were "lovers of money." They were adepts at fitting in the lust of acquisitiveness with their religion. This bald simplicity of Jesus' alternative, "either God or mammon, but not both," aroused their scornful contempt. They had been choosing both all their lives.

Doctor Moffatt has done well to give this word "sneer" a place in the New Testament, for it has had a large place in Christian history from the very opening of Jesus' ministry. It is one of the most unlovely words in the language; and that is fitting, for it is one of the most unlovely things in the world. It has been one of the most destructive and malicious enemies of Christianity. It is not an open fighter's weapon but the favorite dagger of the coward and the snob.

Always used at every stage of Christian history, it has never been more popular or widely used than to-day. That is one reason why this word of Moffatt's brings such a timely insight. It links across nineteen centuries the earliest opposition of Jesus to the latest. The art of the sneer has reached an amazing perfection in our day. The hiss of the sneer is one of the most familiar sounds in our modern medley of noises. A whole literary cult has thrived on the perfection of the technique of the sneer. Some acclaimed as major prophets are simply past masters of the sneer.

A whole school of biography has been founded on the art. These sculptors of life do not work in marble or granite; they work in mud. They count that day lost which does not see "debunked" some figure which has commanded reverence and admiration. This school might well be called the "Three Sneers for Anybody" school of biography. These sophisticated minds do not live by such ridiculous things as admiration, hope, and love; wit, mockery, and slander are so much more clever and modern. One of our own American poets has thus described these apostles of the sneer:

"They trample on their youth, and faith and love.
  They cast their hope of human kind away.
 With heaven's clear messages they madly strove
  And conquered—and their spirits turned to clay."

There are many reasons for the vogue of the sneer.

It is *inarticulate*. It does not deal in reasons, but in epithets. Paley well asks, "Who can refute a sneer?" It is vague, like a fog, and just as deadly. It creates an atmosphere of reproach.

To sneer is *easy*. It is not a mental operation. It requires no mastery of knowledge or skill in reasoning. A sneer begs every question. It is more like a physical operation, which any mind, no matter how shallow, can readily manage, like sticking out the tongue in derision.

The sneer ministers to *conceit* in the one who uses it. It gives that feeling, rated so highly among life's tickling sensations by many, "How much smarter I am than these poor simpletons!"

Accordingly, it gives a reputation for wit, that chief end of man according to the shorter catechism of to-day.

Three times this word "sneer" is used in Luke and Acts. Each occasion interprets a current trend of our own time.

1. There was the sneer at *ethical loyalties*. That clear division between allegiance to the righteousness of God and the serving of mammon was sneered at by lovers of money. In A. D. 1928 as in A. D. 30 it may be called "The Golden Sneer." Confronted with a choice between God and mammon an easy ethical inclusiveness says, "Take them

both." Three of the vital issues before the church to-day—God against materialism, Christian industry against an old regime, and a warless world against one filled with war—call forth the same contempt. When taking Jesus seriously interferes with the profit side of the ledger the answer is frequently the easy sneer. "Sentimentalists," "idealists"—these words become, by a vicious perversion of values, terms of reproach.

2. There was the sneer at *love and sacrifice*. In Luke 23. 35 we read, in a description of the crowd at the foot of the cross, "The people stood and looked on and even the rulers *sneered* at him." The love of Christ as a motive of life often meets the same response.

3. There was the sneer at the *spiritual foundations* of life. In the presence of the great experience of Pentecost, when the transforming energies of the Spirit of God entered the souls of men and marked a new epoch in the evolution of humanity, "some others *sneered*" (Acts 2. 13)—the same ignorant disdain, unwilling to examine, preferring to flee to the refuge of ignorant contempt. The realities of the spiritual nature of man meet the same reaction in many quarters to-day, both on the score of the content of faith and its expression in practical life. To meet that sneer there is need that the air of apology for our faith be dropped. Jesus Christ is one of the facts of the universe as truly as the elements of chemistry; the experience of religion is as genuine and authentic as the experience of heat and cold. As Dr. Harry Emerson Fosdick well puts it:

Christ must be recognized as a fact just as much as the readily accepted facts of chemistry and mechanics. The

universe is not composed of newts only; it has its New-
tons. Crystals do not make up all of the facts of existence; there is Christ. We must recognize that there
are two worlds existing now, the temporal and the eternal.

But the sneer is futile. It has always proved
so and the sneers which are the fads of the hour
will prove equally so. To Paley's question, Who can
refute a sneer? there is one devastating answer.
Time can refute a sneer. The trail of the years is
scattered with the remains of the forgotten sneers
of yesterday.

❧ ❧ ❧

THE FINE ART OF PESTERING

I will give her justice to prevent her from *constantly
coming to pester me.—Luke 18. 5* (Weymouth).

JESUS told this story as an encouragement to
prayer. But its insight into human motives and
human nature make it an encouragement to persistent pestering for justice as well.

A great many steps in human progress have been
reluctantly taken by people who did not particularly revere God or respect man but who did respect
"pestering." The judge in Jesus' story well stands
for officials of every sort, from kings and emperors
down to the corner policeman. They have one
important trait in common—an aversion to being
pestered. They have to get on with the job in
some fashion, and their love of justice is frequently
far less conspicuous than their love of quiet. A

"pest" is a nuisance, an embarrassment, and may precipitate a crisis. Consequently, wrongs have been frequently remedied, not at the command of a troubled conscience, but on account of a troubled ease.

William Lloyd Garrison is one of the notable examples of a man with a genius for constantly pestering. Even the theoretical opponents of slavery as well as its defenders, as a rule, regarded him as a "pest." He was a fanatic, and contemporary records do not paint him as an altogether pleasant man to live with. But he did not worry about being pleasant any more than this "unreasonable" widow did. Both got things done. In the whole field of social progress the degree of Doctor of Philosophy is frequently of less use than that of Master of Arts of Pestering.

❧ ❧ ❧

THE APPETITE FOR SALUTES

They are *fond of getting saluted.*—*Luke 20. 46* (Moffatt).

THESE words are translated in the King James Version of the Gospel of Luke as "They love greetings in the markets." Obviously, that might be taken as a wholly innocent and commendable fondness for the friendly talk of the market place. Moffatt's translation makes clear the kind of greetings the scribes hankered for. It was not the hail of fellowship but the salute to a superior in rank.

How fond of that exhilaration one can become!

Good morning, Doctor!
How do you do, Colonel!
You're looking well, Bishop!
I'm proud to know you, Senator!

Salutes! They are among the most corrupting words in the world. The love of salutes has wrecked more careers and more good causes than almost any other obstacle or opposition. "Give us this day our daily salute," becomes the prayer of multitudes. The salute is more necessary than bread.

The lust for pre-eminence, for flattering recognition, is deadly because it is a habit-forming drug. Alfred Austin counsels,

> "Friend, be not fretful if the voice of fame
>   Along the narrow way of hurrying men,
>   Where echo unto echo shouts again,
>   Be all day long not noisy with your name."[1]

And he describes just what happens in a distressingly large number of cases—the one whose ear does not catch the echo of his name "frets." And a fretter is a poor fighter in any cause. He is too preoccupied with "fretting" to make any effective moves against the enemy. Again and again throughout Jesus' training of his disciples it appears that one of his chief cares is to prevent their preoccupation with other things, things which would prevent concentration on the kingdom of God. Three possible preoccupations are stressed—worry, the love of money, and the desire for pre-eminence. Those three pitfalls occupy a surprisingly large portion of his teaching. The reason is plain—he needed in

---

[1] From "The Door of Humility." The Macmillan Company, publishers. Used by permission.

his disciples one great preoccupation and one only
—Seek ye first the Kingdom.

The lust of salutes, titles, precedence, destroys
the effectiveness of a disciple's work for the cause
of Christ, as does any other kind of lust. It becomes an end in itself; it becomes a substitute for
real achievement. Moreover, the craving for salutes,
the manipulating to get them, has demoralized the
working force of the Kingdom, and with ruinous
results.

He that findeth his life must lose his dependence
on flattering recognition. Emily Dickinson, in a
characteristically humorous verse, laughs at this
itch for honors:

> "I'm nobody! Who are you?
> Are you nobody too?
> Then there's a pair of us—don't tell!
> They'd banish us, you know.
> How dreary to be somebody!
> How public, like a frog,
> To tell your name the livelong day
> To an admiring bog!"

Jesus offers two sure cures for this enervating
disease: the grip of his great enterprise itself upon
the mind and heart and the enlistment of the disciples to win a far higher order of merit, the most
glittering decoration and title ever worn by any
one—"I have called you friends." That, in the
most literal sense of the words, is a Distinguished
Service Cross.

❧ ❧ ❧

SOPORIFICS

From *hour to hour keep awake.—Luke 21. 36* (Moffatt).

ONE of the finest and most difficult arts of life —that of keeping awake. There are so many opiates and soporifics, "knock-out drops," which deaden and cloud the spirit and lull it to sleep. Keeping the soul awake is a continuous vigil. It cannot be done by a sudden or even frantic arousement every thirty days or every seven days. It is only to be done "hour by hour." Doctor Moffatt's expansion of the word "always," a word we tend to pass over lightly, into the detailed and picturesque, "hour by hour," gives a real insight into one of life's persistent problems.

There are in literature two striking pictures of the liability of the soul to be deadened by opiates and the senses to be narcotized. They are both cases where this is done by a false sense of attainment and arrival, perhaps the most subtle opiate of all life's experiences. One is Bunyan's chapter on "The Enchanted Ground" in *The Pilgrim's Progress*, where the onward push of the pilgrims is lulled into a drowse. The other is Tennyson's "Lotus Eaters."

The success of a transatlantic air flight depends not only on wind and weather, or on the engine's going for forty hours without missing a beat. It depends supremely on whether the pilot can keep awake. The net result of the longer flight of life depends on the same variable factor.

Most anything has possibilities of becoming a soporific to the spirit and making it oblivious both of dangers and high possibilities. We must be adept workers of magic and exorcism. We need to exorcise the yawn, for the yawn is one of the most evil demons we will ever meet.

Habit is the most common narcotic to the alertness of the spirit and senses. It comes as an old familiar friend. More than that, it *is* a friend. Almost every advance in psychology is a new chapter in the amazing story of how habit makes life, in the human sense, possible. Without the help of habit we would never emerge from helpless infancy. Life would be consumed in buttoning and unbuttoning buttons. But habit will take over everything in life instead of merely the physical basis of life, if we let it. It can smother the higher centers of the brain like coal gas. That is what has happened again and again. Many people "think" with their spinal column, not with their brain. Their responses have become instinctive. The enterprise of their life is conducted like a business of which the head is absent, ordered to a sanitarium perhaps. Nothing is referred to the head of the firm; everything is handled by a lower department. "There is plenty of room at the top" —of the spinal column. Hour by hour—use it!

The fallacy of arrival drugs the aspiration of the soul like a field of poppies. The premature satisfaction, the mistaking the means for the end, the beginning for the conclusion, the blue print for the finished building—these things have snuffed out the achievement of many a promising life, when the life had barely started. This is the picture drawn, as has been indicated, both by Bunyan and Tennyson. There is only one safe tense to the verb "arrive"—the future. Browning uses it in the only way it should be used:

"I go to prove my soul. . . .
. . . I *shall arrive*."

When we use it in life in either the present or
past, life withers.

Popularity is a habit-forming drug which, like
many other poisons, paralyzes the higher centers
of the brain. It beclouds the mind like alcohol.
Trying to get a clear vision of the world while
intoxicated with adulation is like trying to look
out on a landscape through a mirror. The subtle
danger of this kind of opiate to the man who deals
with crowds is well pictured in an incident told in
the life of Silvester Horne.

Once when Mr. Horne was a boy he had gone to see
Doctor Dale, in the vestry of a church where he was
preaching, bearing a letter from his father hinting at
Silvester Horne's inclination toward the ministry.

"My lad," said Dale, looking kindly down at me, "remember our temptation is not, as a rule, money." Then
he pointed through the open door to the church, where
the crowds of people were still slowly straggling down
the aisles: "*That* is our temptation." Boy as I was, I
felt instinctively what he meant; and a curious surprise
came over me that he should feel the snares of popularity so keenly.[1]

The *easy chair* lulls to sleep, spiritually as well as
physically. Try reading a solid book, that requires
close thinking, in a soft, friendly reclining chair.
Your wits sink back with an easy sprawl as well
as your body. Ambition must be made of sterner
stuff. Wealth, the pursuit of comfort, absorption

---

[1] From *The Life of Charles Silvester Horne*, by W. R. Selbie.
George H. Doran Company, publishers. Used by permission.

in the pillows and upholstery of life show down the eager movements of the spirit.

The *eye turned inward*, afflicting our vision of the world, like a cataract on the eye, dulls the divine powers of sympathy.

"From hour to hour keep awake *praying*"—there opens the avenue of escape. It is life's crowning miracle, and yet a daily miracle that the mind can so open itself to the quickening of the spirit—that it moves alive and awake. Carlyle, in words of rare and beautiful tenderness, has recorded the wonder of the miracle:

Daily I am taught again the unfathomable mystery of what we call a soul radiant with Heaven even while capable of being overclouded and, as it were, swallowed up by the bottomless mud it has to live in in this world.

❧ ❧ ❧

THE COMMUTER'S SERMON

His habit at this time *was* to *teach in the Temple by day*, but *to go out and spend the night on the Mount* called the Oliveyard.—*Luke 21. 37* (Weymouth).

FOR the last week of his life Jesus was a commuter. Every morning he went into the city to do his work. Every evening he went back to the little quiet place in the country to spend the night. It may seem an act of violence to use such a distinctively modern word as "commuting" to describe the daily journeys of Jesus. Yet in this physical aspect of his life he followed exactly the habits of that great, thronging modern tribe of suburbanites who flock into the city to work in the morning and at five or six in the evening go out again to the little village on the outskirts of the city.

Here is an aspect of Jesus' last week which comes home very closely to a great army of hurrying, thronging people. The trains, the street cars, busses and ferries bring into the cities every day millions of people whose regular movements on the shuttle of traffic are exactly those of Jesus as he journeyed back and forth from the hillside of Olivet to the crowded streets of Jerusalem.

If we look closely at the life of Jesus during these days and nights, we find more than a physical resemblance to the motions of the modern suburbanite. His life has, in those last five days, a peculiar message to those who go back and forth. He avoided the peculiar temptations of the commuter.

To look at just one aspect of the moral risks of living in the suburbs we may truly say that the great danger of the commuter is that he may avoid responsibilities at both ends of his trip. The railway train may be used—unconsciously at times—as a way of escape from burdens and responsibilities, both in the city and at home. Jesus bore the burdens and responsibilities at both places.

The suburbanite easily finds an excuse for slipping out of responsibilities in the city to which he goes to work. He does not live there. He merely pays a daily visit. His church is not there. His family and friends, for the large part, are not there. The social problems of the city, its needs, its appeals, come to have the character of things afar off. He does not know how "the other half lives." It is easy not to care. He is in a hurry to catch the five-fifteen.

At the other end of the line the process of side-stepping is just as easy and insidious. Listen to snatches of conversation painfully familiar to every pastor in a suburban town: "I'm so tired when I get back from the city that I really can't take up any work here"; "I moved out here to rest"; "I was active in the church in the city for fifteen years but I really can't start in again out here." And so it goes through the whole catalogue.

The tasks of the Kingdom remain undone for the lack of energy that is lost somewhere on the road between the two points. Many a suburbanite is truly "a lost soul" as far as any genuine participation in the causes of human welfare are concerned, outside of his own business affairs.

The road between Jerusalem and the Mount of Olives was not a road of evasion for Jesus. He gave himself supremely in both places.

After the great earthquake of a few years ago in Tokyo no one was admitted into the city unless he came bearing rice and a candle; in other words, food and light. There was no room for merely another person to be carried. That same passport ought to be ours whether we come into the bustling city or the quiet countryside—food and light—strength and sympathy, skill, brought and shared.

❧ ❧ ❧

DELIGHTED TO SEE JESUS!

Herod was *greatly delighted* to see Jesus.—*Luke 23. 8* (Moffatt).

THE word "delighted" expresses exactly the super- ficiality of Herod. The word is ordinarily used of such trivial affairs, and it is fitting here, for every event in Herod's life is a trivial affair. He could not have any other kind. He is the perfect example of the genial, superficial curiosity seeker.

Of course he was delighted to see Jesus. It was a sort of picnic for him. You can just see him rushing about rubbing his hands in anticipation. "Isn't Jerusalem the most interesting place. Here one meets all the interesting types. Perhaps he'll do a miracle for us. Wouldn't that be exciting!" And he chatters, chatters on, empty-headed fool that he is. There is not to be found in literature anywhere a more powerfully dramatic scene than this loquacious empty-pated chatterbox confronted with the regal silence of Jesus. The silence of Jesus is the perfect tribute to utter insignificance.

John Masefield, in his noble and reverent play, "The Trial of Jesus," takes exactly this conception of Herod as a superficial chatterer, curious over the latest sensation. Herod is quite irritated that Jesus refuses to work a miracle for him.

As we read the story, far away and incredible it all seems, that a man should try to use Jesus as an entertainer, that a man could look him fairly in the face and never get any conception of the greatness of the man. Pilate, at least, had the mentality and judgment to escape that ignominy.

And yet, is it so far away? Are there not people

like Herod, many of them, some in the ranks of
Jesus' professed followers, light-minded chatterers
who never remotely understand the stupendous
meaning of Jesus? Just as Jesus was the latest
curiosity and Herod was delighted to see him, so
He has become a fashion. There are multitudes
on whom the crucifixion of Jesus and the whole
sacrificial conception of life have made no real
impression at all. Jesus' uncompromising claims
are treated with an unconscious indifference. Like
Herod, they are delighted to see Jesus; like Herod,
they never see him at all.

It is so easy to say "they" in the preceding
sentence. Had we not better say "we"?

* * *

PILATE'S COMPROMISE

I shall release him with a *whipping.—Luke 23. 16*
(Moffatt).

I will *teach him a lesson* (Goodspeed).

I will . . . give him a *light punishment* (Weymouth).

THE alternatives before Pilate in the trial of
Jesus were simple and plain—either condemnation
or release. Pilate tried to straddle them. His
real desire, of course, was to release Jesus. But
he didn't have the moral character for that. He
reasoned, rather: "*I can't* condemn him. *I won't*
champion him. I'll just insult him and thus make
a compromise between the two. I'll release him
with a whipping. That will be a sop both to my
conscience and to the Jews!"

What a cheap attitude it was!

Yet what a common attitude to Jesus!

It is exactly the attitude of many whose actions, if not their conscious reassuring, proclaim: "I can't condemn Jesus. I won't acclaim him. I'll just strike a cross between the two. I'll give him the moral equivalent of a light whipping. I'll give him some fair words and throw him out."

"Fair words and throw him out"—this modern equivalent of Pilate's action is so common that it has almost become standardized. There has been worked out for it, in our day, a well-recognized technique. The very form of words with which it is done have almost become a ritual.

The modern form of this shuffling compromise in regard to Jesus which will neither condemn nor loyally follow takes several forms.

One of the most common is that impertinent patronage of Jesus which pays formal tribute to his teachings and then disdainfully dismisses them as impractical, visionary, "idealistic." Why idealistic should be an adjective of contempt is a mystery, but it is so. The company who take this position welcome Jesus to the front door with protestations of hospitality, and once in the house, roughly throw him out the back door as an encumbrance, a fanatic touched in the head, a troublemaker, and a bore. The apology for this is the well-worn sophistry, "We live in a practical world."

A frequent modern parallel to Pilate's compromise is: "I'll allow Jesus a small place in my life—in the show window. But I'll keep him cooped up there and never let him get loose in the whole house." So men give him one day and fence off the other six secure from his trespassing. They admit him to rule over minor etiquettes but give him no vote in the decisions on the major issues of life.

An orthodox form of Pilate's heresy is the attitude, happily growing less common, which says: "I'll grant Jesus jurisdiction over individual conduct, but let him keep away from society. When he tries to enter where he does not belong he needs to be scourged."

Rome has passed into history. Pilate, with his cowardly compromise on the case of Jesus Christ, remains.

❧ ❧ ❧

"NONSENSE!"

But this story of the women seemed in their opinion to be *nonsense.—Luke 24. 11* (Moffatt-Goodspeed).

THIS was the first verdict on the resurrection of Jesus—Nonsense! Yet with the words scarcely out of his mouth Peter gets up and starts on a breakneck run to the tomb to look into this nonsense! The wild hope proved too much for the first snap judgment of "Nonsense!"

That experience of Peter's is a symbol of the experience of the race. "What? Resurrection— Immortality—Life after Death?" has been the incredulous question. "Nonsense!" comes the ready answer.

And then humanity, like Peter, has rushed to meet the wild hope. The urging within the breast of man has been an explosive, propulsive force sending him with a leap to the great faith.

Bliss Perry in a noble sentence has described the movement of mind and heart in Peter and in the heart of humanity. "Easter," he says, "like all deep things, begins in mystery and it ends, like all high things, in a great courage."

The mystery is so deep that the first verdict is nonsense. And without the background and foundation of the God and Father of our Lord Jesus Christ, even the final verdict may well be "nonsense." But with that foundation, life takes on the high courage of a great faith.

What changed the mystery of the resurrection for Peter from nonsense into reality? One thing only—experience. It is the experience of God in Christ which throws out the first verdict. There is no other altogether sufficient evidence. We can listen to all the banging tambourines in the dark-rooms of mediums and still render the verdict— "Nonsense!" We can listen to the well-worn analogy of the butterfly emerging from the cocoon and remain unmoved. The resurrection is to be proved from Jesus Christ and not Christ from the resurrection. It is from the experience of what God is that we hold the faith in our immortal destiny. "Even if Christ had shown himself to no one after his death," declares Dean Inge, "we might still be sure that he has risen. *Being what he is*, he could not be beholden to death. And the same applies to our immortality. Because we are spiritual beings we cannot wholly perish."

The question of our immortality is not so much a matter of God by a special exertion rescuing us from extinction and oblivion, but whether, quite aside from the body, we are possessed of life such that, by its very nature, it is inextinguishable, inherently eternal; whether our spirits have become so possessed with the spirit of God that we cannot be canceled out, so long as God lasts.

When we think deeply, it is the "faith of unbelief" which is nearer "nonsense" than the faith in God as revealed in Christ. To believe in a blank meaningless universe requires a far more staggering act of faith than to believe in a universe through which runs an increasing purpose of God.

Dr. T. H. Martin, of Liverpool, has put this burden of the faith of denial in a paragraph so strong that it cries for quotation:

Man in his primitive state, gross and sensual, nevertheless laying hold of great ideals, believing in an eternal right, an eternal truth, an eternal justice, an everlasting goodness and love, making great ventures for it, and sublime sacrifices because of it, and at the end, thinking over it all, trying to understand it all, talking about "God." So unpromising a beginning, so glorious an end! How came this to be? Where did he get the idea from? Can science tell us? Is it blind force or chance? Is it the result of a fortuitous assemblage of atoms? And Jesus, the top and crown of things, in whom we see the very face of God—can he be explained so? Only an idiot could think or believe that. Our old earth is more than matter, or force, or atoms. Something calls, constrains, pulls, draws, holds, lifts, saves, satisfies, cares. Someone is out there in the distant, here in the near, who speaks, subdues, silences me. God! Is it really so? And the answer comes gentle and low: "E'en so: it is so!"[1]

---

[1] Quoted in *The Christian Century*.

So on the foundation of the God of Jesus—as revealed in Jesus, the mystery ends in the high courage expressed in the words of Walt Whitman:

"I know I am deathless.
  I know this orbit of mine cannot be swept with a car-
    penter's compass,
  I know I shall not pass like a child's curlicue cut with a
    burnt stick at night."

❦　❦　❦

THE FIRST CHRISTIAN EXPERIENCE MEETING

Then they related their own *experience.—Luke 24. 35* (Moffatt).

HERE, on the evening of the day of resurrection, the first institution of Christianity came into existence. It was not baptism, not the Lord's Supper, not the mass, not even formal Christian worship. It was an experience meeting. "Then they related their own experience" of meeting Christ. It was a little prayer meeting—and its sole content was the relation by those present of how Christ had appeared to them. It was not argument; it was not eloquence, save for that supreme "eloquence" of Christian experience.

It was not merely the first Christian institution. It was more. It was and is the only permanently effective Christian institution—the recital of actual experience of Christ. It was the first demonstration of the methods by which the Christian faith and life were to spread and did spread. It was also the first demonstration of the method by which it

must always win its way, if it is to be more than
a thin veneer on the surface of life, more than a
pitifully transparent coat of paint over a foundation
of paganism.

"They related their own experience." That is
the unfailing Christian apologetic, and the gates
of hell cannot prevail against it. It is the one sure
basis of Christian conquest.

From the very birthday of the Christian Church
there comes across the centuries a tremendously
timely and urgent message for our own time.

This Easter evening experience meeting points
the way to the answer to the great bewilderment
and search of multitudes of our day—the need for
an unshakable authority and certainty in religion.
Many of the conventional foundations of authority
are no longer adequate for men of the modern world.

An infallible church, an authoritative creed, a
literally inspired Book—all of these sources of
authority are still offered the world by Catholic
and Protestant dogmatists. Yet these cannot meet
the needs of earnest multitudes. As Dr. Raymond
Calkins says, "The gravest religious problem of
our modern world is the discovery of the grounds
of religious certainty, apart from Roman Cathol-
icism, on the one hand, or of unscientific dogmatism, on the other."[1]

Here it is—Christianity's endowment on its
birthday. In the first chapter of *The Eloquence of
Christian Experience* Dr. Raymond Calkins gives an
impressive and moving study of the religious certainty of the early Christian fellowship in the New
Testament, showing that it was just what came

[1] The Macmillan Company, publishers. Used by permission.

into being at this first Easter prayer meeting—the disciples' experience of Christ.

That amazing certainty and assurance which glows in the book of Acts and the Epistles had this unfailing basis. The certainty and authority was not in the *church*. There was no church. It was not founded on an authoritative *creed*. There was no creed. It was not founded on an inspired and infallible *book*. The New Testament did not exist.

The ground of their assurance was their experience of God in and through the historical Jesus. This the New Testament affirms is the unshakable and immovable reality. Here we seem to have touched bottom. These New Testament writers have found solid ground for religious certainty.

The Christian experience of God is the one thing needful. It is the one thing that we can positively least afford to lose. The practical wisdom of men of affairs, the philosophy of our universities, the culture of our schools—these are all a necessary and important part of our equipment as ministers of Jesus Christ. . . . Underneath every other discipline of mind and body there must be a deep, warm, passionate experience of God in Jesus Christ. Paul well calls this a sacred deposit, a holy treasure, a priceless possession. The Christian experience of God alone answers the quest of the human soul for certainty. It alone is the unshakable ground of Christian faith and of Christian knowledge.[1]

This little company of a few souls, met in the gathering dusk of eventide on the first Easter, found the sure foundation not only of New Testament preaching, but of Christian achievement always and everywhere.

[1] From *The Eloquence of Christian Experience*, by Raymond Calkins. The Macmillan Company, publishers. Used by permission.

BUBBLES

Bethesda, . . . where a crowd of invalids used to lie,
. . . *waiting for the water to bubble.—John 5. 3* (Moffatt).

THE healing of the impotent man at the Pool of
Bethesda has many values for thought and action.
But among them one thing stands out clearly—
here were a group of invalids depending for their
cure on some external commotion. They put all
their trust in "bubbles." They sat there waiting
to seize the periodic disturbance and bubbling of
the pool to plunge in and be saved.

It is not pressing an allegory too far to catch in
this company of folk, eagerly scanning the surface
of the pool for bubbles, a suggestion or picture of
a church, or those within it, hoping to find, in the
coming of some new craze or agitation, the means
of supplying a deficiency in its own inner life. The
weakness portrayed is a dependence on externalism,
a superficial opportunism which looks to the stirrings of popular interest, the rise of a new fashion
of the hour, with the hope of exploiting it. It is a
faith in bubbles on the surface of life.

Society is very much like a boiling spring. It
has its periodic fashions and crazes. A new word,
a new interest, leaps into prominence; the surface
of the pool of life is disturbed; it bubbles. And a
church, in a mood of invalidism, sees the new upheaval, and says, "Lo, here! This is the thing
which will put me on my feet. I can jump into
the center of these bubbles and grow strong again!"

Now, of course, it is not to be denied that there
have been great periodic movements in the minds
of men which have been tides which, taken at the

flood, lead on to fortune. There were such deep stirrings of the world's mind in the first Christian century, in the Reformation and the evangelical revival of the eighteenth century. But these have not been bubbles on the surface. They were not external, not mere fashions, but veritable gales of the Spirit of God which bloweth where it listeth and we see the effects.

Faith in bubbles is quite another thing.

One recent pathetic instance of trust in external commotion to bring results which can be secured only by inward renewal of life and power was the Great War. Only by going back to the contemporary records, the newspapers, magazines, pamphlets, and books of 1914 and 1915 can we realize the hopes and expectations which multitudes of people had of what the war was going to do for religion. The war was the most agitated bubbling which has ever disturbed the pool of the world's life. Superficial thinkers, interpreting certain manifestations in the light of their own hopes, said: "Here it is. Here is an agitation that will turn people to God. The war will save religion and the church. The bubbles will be our cure."

It is too early to measure the effect of the war on Christianity. A balance sheet of assets and liabilities cannot be struck. Forces good and bad have been set in motion which will run for years. But it is not too early to realize that the expectation that the upheaval of the war would result in an increase of spiritual life and power, in salvation for the church, was a tragic illusion. The tumult and the shouting die and the war left what it always leaves—blight, devastation, death. The disturbance

passes, and, like the poor man at the pool, we are
not saved by it.

Each new intellectual fashion which agitates the
minds of men is seen by some as a way of salvation.
There is a great overestimation of what such new
interests and developments can do. The new
trends in religious education have been greeted, not
for what they are, legitimate aids to religious life,
but as wonder-working panaceas which would effect
an automatic salvation. "Jump into this pool and
all our troubles will be over." Take the word
"community," for example. It has had an immense vogue. Some have vainly imagined that by
baptizing their church with a new name and calling
it a "community church" they would be rid of all
the ills a church is heir to.

So with the stunts and tricks constituting that
modern form of unfaith which is so besetting a sin
to preachers who must proclaim the gospel to a
motion-picture age. "We will plunge into this
pool and be saved," a great many bewildered
preachers and churches have said, as they have
grasped at the showman's tricks. It is a form of
exchange of faith in the living God for faith in
bubbles.

The man at the pool was saved not by the coming of an external disturbance but by the advent
of a Person. It is the advent of Jesus Christ into
the midst of our life which is the one hope of salvation. By faith are we saved—faith in the meaning
of that fine definition of it given by Doctor DuBose
—"the setting of our entire selves Godward."

The kingdom of heaven cometh not with observation of bubbles.

THE TRAFFIC JAM

The man who had been cured did not know who it was; for *Jesus had passed out unnoticed*, there being a crowd in the place.—*John 5. 13* (Weymouth).

WHAT a theme for a crowded age—the unnoticed Jesus—"there being a crowd in the place!" How perilously closely it fits large aspects of our world —the Son of man lost in a traffic jam! So dense a crowd, such a weaving to and fro that even the one who was the most in debt to Jesus lost sight of him.

This word of Weymouth's translation expresses the most formidable and characteristic obstacle to the Christian faith in our day. The opposition to Jesus most often met is not of the kind typified by the crucifixion or the relentless antagonism of the Pharisees. These still exist. But it is, rather, here, tucked away in an incident of the day's work of Jesus, that we find the supreme hindrance to the cause of Christ. He was simply lost from view in the crowd.

In it is a shaft of light which illuminates great stretches of history, both personal, political, and ecclesiastical. Jesus' work done, he is allowed to be elbowed out to obscurity. Indeed, both in individual and social life Jesus often suffers the fate of that very familiar figure of the modern newspaper world—the person whose name and story fills the front page for a few days and then drops back to smaller type on page six.

This is especially true in these years of the twentieth century in the most fabulously prosperous land under the sun—the United States.

There is such a staggering crowd of things in

the world's show windows that it is easy for men not to notice Jesus.

The enormous hodgepodge of things has served also to crowd Jesus out of many minds and lives. He is not so much thrown out by set purpose as dropped out. He cannot be kept amid the clutter of interests.

On a much higher level of life the same crowding out process goes on simply through the mere accumulation of knowledge and facts and data of all kinds. Some have even feared that the mass of facts has become too great for the mind to carry. Richard Roberts has said:

The mind is breaking down under the weight of its own achievements. With the growth of the world's population, the facts, external and internal, that have to be dealt with are too numerous for any single brain. Salvation by knowledge is becoming a desperate undertaking. The paths of education are blocked by mountains of books. There will have to be greater specialization and a return to the elemental facts of existence.

The scientific approach to life—so dominant an influence to-day—has the effect of crowding God off the main avenue of life into a corner. Many people have come to feel that in knowing and obeying scientific laws they have no further needs. They leave no place, because they really feel no need of personal relationship to God. The idea of a life sustained and renewed through fellowship is foreign to them.

Shall this be the verdict on our time and our society—"And Jesus passed out unnoticed, there being a crowd in the place"?

Shall it be the verdict on our lives?

Whether written of a nation or a person, it is a verdict of doom—an epitaph.

❧ ❧ ❧

CONTEMPT FOR THE MOB

As for this mob . . . —*John 7. 49* (Moffatt).
This rabble . . . (Weymouth).

THERE spoke the snob.   The words voice the contemptuous scorn of the aristocrats of the San-hedrin for the common people of the nation.   You can almost see the curl of the lips as the words are spoken: "This mob—this rabble, these ignorant louts unversed in the niceties of the law—they are accursed."

That same snobbery for the great mass of hu-manity has always been manifest, but it is active in new and vicious form to-day.   It has become so much a fashion that it constitutes a real moral, intellectual and spiritual pitfall for our time.   A recent novelist has thus described the expression of one of his characters, "His eyes seemed fashioned for small contempts."   That description would stand for a large number of self-constituted Sanhe-drins to-day.

There are many causes for this rising tide of snobbery in these present days.   One is unques-tionably the apparent justification for it furnished by statistics.   We have taken to tests and statis-tics with all the eagerness of a child for a new toy. And the far-reaching generalizations made on the basis of arbitrary tests are frequently those of a child with a toy that he does not know exactly how to work. On the basis of the army tests made on soldiers in training during the World War, we have learned that the intellectual attainments of the so-called average man make a showing that came with a shock of surprise. We have learned such facts as these:

The average man leaves school at the eighth grade. He has a smattering of local geography, and knows a little bit about history and a few elementary facts of physiology. In spite of the fact that he is to be accepted as a citizen, he has no general knowledge of civics, science, politics, or literature. He is able to speak one language only. On a standardized intelligence test he makes about the same score as does an average boy of fourteen. He never develops the intelligence required for satisfactory high-school work.

These facts regarding the scholastic attainments of the average man have been made, in a wholly unjustifiable manner, the basis for a whole school of contempt for the rank and file of the nation. A Eugenic Conference held in New York a few years ago exhibited a chart which indicated that thirty billion persons had been reared to maturity in civilized countries since the dawn of history eight or ten thousand years ago, and adds that the thing of unique interest which the chart pointed out was that only about five thousand persons out of the whole thirty billion ever "amounted to much."

A. E. Wiggam, one of the high priests of this cult of contempt for the mob, thus sums up the truth as he sees it: "The strength of mind and body, of soul and spirit, of these few precious people is worth more than all the rest of humanity put together."[1]

Three things should be remembered about this modern expression of the old contempt of the Sanhedrin for the "rabble."

1. It is the refuge of every autocratic force in society, of every reactionary, of every exploiter.

2. It has been historically and is to-day the "defense mechanism" of empty conceit and privilege frantically grasping its advantages.

3. It is a vicious denial of the spirit of Jesus and the Christian gospel.

The pretensions of this modern cult of aristocracy demand a new understanding and proclamation of the attitude of Jesus to this same "mob" and "rabble" on which the Sanhedrin poured its cynical contempt and loathing. His sympathy for people knew no limits and his faith in the possibilities of mankind was unwavering. His central teaching of the sacredness of personality and the worth of man is the charter of democracy and human freedom.

That great faith of Jesus is quaintly and beautifully but with profound truth expressed in the words of that Negro spiritual, "All God's Chillun Got Wings."

This is not the affirmation of a sentimental blindness to the facts of human evil. It is not a superficial estimate of humanity seen through rose-colored glasses. It is a simple and noble expression

---

[1] From *The New Decalogue of Science*. Copyright, 1922–23. Used by permission of the publishers, The Bobbs-Merrill Company.

of the spiritual capacity of man. It is a melodious declaration of the truth that "To as many as received him, to them gave he power to become the sons of God." John Wesley records somewhere in his *Journal* that he preached on the text just quoted and he adds the note, "They seemed greatly encouraged." Small wonder! The only bit of encouragement that can come to the human soul strong enough to outlast every vicissitude is the assurance that he is the child of God with divine possibilities.

Days such as ours need the assertion of the faith that is embedded in the gospel in the possibilities of man through the action of the Spirit of God. The faith expressed in the words, "All God's chillun got wings" is also timely in that it asserts the sacredness and value of human personality at a time when a rampant materialism puts property values before the values of the soul.

❧ ❧ ❧

A SPECTACLE OR A PERSON?

Those to whom he had been a *familiar sight* as a beggar.—*John 9. 8* (Moffatt).
A familiar *object* (Weymouth).

THESE townsmen had seen this beggar for years as an "object," a "sight," a familiar spectacle of the village life. Jesus was the first one, apparently, ever to see him as a *person*. In other words, they had never really seen him at all. He was merely part of the landscape.

The way of these villagers in regarding a man as

a sort of depersonalized object or spectacle points out a continual danger to which our power of selective attention lays us open. We develop very readily an ability to blot out from our conscious vision things to which we are not giving our immediate and intense attention. We cross a crowded street and the blazing electric sign in front of our eyes does not really exist for us. Neither does the crowd of hurrying individuals a hundred yards away. If we could not do this, we would soon be killed, no doubt. While letting our eyes roam indiscriminately an automobile or street car would pick us off.

But while this power of partial or voluntary blindness makes for physical safety, it carries grave moral and spiritual dangers. It is the danger of failing to put ourselves in the place of another and really see him as a person. To the neighbors of this man he was only a sight; to the disciples of Jesus he was an interesting theme for theological discussion. Only to Jesus was he a brother in need.

It is so easy to get that way. Bishop Francis J. McConnell shows this very strikingly in telling of the terrible pull on one's sympathies which the coughing of the tubercular coolies who pull jinrickshas in Chinese cities makes on one. He says that for the first few nights he could hardly sleep at all. At the end of thirty days the coughing becomes so familiar one hardly hears it.

The same process goes on in regard to the major portion of life with many people. Persons with peculiar characteristics and needs have become just "spectacles" or "types." Let us beware of the word "type." It is one of the most vicious

words in the English language. It is the perfect
astringent on sympathy. When we get to regarding
people as "types" of this or that, the sensitive soul
has died. An American visitor to London wrote
home to a friend: "You must visit the Victoria
embankment and see the people sleeping on benches.
There are the most interesting 'types.'" That
heart-breaking panorama of aching, homeless woe
was just a child's peep box of "types" to her. An
extreme instance of the same callousness of this
Palestinian village is that of a great architect, on
the deck of a ferry boat in the Hudson River,
when a stoker fell from the stern of a tug and was
smashed by its screw to pulp that left on the
waters a lacquer of bloody oil. He merely cried,
"What *color!*"

☙ ☙ ☙

PUTTING JESUS INTO A PIGEON HOLE

We do not know *where this fellow comes from.—John
9. 30* (Weymouth).

THE fundamental objection to Jesus on the part
of many was that he would not fit into a pigeonhole. The Pharisees had a cut-and-dried universe.
Things went into arbitrary and traditional classifications. They could get around in that kind of
a world. Here they are trying to fit Jesus into two
of their most standardized classifications—the geographical pigeonhole and the hereditary one. They
are nettled because they cannot "place him." All
their holes were round. Jesus would not fit into

them.   He was a square peg.   He could not be
disposed of as just another stock sample of a familiar
class.   To understand him they had to think.   They
didn't like to think.   They didn't know how.   They
wouldn't learn.   Pilate is trying the same thing
when he demands of Jesus, "Where do you come
from?"   He was trying to evaluate Jesus on the
basis of a geographical pigeonhole.

It is a very common state of mind.   It led eventually to the crucifixion and leads to much of the
evil and tragedy of the world.

We cannot pigeonhole Jesus.   We cannot force
him into any conventional classification.   He is
unique.   We cannot tie him up with any number
of individuals as just "another sample of the same
thing."   There are no other samples of the same
thing.   Jesus, to use Edwin Arlington Robinson's
fine phrase in "Merlin," is

> "The man who had made other men
>   As ordinary as arithmetic."

When Jesus becomes to us merely one of any
group he becomes nothing.

*   *   *

LIFE TO THE FULL

I have come that they may have *life . . . to the full.*—
John 10. 10 (Moffatt).

ONE of the many vivid pictures in the writings
of William James is his comparison of the position
of man in the universe to that of a dog in a draw-

ing room. He says that just as there is a world
of powers, ideas, and values quite beyond the dog's
sight, so there is a world of experience and values
beyond the world that is obvious to our eyes.

The mark of the abundant life, the "life *to the
full*," to the limit of our possibilities, which Jesus
desired to bring to men, is awareness and grasp of
that world of values and ideas and powers beyond
the elementary senses. That world is called "life"
in the Gospel of John. It covers much that is
called the "kingdom of heaven" and "the kingdom
of God" in the synoptic Gospels.

The problem of life, then, is to get out of the
realm of fractions; to cease to live on a mere fraction of our inheritance and powers, and to live *to
the full*.

The truth that ordinarily man does not live
more than a fraction of his possible life is made
clearer with every advance in the study of the
mind. Many lives are like a ship, creeping along
slowly on one small auxiliary engine, with the main
engines out of commission, giving none of the powerful drive of which they are capable.

Modern psychology brings real light to this
problem of living to the full of our possible powers.
It supports the theory that the chief cause of
fatigue is not exhaustion. When our energies fail
t is not because our definite, limited supply of
energy is used up. That was the old physical
theory of energy, now pretty largely abandoned.
The present new theory is that there are "resources
of power whose existence we do not ordinarily recognize, but which can be made available for the
purposes of our daily life."

Dr. J. A. Hadfield gives some remarkable instances of persons making available untapped resources of power:

A corporal, whose courage won the V. C., was for several days cut off from our troops, was exposed the whole time to bombardment (subsisting meanwhile on the barest rations), and yet, in spite of the awful strain, he came out feeling cheerful, elated, and without fatigue. Several men with him had the endurance to pass through the same experience, but at the end were exhausted and broke down. The corporal had evidently discovered sources of power which were not exhausted by the terrible strain he underwent, but provided an ample resupply.

Four years ago, at midnight, I witnessed an explosion at a great munition factory, and afterward heard that a woman, after her day's work, had risen from bed and, in anxiety for the safety of her husband and son, had run practically the whole distance of seven miles to the scene of the explosion in an incredibly short time.

We tend to live on a mere fraction of our possibilities not only in regard to energy and power but in regard to *joy*. Jesus expressly emphasized that normal result of the life he could impart—"I have spoken to you, . . . and that your joy may become perfect." It requires no labored assemblage of evidence to convince us that in our civilization, overflowing with opulence, the supply of joy is tragically depleted. Our rightful inheritance seems to be tied up in chancery. We can't get at it. The stupendous and brilliant feats of our civilization bring us no deep joy or content. Our buildings are higher but our joy is not more profound. As one has said, "We have machinery to manufacture everything except the peace which passeth understanding."

In a letter to the New York World a writer has described in picturesque detail people living on a fraction of life's energy and content vainly reaching out for impossible material panaceas:

All over the country there are muddled people seeking a sad Carlylian entrance to light. Everywhere you turn there are fuzzy-minded incompetents, unhappy idealists, and pathetically ambitious idiots who are looking for panaceas which will enable them to face life—the Darwinian unfit, seeking frantically for miracles with which to save themselves. These go in for beauty clays, gland treatments, miracle foods, mental sciences, and psychoanalysis indiscriminately. They don't go in for Roentgenanalysis or operations. They want something dazzling and infallible.

Our age has given great study to the task of adding years to our life and has succeeded marvelously. In the last fifty years the span of the average life has been increased by fifteen years. But the deepest problem is not to add years to our life but *life to our years*. That is the gift Jesus came to impart—*"life* to the full."

It cannot be acquired by a frantic plunge after acquisition of either things or sensations. That is a popular modern method. A character in one of William J. Locke's novels expresses this conception perfectly—"I would like to take life by the throat and *choke* something out of it." Life to the full never comes by choking; it must grow.

It is in contact with the Spirit of God that the gates are opened by which a liberating divine energy and joy come into life. The New Testament experience of the Spirit of God brought and brings the power of living life to the full. We cannot go through the New Testament without being struck again and again by the truth that the normal Christian experience brought a new increase of power. "I have strength through him who gives me power."

Love of God brings a unifying power to life. It harmonizes the emotions of the soul, bringing chaos into one inspiring purpose, and abolishing conflict. But it must be a love that shakes the whole life. That pale kind of emotion suggested by Matthew Arnold's unconsciously satiric definition of religion as "Morality tinged with emotion" will never do it. A "tinge" will not bring life to the full or turn the world upside down.

Sacrificial love to man brings strange recreative power. As the author of *The Lady of the Decoration* says in words worthy of a place in the New Testament: "The most miserable, pitifully smashed up life could blossom again if it would only blossom for others."

⚜ ⚜ ⚜

SAVE OUR HOLY PLACE!

The Romans will come and *suppress our holy Place.—John 11. 48* (Moffatt).

No wonder the Pharisee wanted to hustle Jesus off the scene. In these words the *real* reasons for their antagonism to Jesus crop out as opposed to the many *good* reasons, piously put forward by many to justify their conspiracy against him. In these words it is as though an unexpected gust of wind blows aside the curtain from the inside room of their mind and discloses the interested, material reasons for their fear and hatred of Jesus.

"We do not want our Holy Place disturbed." No doubt it was partly a religious fear. But it was also a disinclination to be jolted loose from a special privilege and order which paid them well.

They didn't want the established order upset.

That is an eternal objection to Jesus. We can hear the same angry and fearful cries flying through the air to-day from all parties, orders, Sanhedrins, whose settled advantages would be disturbed by the real dominion of Jesus over life.

"Our Holy Place," runs the real argument, no matter how plausibly it may be dressed up for show purposes—"our sacred twenty-per-cent interest, our traditional power over the lives of men, our war system, our race supremacy—will be suppressed!"

"Away with such a fellow!"

⁂ ⁂ ⁂

GET IT FINISHED SOMEHOW

Pilate *came outside* to them.—*John 18. 29* (Moffatt).

A CLOSE study of Pilate's movements during the trial of Jesus gives an overwhelming impression of *fidgets*. Pilate bobs in and out through the curtain like a nervous wreck. Now you see him and now you don't. He rushes out to the porch to bargain

with the crowd. Then he rushes back into the
house to work out a new scheme to get Jesus off
his hands. For that was the one idea behind all
this dashing back and forth—get rid of him somehow!

Six times he goes in and out between the crowd
and Jesus in the court room: (1) John 18. 29; (2)
John 18. 33; (3) John 18. 38; (4) John 19. 4; (5) John
19. 8; (6) John 19. 13. In that last passage he
reaches the end of his tortuous path of shuffling
evasions. He gets rid of the bothersome nuisance
at last. "Then Pilate handed him over to them to
be crucified. So they took Jesus" (John 19. 16, 17,
Moffatt).

So they took him away, did they? That was
what Pilate wanted, just to put Jesus down somewhere and be rid of him.

Took him away, did they? In that last scene in
this sordid drama of six acts the soldiers tied Pilate
so tightly to Jesus that all the centuries of a million
years will not dissolve the bonds. "Crucified by
Pontius Pilate." Who ever achieved an immortality like that?

This nervous, irritated effort of Pilate's to get
Jesus' case disposed of somehow is not merely one
man's tragedy. It is a picture of a way of meeting
responsibilities that is deeply embedded in human
life, which goes on endlessly. The white light
which beats about Calvary reveals where it leads to.

Get rid of it somehow! That becomes the ruling
motive or mood of many in dealing with problems
and responsibilities. Like Pilate, they have a
genuine desire to deal with them justly. But if
the problems hang on long enough, that first motive

is lost in a feeling of irritation and the chief desire becomes to shake loose from the problem some way —any way—as long as the thing is settled, and we escape the responsibility!

When a responsibility, a burden, a problem, gets on our *nerves* rather than on our mind or our heart or conscience, we are lost, as Pilate was. Watch your "nerves"! They are the most impertinent members of your whole being. They will usurp the seat of judgment. Pilate allowed Jesus to get "on his nerves." His "nerves" usurped the place of his mind, his heart, his conscience. Our own "nerves" will do the same if we allow them the run of the house instead of holding them to their legitimate place of service.

A major problem in the growth of character and the ordering of life is to refuse to allow the judgment to be stampeded by irritations, or the impatient insistence to get rid of the bother some way. For it was just that which led to Calvary. It always leads to some kind of a cowardly evasion.

❧ ❧ ❧

EACH GIVING A BLOW

And they marched up to him, . . . each *one giving him a blow.*—*John 19. 3* (Goodspeed).

Doctor Goodspeed individualizes the scourging and torture of Jesus by stressing the particular blow given by each one. It not only adds to the grimness and horror of the scourging; it is also a vivid reminder of individual responsibility. Jesus did not suffer any general indignity. There is no such thing. He suffered a succession of particular insults and assaults—each one as definite and responsible as if it stood alone.

Try to imagine this grim parade of roistering soldiers marching up to Jesus—one by one—and each one weighing the question—"Where shall I strike him—on the head or over the heart? Shall I give him a blow with the bare hand or a club?"

It is not mere imagination. These questions did flash through the minds of these men.

It is not a pleasant thing to run through one's mind, for it has another question trailing after it —what kind of a particular blow do *we* give Jesus? What is our special peculiar way of striking Jesus and his cause?

Several considerations come to mind as we think of ourselves as possible members of this company.

Some undoubtedly must have struck Jesus merely because they were in a parade where it was the fashion. That is the subtle danger of fashion parades.

It is inconceivable that each one of these men had a definite reasoned animosity to Jesus. It is very probable that none of them had. Brutality had merely become a thoughtless tradition, a bar-rack-room sport. The crucifixion was a sport event —of a sort—to the guard. The parade formed, marched past Jesus—the blows started, and each one, following along the almost automatic march, delivered his own personal blow.

The parade still goes on. We follow modes of life, indulge in ways of thinking, which are cruel blows to Jesus, to all that he stands for in the world's hope, to all that he died to accomplish. We do not choose deliberately to do it. We are in a fashion parade. We take our cue from the crowd.

These men struck Jesus publicly. Alas that so many of our blows are given in secret! We do not repudiate him publicly. But in the secret places of the heart—in the depths of life where motives are formed and the costs of sacrifices are weighed—we strike.

We cannot forget that the disloyalties of Jesus' disciples hurt more than the rough, crude assaults of enemies. The blow that hurt Jesus most was one that never touched him physically. It was not a blow on the head. It was a thrust through the heart. Can we imagine that any cruel stinging blow on the mouth given by a soldier hurt Jesus as did the denial of Peter?

"I never saw the man," cried Peter.

"Yes, I'm a Christian, but I don't really take it seriously," is the modern echo of Peter's words.

We do not say the words. We merely act them. "Each one." . . .

       ❧ ❧ ❧

FINDING A WAY AND MAKING ONE

This made Pilate try *to find a way* to let him go, but . . —*John 19. 12* (Goodspeed).

WHAT was needed was to *make* a way to let Jesus go. Pilate merely tried to *find* one. Pilate lived by finding things. He dodged all over the place looking for a way out of the responsibility of dealing with Jesus. He was pathetically eager to find a way. He did not lift a finger to make one.

When he couldn't find an easy, ready-made way of duty, instead of making one, he set out to *find* something else, a ready-made excuse, an alibi.

Josephine Daskam Bacon, in a sharp little portrait called "Pilate's Wife," has drawn this search of Pilate, first for the easy way of disposing of Jesus justly, and failing that, for the excuse consoling to his conscience. Pilate's wife is speaking of the crucifixion of Jesus:

"I have been worried, ever since his death,
  About my husband.
  I warned him many times of that young Jew—
  'Don't let those ignorant natives kill him,' I begged,
  'You will be bitterly blamed for it,
  Sometime, somewhere!'
  He was too fair, too logical, my husband.
  'But think,' he said, 'what I am bound to do,
  In these outlandish districts!
  Rome rules by tact, by suppleness, by smoothness.
  It seems they want to kill him—we must let them.
  Bloodthirsty rabble!'
   He washed his hands in water before them, later.
  They were so crude, one spoke to them in pictures—"[1]

This text throws into bright light two types of character—two ways of living.

There is the haphazard, impersonal, lucky way of *finding* something.

There is the personal, costly, creative way of *making* something.

[1] From *Truth o' Women*. D. Appleton & Company, New York, publishers. Used by permission.

Unconsciously or consciously we choose one or the other method of life.

We find plenty of things in life. Even Pilate finally found a way of getting rid of Jesus. But the ways we find are like the way Pilate found; they lead to nothing or they lead downward.

We never find a way to real achievement. We speak of Columbus finding a way to America. He didn't find a way. He made it. Goodyear didn't find a way to manufacture rubber. He made it, through a weary road of endless obstacles.

We do not find a way to character or great service. True, life has its great surprises and we find chances and opportunities, as Jesus portrayed in the parable of the man finding the treasure in the field. To get it, however, he had to sell all and fashion life into the deliberate business of winning it by a great concentration.

Mankind will never find a way out of great social evils. We must make it, through toil and tribulation. One of the greatest obstacles to social betterment has been the lazy, blind optimism that in some way the world will accidentally stumble on to an easy, painless way out of the wrong. One of the striking things in Beard's *Rise of American Civilization* is the recital of the manner in which politicians both of the North and South, for a whole generation before the Civil War, refused honestly to face the slavery issue, and clung to the vague, baseless hope that some way of settling the issue would appear out of the clouds.

Many now take the same attitude to war. Every one would be glad to find a way to get rid of it. No way will ever be found; it must be made. One

of the great soldiers of our time, Foch, in one of
his principles of war, has indicated a first principle
of peace-making: "We must always seek to create
events, not merely to suffer them."

❧ ❧ ❧

THE LEGACY OF A LIFE

The upper room where they were *in the habit* of meeting.—*Acts 1. 13* (Moffatt).

A MODERN realist attempting to assess what
Christianity actually was in the world in these first
days of its existence would have presented a rather
sorry invoice. To the materialistic eye it was not
much more than is contained in this verse—a
rather loosely formed habit among a few obscure
and insignificant people from among the lower
strata of Jerusalem society. The whole crowd,
including the fringe, was a hundred and twenty
altogether. There was no "program" or organization. The paraphernalia of a modern "movement" were absent.

It was a very tenuous and slender legacy which
Jesus left in the world—just a few people with
personal devotion and a few reminiscences.

No great character ever left so *little*.

No one ever left so *much*.

It was enough to transform the world.

One striking thing about this legacy of Jesus is
that it is just what most of us leave when we pass
out of this world—a few devoted friends and some
reminiscences—a pathetically meager legacy. And

yet it all depends on the quality of the reminiscences. If the quality is fine and strong, this same legacy which Jesus left and which we leave may be a real transforming and abiding force.

Some men leave more and other than this. Some have left a large estate, to bless or curse. A very few men have left a compact body of thought as their gift to the world. Some have left a name or an institution. Jesus, from one point of view, left what we all do—friends, on whom the quality of our lives has made some impress and the abiding memory of our spirit.

The force of a sunbeam, modern science tells us, gives the world as real a push as dropping a stone upon it. The force of a particular beam is infinitesimal but real and perceptible.

Is there light enough in us to give the world any kind of a push?

❧ ❧ ❧

THE PIONEER OF LIFE

You killed the *pioneer of Life.*—*Acts 3. 15* (Moffatt).

THIS description of Jesus, "the pioneer of life," is one of the great poetic insights of Doctor Moffatt. It is a great service to launch into the stream of thought such a truly illuminating and inspiring phrase. It is one of those great phrases described by Professor Simon N. Patten as being worth more than books because "they work harder and live longer."

A pioneer is one who enlarges the possible area of
life, one who pushes back horizons and blazes the
trail into new habitations for humanity. The word
catches many of the essential and unique meanings
of Jesus for the world. He, above all others, was
the great enlarger of life; the one who pushed back
the horizons of men's minds, sympathies and lives;
the trail breaker to new heights.

The greatest thrills of history lie in the glory
of the world's pioneers, from Abraham on his westward hazard of faith, pushing out into unknown
domains, down to the lonely flyer making the first
trail through the air across the seas. The great
human epic is the long daring trek of humanity
pushing steadily westward. Tennyson puts into the
mouth of Ulysses the very spirit of those great
pioneer souls who have led the parade:

"For my purpose holds to sail beyond the sunset
And the baths of all the western stars
Until I die."

Steadily through the centuries have pushed the
pioneers across the Atlantic, over the mountain
ridges into the great central plain of America; then
on over the prairies and deserts to the path of the
western stars in the Pacific. The Santa Maria and
the Mayflower, Magellan and Drake, Daniel Boone,
Lewis and Clark, and Livingstone—pioneers!

There is a deeper thrill in "the pioneer of *life*"—
Jesus. He was not merely a horizontal pioneer,
pushing back the horizons of continents. He was
a vertical pioneer, opening up a way into the high
heavens and the depths of the human heart.

Jesus pioneered a new and living way into the heart of the Father. He threw open a new home to the race—in the very heart of God himself. Because he was the way, we may follow. "Where I am, there ye may be also." "From God, *who is our home*," says Wordsworth.

Jesus opened up a new quality of life; he led men into new regions of power. That new habitation which he pioneered Paul well described. "The life I now live . . . I live by the faith in the Son of God."

Jesus crossed old frontiers. The ancient barriers of race and clan and color and class, with all their fearful taboos, with their high walls of exclusion, had no meaning for him. The whole course of social betterment has been but following the footsteps of Jesus through the wilderness of human suffering and need. Still, he is far ahead in the unconquered wastes of life.

This conception of Jesus as the pioneer of life saves Christianity from being merely a refuge. Christianity has been too much regarded as a harbor from storms, a refuge—a retreat from the conflicts of life. To escape from penalties and dangers and risks of life has been regarded as the chief end of a Christian. Many have learned only one hymn:

> "Hide me, O my Saviour, hide,
>   Till the storm of life be past,
>   Safe into the haven guide,
>   O receive my soul at last!"

Glorious as that is, deep and genuine as the need which it expresses is, it is inadequate. Chris-

tianity is an achievement, a venture, a discovery.
Its motto cannot be "Safety first." It must pioneer
to open up new achievements in living together.

> "The men of the East may watch the stars
>   And signs and seasons mark,
>   But the men signed with the cross of Christ
>   Go gaily in the dark."

To-day this conception of Jesus comes as a
needed impetus to the spirit of daring and risk, so
sadly waning in many quarters. Dr. Francis Green-
wood Peabody has described a prevailing mood
among us, even among Christ's disciples:

> Most of us devote a great part of our time to insuring
> ourselves against the risks of life. We accumulate money;
> we fortify health; we guard ourselves against uncertainty;
> we lay our plans for leisure, comfort, and old age. Abra-
> ham going out, not knowing whither he was going, Pil-
> grims launching forth into a stormy sea, soldiers risking
> all in the great adventure, Jesus Christ finding peace and
> joy at the end of his short career—all these seem remote
> from a prudent and judicious way of life. An assured
> income, a good digestion, an undisturbed conformity to a
> venerable creed—what can make one safer than these?

This is emphatically not the mood or spirit of a
pioneer. And it is emphatically not the mood or
spirit of Jesus.

The great aspiration needed to lift life to Jesus'
level of courage and the risk represented by the
cross is put into a remarkable modern prayer first
printed in the London *Spectator*. It worships Jesus,
the pioneer of life.

"Jesus, whose lot with us was cast,
  Who saw it out, from first to last:
Patient and fearless, tender, true,
Carpenter, vagabond, felon, Jew:
Whose humorous eye took in each phase
Of full rich life this world displays,
Yet ever more kept fast in view
The far-off goal it leads us to:
Who, as your hour neared, did not fail,
The world's fate trembling in the scale,
With your half-hearted band to dine
And chat across the bread and wine,
Then went out firm to face the end
Alone without a single friend:
Who felt, as your last words confessed,
Wrung from a proud unflinching breast
By hours of dull ignoble pain,
Your whole life's fight was fought in vain;
Would I could win and keep and feel
That heart of love, that spirit of steel."

❧ ❧ ❧

ANNOYED OR AMAZED?

The priests, the commander of the Temple, and the
Sadducees, *who were annoyed* at them teaching the people
and proclaiming Jesus.—*Acts 4. 2* (Moffatt).
Greatly disturbed (Goodspeed).

THERE are two kinds of people in the world,
judged by their characteristic reactions to life.

One kind is annoyed by incidental things. Their
prestige is not enhanced, their comfort is disturbed,
their routine is broken up, their exaggerated sense

of order is outraged. They are annoyed, because they live mainly for these things.

Another kind is too gripped with amazement over life's wonders, its surprising graces, its positive good, to waste nervous energy in fussy explosions over inconveniences or incidentals.

The crowd in the Temple praised God for the astounding miracle of abundant life, in the healing of the cripple and the preaching of Jesus the life-giver.

The Temple bureaucrats were annoyed. They had not seen anything but "disorder" and a blow to their self-esteem.

What is your most characteristic mood—annoyance or amazement? They are the opposite poles of life.

❧　❧　❧

OUTSIDERS

"By what authority, in whose name, have *men like you* done this?"—*Acts 4. 7* (Moffatt).

THE translation "men like you" is a bit of very dramatic interpretation found in a note of Doctor Moffatt's on this verse. He says, "With a touch of superciliousness ('men like you!'), which is perhaps better expressed in reading aloud than by any verbal periphrasis."

It is a feeling of snobbish contempt for an outsider, without ordination, without the authority of the religious caste. It is better expressed by a gesture than by a word. Indeed, the word "superciliousness" is a gesture originally. It comes from the Latin word *supercilium*, meaning "eyebrow." It is a lifting of the eyebrow in haughtiness and disdain.

The eyebrow is a fine test of mental quality and moral character. It can be lifted in disdain or lowered in thinking. These Temple aristocrats never lowered their eyebrows in real thinking over a new force or event. They were supercilious— eyebrow lifters. Snobbish contempt was so much easier than open-minded study.

Here was the haughty pride in being an insider, in being ordained, in being regular—ecclesiastical caste. You can see the arrogance in the expression accompanying the expression, "men like you!" "How could the grace of God possibly come to the world outside of the regular official channel?"

You can hear the sneer of the official insider all down the centuries. There is something very ironical in this conversation. Here was Peter, on whom the whole structure of apostolic succession depends, being challenged because he didn't have it!

"Men like you" has the sneer of official priestly complacency, flung at every prophet with the living word of God in his heart and on his lips, men who have come in from the outside with no diploma of official sanction—men like Martin Luther, George Fox, John Wesley, Roger Williams, William Booth, the woman Anne Hutchinson, and the whole company of God's Irregular Volunteers.

This sneer at "outsiders," directed against men who were furthest on the inside of the *mind* of Christ of any men who ever lived, ought to check our easy habit of testing the value of a prophet's message by its source rather than by its contents.

This chapter of New Testament history should teach us to beware how we call anybody an outsider. A person may be on the outside of every ecclesiastical caste and tradition and be on the inside of God's purpose and revelation. It should warn us effectively—a warning continually needed —of taking regularity of order or opinion or procedure too seriously. God has never appeared to notice it at all. God's revelations frequently come outside of the regularly appointed channels. This has happened often because the channels were closed, through arrogant complacency and contempt akin to that of these rulers, elders, and scribes.

That was one of the deep truths manifested in the birth of Jesus in a barn—a truth so easily forgotten.

* * *

WHAT WILL HAPPEN NEXT?

Wondering *what would happen next.*—*Acts 5. 24* (Weymouth).

As long as the church had the world on the *qui vive* it had measureless power. These Roman soldiers and officials after Peter's escape from jail were in a state of baffled expectancy. They couldn't figure where some strange unknown power would break loose next. But they paid the little church the magnificent tribute of expecting something to happen. It was a company in which things happened.

That attribute of throwing the world into amazed
expectancy was one of the secrets of its vital power.
It is always an indispensable secret of power. The
church has reached the bankruptcy court when the
world expects nothing to happen, when its life
flows on in placid routine from which no great
upheaval is looked for.

This wonderment which the church of the apostolic age caused affords a good test with which to
measure the church of our own time and our own
lives. Is there such an abounding vigor and resource-
fulness of Christian faith in us that the world is
constantly wondering what the next manifestation
of power will be? Alas, to ask the question is frequently to answer it that the world doesn't expect
anything to happen. We are not in the business
of producing amazement. We grow tame. We
slide into routine about which the prediction of an
unheroic sameness is only too easy.

Dr. H. R. L. Sheppard, the beloved rector who
served Saint Martin's-in-the-Fields, London, for
many years, and who in his own person and message possessed just this power of apostolic amazement, has said recently in a characteristic utterance:

Many onlookers "find our brave assertions and poor
achievements irreconcilable. . . . We appear to them like
Alpine climbers who, after boasting of the height they
were about to scale, take their ice-axe, rope, and other
equipment, and are discovered later proceeding cautiously up Ludgate Hill."

This power of creating amazed expectancy cannot
be acquired by a spurious sensationalism. It is
not outward sensationalism in the apostolic church

but a startling wealth of inner power and conviction that made the world wonder. The church cannot rally the world by blowing on a penny whistle, as is the superficial practice of many.

The real reason why the world does not expect more to happen *through* us is that so little has happened *in* us. Dr. James Denny put a finger on the creeping paralysis when he observed, "The number of people who suppose that they are Christians while it is all the same to them if Christ had never lived is appalling."

Christendom in the Middle Ages united in crusades to recover a lost tomb. Is there not a finer quest for our day—to recover a lost question mark? Not a question mark concerning the gospel's power or the church's mission, but the search for that abundant spiritual life and daring, that the world may continually ask the old question, "What will these astounding Christians do next?"

§ §§ §§

AND AT HOME

Not for a single day did they cease to teach and preach . . . in the Temple *and at home.*—Acts 5. 42 (Moffatt).

WE have not ceased to preach at the temple. But we have, rather largely, ceased to do it *at home*. And therein lies one of the major differences between the church of the book of Acts and the church of our own day.

Preaching at the temple is not enough. Indeed,

it is rather apt to be sort of futile unless there is the teaching *"at home."*

It is an urgent and timely word which comes from this exhilarated, creative day and company of the first Christian church at Jerusalem. Here was a secret, a largely forgotten secret of our time. Its recovery transcends many other much more imposing "programs" set before the church of our time.

Nothing can be a substitute for the shaping of Christian character at home. George Santayana, the poet and philosopher, a master of exquisite English, though born in Spain, writes with great insight concerning his use of the language. "The roots of the language," he says, "do not quite reach to my center. I never drank in in childhood the homely cadences and ditties which in pure spontaneous poetry set the essential key."[1] How beautifully and truly these words fit the spiritual experiences of millions of Christian homes! "The pure spontaneous poetry" of the Christian gospel has set the essential key of life—and the note has never been lost. The homely cadences of a faith learned and experienced in childhood can never be matched.

That apostolic age was much like ours in the deadliness of things which swarm in to crowd out religion from the life. It is a sobering thing to ask, "What will a generation be like which has grown up with no Christian teaching and molding at home?" Henry Seidel Canby asks the alarming question:

---

[1] Charles Scribner's Sons, publishers. Used by permission.

In the last war there were regiments of poor, stunted devils, syphilitic, tubercular, crooked in body, incapable of anything but menial work and the kind of fighting where hopeless endurance counts. They were the grandchildren of the factory slaves. What will the grandchildren of the tabloid readers be like? Healthy of body perhaps, for this exploitation is by flattery; not poor, not oppressed, for it is their economic power which makes them exploitable; but in emotions, ideals, intelligence, either wrought into fantastic shapes or burnt out altogether. Soiled minds, rotten before they are ripe.

In the face of such liabilities, shall we lightly let slip out the *"and at home"* part of that grand strategy of the apostolic age?

The question is far more serious than that—we are *already* doing it. The only question is, Shall we go on doing it?

❦ ❦ ❦

THE EARTHQUAKE PRAYER

Enable thy servants to proclaim thy message with *fearless courage.*—*Acts 4. 29* (Weymouth).

HERE was a prayer that shook the place like an earthquake. It was a prayer for just one thing— fearless courage. When a church prays for that, it always precipitates some kind of an earthquake.

This prayer is the key to an understanding of the abounding vigor and power of the apostolic church. It is a remarkable evidence of an indomitable spirit. After their leader's escape from jail and death, while they all stood in slippery places of peril, they prayed for just one thing—reckless, bold courage. Not a syllable about protection. Not even, in the excitement, a word of thanksgiving—just courage to carry on.

No wonder the house shook. You can lean your ear and heart down close to the fourth chapter of the book of Acts and hear the vibration to this day. It is like the ground swell of a new springtime. And that was exactly what it was—bursting life.

This is one of the first recorded prayers of the Christian Church. Suppose it had been a model of all Christian prayers—forgetful of safety and gain; intent only on the fearless courage of proclaiming Christ.

So many prayers of individuals and churches have the deep bass accompaniment, whatever the air, of "me, me, me"; "Save us from danger; increase us, magnify our organization"—these are rather constant notes in our prayers, not necessarily unchristian, save as they predominate. But this little company were desperately reckless—"Never mind what becomes of us, O Lord, only give us fearless courage!"

What house would not shake with that prayer to-day? Some houses of God do shake with it. Some towers of evil shake before it. Suppose it could be recovered as the normal burden of Christian prayer. What could not be accomplished? The solidified rocks of intrenched evil would experience an earthquake.

The newspapers a few months ago recorded a story of a clergyman in Vermont who recovered his voice and spoke aloud after whispering for seventeen years. Many a disciple of Jesus has need of the same miracle. Many have been "whispering" the message of Jesus for more than seventeen years—such a suave, velvety whisper that it startled or restrained nobody.

Milton's "Areopagitica" contains a strong, inspiring sentence concerning the heroic stand which he took against great odds: "God intended to prove me, whether I durst take up alone a rightful cause against a world of disesteem, and found I durst." This is the great poet's explanation of the heroic stand which he took against the social, political and religious opposition of his day.

"And found I *durst*." What an instinctive response the quaint and noble old English word awakens! It is matched by that simple, modest word of Lindbergh in his story of his flight across the Atlantic. "I decided," he wrote, "that I must not think any more about going back." That was the moment of triumph.

It was the moment of triumph of the little company of disciples and will be the only lasting triumph of any company.

We need to make that the chief burden of prayer, for we are so open to the mounting hesitations of what Wordsworth calls "the uncourageous elder years." Whether we are so elderly or not, we soon meet the uncourageous years. Instead of the assault on the world's evil, so full of risk and toil, we begin to play what is known in sport as "a defensive game."

We need a fearless courage to proclaim a spiritual universe amid a growing fashion of materialism; to proclaim a gospel of moral austerity in a day of tolerated license; to proclaim a gospel of justice and brotherhood in the face of powerful forces of exploitation.

⚜ ⚜ ⚜

THE "HEATHEN"

The Jewish believers . . . were amazed because the gift of the Holy Spirit had been showered *upon the heathen too.*—*Acts 10. 45* (Goodspeed).

AFTER nineteen Christian centuries this is still hard to believe and act upon. For these men of privilege, these Jews, with a strong consciousness of race and national superiority, it was a staggering amazement to be asked to believe that the Holy Spirit had been showered on "the heathen" as well as upon themselves.

Goodspeed's translation of the word usually rendered "Gentiles" as "heathen" undoubtedly better preserves the original values of the word. It gives us more of the emotional content which the word "Gentile" had for the Jew. To our ears there is nothing objectionable in the word "Gentile." It is even a designation that carries a tinge of superiority. But to the Jew it had just the feeling of condescension and implicit arrogance which the word "heathen" has.

This problem raised at the very birth hour of distinctively foreign missions in Christianity is a very timely and momentous one for the present stage of missions.

Can we readily and wholly and gladly admit the

Christian churches of what have been called "heathen" lands to a full equality with us of another race and older privilege?

This is the major question in missions in China and India to-day—as it was a major question in Cæsarea. On the way it is answered depends much of the future of Christianity in the Orient.

The development of a self-directing, self-governing church on mission fields has been proclaimed as an objective of the missionary activity of churches in Western lands. Are we willing to face all the implications of that announced purpose, and do it not grudgingly—with a tight grasp on property that will relax only by force—but eagerly?

Are we, the church at home and missionaries on the field, willing to give over the direction of the church to nationals, to take a subordinate place, to yield authority we have always held, to turn our property, to serve under native direction—in other words, to admit that "the heathen" have been showered with divine grace in as copious a manner as the white race?

The question takes another form: Have we ourselves been showered with enough grace to do it? It will mean renouncing the patronizing attitude to the "heathen" which has been a part of our racial and national inheritance. Kipling's phrase, "half devil and half child," as a description of "new-caught savage peoples," well expresses that patronizing attitude. Indeed the whole poem, "The White Man's Burden," might well serve as a Bible for the cult of Nordic supremacy.

To-day—as in Peter's day—the future of missions hangs in the balance.

BLOCKING THE ROAD TO CHRIST

We ought not to put *fresh difficulties* in the way of those who are turning to God from among the Gentiles.
—*Acts 15. 19* (Moffatt).

We ought not to put *obstacles* (Goodspeed).

Against inflicting *unexpected annoyances* (Weymouth).

HERE was a great principle of Christian faith—a Magna Charta of the church—unhappily so often forgotten. If it had been kept in the high central place to which the apostle James, with a great reach of faith, elevated it in this Christian assembly in Jerusalem, the history of Christianity would have been a far more glorious story. "We have no right," he declares, "to put fresh difficulties, obstacles, unexpected annoyances in the way of those coming to Christ from heathenism."

Circumcision, which was the matter under discussion, was a Jewish rite. It had no place whatever as a requirement for Christian faith and discipleship. It was exactly described in the words, "fresh difficulties" and "unexpected annoyances." It blocked the way like a stone fence erected at the entrance of the house of God. "Believe on the Lord Jesus Christ, and thou shalt be saved" was the sufficient Christian evangel. Rites and tests which were not an essential part of this one great message were an insufferable annoyance. They not only blocked the path to Christ; they obscured him.

Yet down through the centuries to this day men have done the thing here condemned. They have imposed legal and intellectual difficulties and annoyances which are not vital parts of Christian faith. Frequently the essential simplicity of being a

Christian has been lost in the mazes of metaphysical and philosophical speculations to which the convert has been required to subscribe. Frequently wandering around amid these conjectures embodied in creeds and confessions, expressed in the thought forms of other long-past centuries, the simpleminded man has been tempted to cry, "They have taken away the Lord . . . and we know not where they have laid him."

This priceless inheritance from the first days of the church is a charter of liberty, freeing the Christian from burdens and tests which Christ himself did not lay down. We have no right to make it harder to become a member of the church than Jesus made it to become one of his disciples. We have no right to impose burdens which Jesus himself did not impose. The requirements for inclusion in Christ's church have often contained, and in many instances still do contain, elements alien from and additional to essential Christian faith according to Jesus. What an absurdity it has been to make membership in the church depend on things which the apostle Paul himself would not understand and never even heard of. Yet it has often been done.

And how the churches have exported these extra, illegal burdens to non-Christian lands! The relics of old conflicts, of the theological battles of the Middle Ages, of the later physical battles of the Civil War in America, incidentals of the history of Western nations which are saddled on to the Christian faith—though no real part of it—have been carried across the seas and set up as requirements of faith in Christ.

Would anything mean more to the cause of Christ

than that we might recover for our time this faith and vision of James, able to distinguish the essential from the incidental in our gospel, and to present Christ, unencumbered by any "unexpected annoyance"?

❧ ❧ ❧

THE MOB MIND IN THE BOOK OF ACTS

They got hold of some idle rascals *to form a mob.—Acts 17. 5* (Moffatt).

THE book of Acts furnishes a fine field for study of the mob mind in action. In the unthinking mobs which assaulted Paul again and again there is the play of one of the most malignant and destructive forces in the world. About society to-day the old entail of the herd mind still clings and becomes the mob mind, which is one of the most ugly and horrible manifestations of all human nature. It is in truth no mind at all, but a wild, contagious impulse which puts the mind out of action. The mob mind is humanity on a wild, blind buffalo stampede.

Any real progress which the world may make in the future depends on the liberation of mankind from the herd mind. This involves substituting thought for blind instinct, stirred by fear, hatred, and prejudice. In a word, it depends on education. It is a help in this process to recognize the blind, irrational action of the mob in the events recorded by the book of Acts, how it is skillfully played upon by all the arguments and incitements so familiar in

our day until it rushes and roars and kills with the
rage and cruelty and blindness of an angry bull.
We see that Christianity here runs the familiar
gauntlet of charges well calculated to stir up the
herd instinct of the mob, that it endangers social
security, is an enemy of the state, is not patriotic,
hurts business, is impious.

The familiar incitement that business will suffer
is made and the inevitable result follows, "The city
was filled with confusion . . . they rushed like one
man."

How many efforts at social betterment to-day
suffer the same frenzied mob cry!

In Acts 16. 20 we find the familiar mob frenzy
stirred up by an appeal to patriotism. The crowd
is urged to stamp out Christianity and mob its
adherents because it is not patriotic! "These fel-
lows are Jews [there was the eternal appeal to race
prejudice] who are making an agitation in our
town. They are proclaiming customs which as
Romans we are not allowed to accept or observe."
They are subverting the empire. It sounds like a
modern blacklist put out by one of our fussy societies
of professional patriots, charging some of the outstanding Christian personalities of the country with
being Bolshevists because they do not take all their
ideas ready made from military bureaucrats.

In John 19. 12 we find this sort of threat was
used very successfully on Pilate during the trial
of Jesus. "If you let him go, you are no friend
of the emperor's!" urged the Jewish politicians.

In Acts 14. 2 "Refractory Jews stirred up and
exasperated the feeling of the Gentiles against the
brothers."

Acts 21. 28 shows the same raucous cry of appeal to race and nationalistic prejudices, making an emotional atmosphere in which straight and fair thinking is impossible. "To the rescue, men of Israel!"

Acts 22. 23. The modern art of camouflage appears. During a heated discussion the enemies of the apostles and of Christianity threw dust in the air to prevent reasoning and to obscure the issues. Compare that blind appeal to chaotic passion with the clear mind, the self-control, the deep wisdom of the town clerk of Ephesus, a man who deserves far more fame than he has ever received. For he represents the hope of the world, that the individual judgment, unclouded by fear or hate, may have growing dominion over that heritage from our subhuman past, the herd mind and the mob mind.

* * *

WHAT IRRITATES YOU?

His soul was *irritated* at the sight of the idols.—*Acts 17. 16* (Moffatt).

ARE you irritable?

Modern science has shown that, in a real sense, to ask this question is equivalent to asking, Are you *alive?*

Irritability, as the word is generally used, is regarded as a defect of character. It is the mark of a runaway nervous system which has gotten out of control. And we are all anxious to avoid a collision with that kind of a runaway. We give the "irritable" person a wide berth—when we can.

But that nervous tendency to explode on the smallest provocation is merely a perverted sensitiveness. It is a degenerate irritability, focused on the wrong objects. Science tells us that irritability is the real glory of life, the essential power which distinguishes life from inert matter. "A living body is an organism," says G. T. W. Patrick, "and the peculiar feature of a living organism is the possession of a group of unique properties, of which the two most conspicuous are *irritability* and reproduction."[1]

Dr. George A. Dorsey thus describes the essential place of *irritability* as the basis of life:

All life is irritable. This irritability inheres in every living cell of every living body. Because of that quality the amoeba is excited to explore its world and man his. That quality leads to the ego in the individual and to culture in the human race.

The enemies of Socrates were so excited that they put him to death. Hunger can so excite an amoeba that it commits cannibalism. Moisture and heat so excite a grain of wheat that it sprouts; if it does not respond to sprouting stimuli it is dead. An amoeba beyond the stage of excitability is dead.

Irritability is in the nature of living things, regardless of size and shape, whether plant or animal, one-celled or many-celled, and of every cell in every living body. Because of this irritability, life responds. Without excitability there could be no response to physical or chemical change in environment.[2]

---

[1] *The World and Its Meaning*, p. 77. Houghton Mifflin Company, publishers. Used by permission.

[2] *Why We Behave Like Human Beings*. Harper & Brothers, publishers. Used by permission.

An amœba without "excitability," "irritability," is dead. So is a human soul.

Paul was alive. His soul was so sensitive that he could be irritated ("exasperated," Goodspeed translates it) by the sight of idols and all that they represented.

One of the chief differences between human beings lies in the kind of things which arouse their irritation. Of course there is perhaps another group whose chief characteristic is torpor, sluggishness of mind and spirit, who don't get irritated or stirred by anything. Their family line seems to draw heavily on the vegetable kingdom. They emulate, amid life's alarms, the fine placidity of the cabbage.

But most people are richly dowered with sensitiveness, capacity to respond, an excitability in the physical sense. Hence the vital question for each of us to face, How does this divine gift of irritability manifest itself? Is it a noble thing like Paul's, which stirred the soul over wrong or injustice or human degradation? Or is it an ignoble thing, a fussy energy which explodes when our coffee is cold, when we miss the morning paper or our self-esteem is wounded?

Paul went through enough hard experiences "to exasperate a saint." The noteworthy thing about that common expression is that the things which are "enough to exasperate a saint" never do exasperate saints. Shipwreck, stoning, imprisonment— none of these things irritated him. The sight of idols did. The vision of the ruin and degradation brought to the sons of God by a pagan ideal of life stirred his whole being.

Here are two men, both endowed with the same

high power of irritability. One is that unlovely
creature, the overgrown baby. He is intensely
"irritable." His prestige, his comfort, his crotchets
and opinions, his "rights"—any invasion of these
things touches off Vesuvius. But great human
injustices, suffering of others, aching needs do not
jar him at all. Another man, like Paul, has so risen
in the scale of life that his irritability is connected
with higher centers of the mind—his sympathies are
stirred and his energies are moved to action.

Where do we stand in the scale of life? Have
we retained a capacity for moral indignation which
Paul here displayed?

Two of the gravest dangers which threaten to
atrophy this high endowment of the soul are cynicism and cloistered selfishness. That latter danger
is well put in a satirical quatrain which recently
won a prize offered by the London Spectator:

> "St. Francis of Assisi
>   Was incapable of taking things easy;
>   That is one of the advances
>   We have made upon St. Francis."

Is our irritability of the Christlike character of
Paul's?

❧ ❧ ❧

ARDOR AND ACCURACY

He preached and taught about Jesus with *ardor and
accuracy.*—Acts 18. 25 (Moffatt).

A DIVINE combination of qualities, twin jewels of

the mind and heart—ardor and accuracy—fire and precision—poetry and geometry!

What a superb ideal for Christian teaching and preaching!

If we wish to realize what an essential combination for the proclamation of the gospel it is, we have only to glance at the ills which follow where one of these qualities appears without the other.

There has been plenty of preaching with ardor, but, alas, with little discernible accuracy. Such a flame is like a fire which has gotten out of control. Such ardor has often come from the hot flames of animosity, of polemical controversy, of unrestrained emotion, or a debauch of exaggerated passion. It has often shown a lack of discernment, condemned, like the Prince in Tennyson's "Princess," to mistake the shadow for the substance.

On the other hand, accuracy alone is often sterile. It may be a soul without a body. The most correct and precise logic on earth can never say to an impotent soul, "In the name of Jesus of Nazareth, rise up and walk." Macaulay has described the best parliamentary oratory as "reason penetrated and made red-hot with passion."

It is the same high fusion of mental qualities which Apollos possessed. Emerson's tribute to ardor is all the more effective from one of his temperament: "The eloquent man is no beautiful speaker but one who is inwardly and desperately drunk with a certain belief."

This description of the preaching of Apollos presents the only ideal which can meet the need of our time—the need of an intelligent faith, quickened and emerged with life-giving emotion.

There is the danger of what has been well called an arid liberalism—so intent on stating the position that the gospel seems to be an academic exercise of intellectual formulation, with no consuming passion or redeeming power. On the other hand, there is the danger of an "inaccurate" gospel, in which the great simplicities of Christ are lost in a confusion of accessories, or smothered in a din of outworn shibboleths.

❧ ❧ ❧

COMMISSIONED TO ATTEST

The commission I received from the Lord Jesus *to attest the gospel* of the grace of God.—*Acts 20. 24* (Moffatt).

To attest is to "certify as true." Paul's commission was to certify the gospel of the grace of God as true, to prove it.

Every disciple's commission is a commission to prove the truth of the gospel, to furnish the evidence from experience by which it can be recognized as true.

This is a much larger commission than to talk about it, to sing about it, or to praise it. Proving it is a more considerable undertaking.

"Come let us *live* the poetry we sing," cries Edwin Markham. That is every man's commission.

It is proof the world waits for. As it is stirringly expressed in the statement of aims of the British Conference on Christian Politics, Economics and Citizenship:

If the Christian ideal vividly expressed and plainly translated into terms of action could be proclaimed, we believe that the new age now opening might be fashioned according to the pattern of Jesus Christ. We Christians can only fail if we are either not intelligent enough to understand our gospel or not honest enough to apply it.

"It is not enough to sit together in heavenly places; we must stand together in unheavenly places."

The only possible method of proof is to furnish in actual experience in individual and collective living, that the unblurred features of Jesus, his mind and spirit, in the words of the text, the very "gospel of the grace of God" shine through.

We frequently succeed, in our efforts to portray Jesus, in giving more of a portrait of ourselves than of him. Philip Guedalla, in *The Second Empire*, says of the Life of Cæsar written by Napoleon III, "The portrait of the artist was excellent but it was less easy to reconcile it with the hard features of Julius Cæsar."[1] A common failure of portraiture, constructing a mirror for the artist instead of a portrait of the subject.

William Lyon Phelps thus notes the same common blunder in portrait painting and another equally fatal one:

A portrait painter may show more of the personality of the artist who copies than of the subject copied. Like stained glass is more conspicuous for its own bright color than for the amount of sunlight it transmits.

He may take more of the accessories than of the person. It is easier to copy incidentals and furnishings.

---

[1] G. P. Putnam's Sons, publishers. Used by permission.

Either of these will cause us to fail in our commission to attest, to prove true, the gospel of God's
grace in Christ.

⁂ ⁂ ⁂

WHEN DO YOU STOP LISTENING?

Until they heard this last statement the people listened
to Paul.—*Acts 22. 22* (Weymouth).

EAGERLY, sympathetically, approvingly these Jews
listened to Paul until he mentioned his being sent
as "an apostle to nations far away"—to the Gentiles, the heathen.

Then it was all over.

Bang went the door of their minds!

Snap went the shutter!

Boom went the explosion!

For in that statement he touched sensitive
nerves—their pet prejudice of aversion to the Gentiles, their sense of race superiority and special
privilege. Nations far away? Disgusting! So the
cordiality of the hearing ended instantaneously
with the cries: "Away with such a fellow from the
earth. He ought not to be permitted to live."

Thus end most challenges to dearly loved pet
prejudices and set opinions.

How modern it all sounds! How like yesterday's
meeting, to-day's conversation, the upheaval over
last Sunday's sermon!

In our hearing of the gospel many of us are
exactly like the Jews in their hearing of it when
it was first proclaimed so many centuries ago. We

listen up to the point where the gospel as preached or taught clashes with our favorite aversion, our cherished animosity, our prejudices, our profit and privilege. Then, inwardly at least, we cry, "Away with such a fellow!"

Max Beerbohm has drawn our picture as well as his own in his humorous confession: "I am a Tory Anarchist. I should like every one to go about doing just as he pleased, short of altering any of the things to which I have grown accustomed." So many are glad to have Jesus Christ go about the world doing exactly as he pleases—short, of course, of *altering any of the things to which they have grown accustomed!*

What is the point at which we stop listening to the teaching of Jesus, and shut the door of our mind with a bang? It is a very humbling but rewarding question to ask ourselves. The very act of asking it and searching honestly and frankly for an answer will be a means of growth in grace.

Sometimes it is this very point at which the Jews flared up in explosion. Some Christians, any more than these first-century Jews, cannot heartily join in carrying the gospel to nations far away.

"I don't believe in foreign missions," and snap goes the shutter of the mind. "We have enough to do at home"—true, far too much for one who talks like that ever to accomplish. Such people do not live on God's globe. They live on a man-made hemisphere, or, worse yet, in a bailiwick, a county, a township. God's love is the equator of the spiritual universe; it circles the whole earth.

Sometimes the prejudice that marks the end of our hearing the gospel is political. When it seems to come to a difference between Cæsar and Christ, the issue to many people is simple and clear. Cæsar always wins.

Sometimes the boiling point is economic. A man can "stand" the gospel as long as it keeps away from business. The sacred customs of the present order in the business world are an ark of the covenant which must not be touched. As long as the preacher sticks to individual morals or theoretical theology he will listen. But let him follow where Jesus leads —into the moral basis of society, social justice—the response is all too frequent. Reinhold Niebuhr has well pictured the difficulty of preaching the gospel in America to-day to an opulent, successful age:

In the history of the world it has probably never been more difficult to preach the gospel than in America in the twentieth century. . . . Your average American is really a pessimist because he is superficially an optimist; he is so thoroughly satisfied with his mechanical achievements that he cannot imagine a world very much better than the one in which he lives. He therefore defends the *status quo* with frantic enthusiasm against every attempt to change it. To such a generation it is not easy to preach repentance. Its people are willing to repent of comparatively insignificant sins, but they are proud of the very limitations of their civilization and tolerance of every effort to make their good seem evil.

In such a world it is very difficult to preach a gospel which demands that we prove our greatness through service and which measures the worth of a man by the contributions which he may be able to make to the spiritual development of his fellow men. There are many pious men in our churches who are perfectly ready to pray with the poorest beggar in the street, but they are not willing to embark upon the adventure of trusting their workingmen and of so organizing their industry that the life of the work and his personality will achieve significance. Many of these men could be won for a Christian adventure in business and industry by careful and courageous Christian pedagogy. But most of them are so proud of the very limitations of our modern life and so oblivious to its sins that they will make short shrift of any teacher of religion who tries to teach them the way of God more perfectly.[1]

When we stop the truth of Christ as soon as it threatens to reach us, we are still living back in B. C. with these Jews and not in A. D., the Year of Our Lord.

FINDING TIME AND MAKING IT

"*When I can find a moment*, I will send for you."—*Acts 24. 25* (Moffatt).

"I will *find time* later" (Goodspeed).

FELIX gives utterance here, in postponing the decision due on Paul's appeal, to one of the oldest and most persistent fallacies of the human mind—that one can ever *find* time. There is a strange delusion which hangs before the mind like a mirage—that we will accidentally stumble against a great big chunk of time that will be available for a hard or disagreeable task which we are trying to escape.

There is this unique characteristic about time which we overlook: we can *lose* time, but we can never *find* it. We have to *make* it.

[1] From The Christian Advocate, March 4, 1926.

This translation introduces a new idea to the familiar version—"When I have a convenient season." It contains that idea and more. It is not merely a convenient moment but *any* moment which cannot be found accidentally, without deliberate and costly effort.

Felix illustrated this perfectly. He found lots of moments for what he wanted to do—to satisfy his curiosity about Paul and open the way for a bribe. We read that he sent for him "pretty frequently" (Acts 24. 26), but he found no moments to face the big issue squarely and render a judgment. Such moments are never found. They must be made.

It is a truth to be especially remembered in an age when such a marvelous new variety of time-filling and time-stealing employments are let loose upon us. "The world is so full of a number of things" that the river of time rushes on like the rapids above Niagara Falls. We are swept irresistibly on unless we anchor ourselves by deliberate choice, as an island is anchored by an unshakable foundation. We live in a time surpassing all others in the multiplication of time-saving devices and inventions. Yet by a strange irony—like one of time's "revenges"—we have less time for many of life's major enterprises, such as self-discovery and the growth of personality, than any previous age. So the very multiplication of mechanical wonders has proved a boomerang in that it defeats often the *use* of time saved.

We have a common bit of advice that runs far deeper into life than usually appears. It is this: "Take your time!" That is, take it *yourself*. Seize it. For if you don't take it yourself and use it, be sure someone else or something else will take it for you.

Felix's vain and vague hope of accidentally finding time is a picture of the measureless amount of the spending of time lavishly by people who make no selective choice in what they buy with it. Life is like going into a department store with a severely and definitely limited amount of money. If you buy this, you *can't* buy that. And the expedition of life—unless planned with a painful and inflexible consecration—turns into a shopping expedition which spends its capital at the first counter. It may happen to be cheap, gaudy beads, but if they catch the eye, that settles it.

Christopher Morley has speculated suggestively about this appalling waste of time—figured statistically by the thoughtful dog hero of *Where the Blue Begins*, Mr. Gissing:

One of the things that struck him about the city was its heedlessness of Time. On every side he saw people spending it without adequate return. Perhaps he was young and doctrinaire: but he devised this theory for himself—all time is wasted that does not give you some awareness of beauty or wonder. In other words, "The days that make us happy make us wise," he said to himself, quoting Masefield's line. On that principle, he asked, how much time is wasted in this city? Well, here are some six million people. To simplify the problem (which is permitted to every philosopher) let us (he said) assume that 2,350,000 of those people have spent a day that could be called, on the whole, happy: a day in which they have had glimpses of reality; a day in which they feel satisfaction. (That was, he felt, a generous allowance.) Very well, then, that leaves 3,650,000 people whose day has been unfruitful: spent in uncongenial work, or in sorrow, suffering, and talking nonsense. This city, then, in one day, has wasted 10,000 years, or 100 centuries. One hundred centuries squandered in a day! It made him feel quite ill, and he tore up the scrap of paper on which he had been figuring.[1]

A feature of our modern life which keeps us from deliberately making time for the highest uses, and betrays us into the old fallacy of Felix, is the note of *strident immediacy* so characteristic of the mood of to-day. So many things must be done right away to keep up with the "swim" that those long processes of growth which are life's finest fruit find no sufficient time to mature. Many have substituted a kind of telegraphic impressionism for long-process fruitage.

William H. Davies has voiced in simple, powerful lines a protest against this ruthless tyranny of external things—a true declaration of independence of the spirit:

"What *is* this life if, full of care,
We have no time to stand and stare?

"No time to stand beneath the boughs
And stare as long as sheep or cows.

"No time to see, in broad daylight,
Streams full of stars, like skies at night.

"No time to turn at beauty's glance,
And watch her feet, how they can dance.

"A poor life this if, full of care,
We have no time to stand and stare."[2]

---

[1] Doubleday, Page & Co., publishers. Used by permission.
[2] *Leisure.* Jonathan Cape, Limited, London, publishers. Used by permission.

Are you a vagrant? A vagrant lives by finding things. Life has no high choices, no seizing of time for creative purposes. A vagrant, in his relation to time, ambles through life a helpless Micawber, hoping time will "turn up." Felix was a vagrant, even though he sat on a throne.

*ﹾ *ﹾ *ﹾ

THE METHOD OF INQUIRY INTO RELI-GION

"I felt *at a loss about the method of inquiry* into such topics."—*Acts 25. 20* (Moffatt).
I was *at a loss as to how to investigate* (Goodspeed).

THE baffling topic to Festus was "a certain Jesus."
Festus is not the only one who has felt at a loss about the method of inquiry into that topic.
There is only one sure method of inquiry, Festus, and you did not find it. Paul told you but you did not listen to him. You asked Agrippa, and he knew nothing about it. The one and only method of inquiry is *experience*. You wish to know whether there is anything in this way—this Jesus? *Try it.* That's the only really scientific method of investigation.
There are many methods of inquiry that have been tried. Men have tried logic. They have discussed Christianity as an academic problem—a thing to be proved or disproved by a clever entanglement of major premise and minor premise and conclusion. But a living thing can never be investigated in a vacuum of formal logic.

Men have "investigated" Christianity by the method of analyzing the physical universe—with physics, chemistry, astronomy, biology they have scrutinized the earth, sea, and sky. They have reported: "The earth is resolvable into so many elements. But our test tubes do not report God or the soul."

So this school of materialistic science has exiled from the universe all unresolvable mystery and wonder. Its revised form of Jane Taylor's "Star" would begin like this:

> "Twinkle, twinkle, giant star,
> I know exactly what you are,
> An incandescent ball of gas
> Condensing to a solid mass.

> "Twinke, twinkle, giant star,
> I need not wonder what you are,
> For seen by spectroscopic ken,
> You're helium and hydrogen."

So by that inquiry God is resolved into a myth. Jesus becomes a bedtime story fit for the race's childhood, and man is told, "You, my dear sir, are nothing but a chemical formula."

There is only one valid method of inquiry—for the Festus of yesterday or to-day. Try it. Try living on the hypothesis that Jesus' revelation of God the Father is true and that his way of life leads into the largest values. That experience will yield *facts* on which to build life.

❧ ❧ ❧

VITAL RELIGION

With a sense of what is vital in religion.—*Rom. 2. 18* (Moffatt).

THIS is Doctor Moffatt's translation of the words rendered in the King James version, "approvest the things that are more excellent." The phrase is put forward in Romans as one of the chief glories of the Jew in his religious heritage.

What a chief glory it is in Christian faith and experience, "a sense of what is vital in religion"! It is surely one of the highest endowments of mind and personality—an instinct for the essential, a discernment between the incidental and the living heart. Indeed, most of the evils, the blunders, the failures of the church through all history have come from a tragic absence of just this sense of the vital. The days when the church has specialized in irrelevancies have been the Dark Ages, no matter at what date they have appeared on the calendar.

What a gift for our confused day this would be —a wide acquirement of this high power of discerning the vital in religion! It is true that the longer the course of Christian history the greater the need for this sense, for the obvious reason that there are more accumulations to discriminate between; in the long years of its history Christianity, like a river, has made vast accumulations from the territory and years through which it has passed. Some of these accretions are true wealth; some are impediments. They are of many kinds, forms, organizations, formulations of beliefs, made at different periods. Without a keen sense of the vital, we are hopelessly encumbered with accumulations and are unfitted for the battle of faith to win the world.

We need, especially in America perhaps, to be on our guard against an external and superficial understanding of this over-worked word "vital." Vitality is frequently confused with vehement action. People who externalize their restlessness or energy are regarded as "vital." As a matter of fact, they may be merely noisy or fidgety. A man may have plenty of vitality and yet keep still. By the same token, he may be exuberantly noisy and have little real vitality. American "vitality" often expresses itself in terms of speeding automobiles, of crowds, speeches, drives, slogans.

The vital in religion is not the elaborate or the spectacular or the noisy. It is the essential source of life. It resides in the elements without which religion dies or becomes paralyzed.

Jesus' revelation of God is a vital center of the Christian religion. The truth that God is Christlike is, as Bishop Francis J. McConnell insists in *The Christlike God*, the vital center of the Christian faith. Everything in the Christian tradition must be brought to that test.

Likewise the central thing in our religion is the person of Jesus, not any theory about him. Theology has often missed this point. Jesus sometimes has been made a figure without life or beauty. As Dr. Herbert Gray has said, "He is used as a support for difficult and involved terms, such as 'the Incarnate Deity,' 'Very God of Very God,' 'the Logos,' 'the Second Person in the Trinity.' He is made the central figure in a transaction called the 'atonement,' to which many differing theories attach themselves. The central thing is the person of Jesus, and what matters more than anything else is to see him and know him, and then to love him."

Jesus' way of life, his ethics as incarnated in his person and life, are vital in Christianity. Almost everything conceivable has been substituted for this. Wearied with the substitution of superfine spirituality for the elementary business of Christian living, John Wesley cried out in his Journal:

My soul is sick of this sublime divinity. Let me think and speak as a little child! Let my religion be plain, artless, simple! Meekness, temperance, patience, faith, and love be my highest gifts; and let the highest words wherein I teach them be those I learn from the Book of God!

Sharing Jesus' compassionate sacrificial sympathy with the whole human brotherhood and all human need is a vital part of Christianity. Professor Blakie had it:

"On me nor Priest nor Presbyter nor Pope,
    Bishop nor Dean may stamp a party name;
But Jesus, with his largely human scope,
    The service of my human life may claim.
Let prideful priests do battle about creeds,
The church is mine that does most Christlike deeds."

❧ ❧ ❧

ENDURANCE PRODUCES CHARACTER

Endurance produces character.—*Rom.* 5. 4 (Moffatt).

Both these translations bring to light a larger principle of life than the more familiar words "tribulation worketh patience." "Patience" covers a much smaller area of the moral life than "character"; and "endurance," likewise, has a much larger significance as a way of life than the more detailed and specific word "tribulations."

As here translated, there is a truth as indisputable as the law of gravitation or the law of harvest, and as large as life itself. It is the law of harvest in the moral and spiritual realm. Character is the accumulated result of a long-period investment. It is not a mysterious "gift," as lawless and irrational as the gift of a fairy godmother in Grimm's Fairy Tales. It is not a mushroom which springs up after a summer rain. It is not produced by a clever trick, like the manipulation of a sleight-of-hand performer. Character comes from endurance, from fortitude. As Booker T. Washington said finely, "Character is the sum of all we struggle against."

Insistence on this great law of moral growth is always necessary, but never perhaps has it had a greater timeliness and urgency than to-day. For "endurance," to say the least, is not one of the favorite ideals of a large section of our generation. To escape the discipline of endurance has become the chief end of man. To substitute the short-cut, the clever evasion, for the hard and grueling discipline of obedience is the vogue of the moment. On the other hand, character to-day seems to many a prize of doubtful value, hardly worth the painful and costly striving of the years. To multitudes in the full flush of the gospel of self-expression, character is no longer life's pearl of great price, but a tarnished jewel left over from quaint Victorian days. So both the ripe fruit of character and its rigorous method of production have been discounted.

A popular mood of the hour is the exaltation of cleverness. Let a thing be bright enough, modish enough, and in the dazzle its moral quality is overlooked as inconsequential. As has been said of a certain section of British society on the Riviera, "They have no God and Michael Arlen is their prophet." This sort of cleverness as an ideal of life is the very opposite of what Paul here terms endurance or fortitude.

It is no wonder that this cult of the flashing, the stimulating, the superficial smartness has resulted in a lack of *staying power*. Without fortitude, endurance, staying power, life consists of many dashing starts and futile abandonments. Arnold Bennett says of novel-writing, "*Anybody* can write a good *first* chapter." Then comes the really difficult time for the conscientious writer. Then it is that if there is to be any character it must come through endurance. To carry life through to the working out of any significant plot, to the growth of any ripe fruit, the same quality of endurance must find play.

Lines of least resistance are lines leading away from character. The substitution of pleasure for discipline as the end of all our seeking, inevitably makes thin souls. There are not enough rigid vertebræ in the backbone to support a full soul. The shriveled fruit of pleasure and the emptiness of its rewards is well described in Robert B. Hamilton's famous lines:

"I walked a mile with Pleasure;
    She chattered all the way.
But I am none the wiser
    For all she had to say.

"I walked a mile with Sorrow,
    And ne'er a word said she.
But, oh, the things I learned from her,
    When Sorrow walked with me!"

The painful superficiality of many lives to-day comes from the unlearned lessons that fortitude, in the face of hard and rough conditions, depends on tribulation, endurance for the sake of a great ideal. It is disturbing to think of the appalling extent to which the rugged school of character described with such warm sincerity, born of personal experience, by Richard Hovey, has dropped out of millions of lives:

"Thank God for poverty
    That makes and keeps us free.
And lets us go our unobtrusive way,
Glad of the sun and rain,
Upright, serene, humane,
Contented with the fortune of a day."[1]

We cannot artificially create the material environment of other days which so often ministered to the growth of character by endurance, a ministration not produced by our present environment. But we can do much so to kindle the aspiration for Christian character that endurance and fortitude

---

against all the withering influences of modern life
will seem overwhelmingly worth while.

※ ※ ※

GOD WORKS WITH THOSE WHO LOVE HIM

We know also that those who love God, those who
have been called in terms of his purpose, *have his aid and
interest in everything.—Rom. 8. 28* (Moffatt).

We know that in everything *God works with those who
love him* (Goodspeed).

IT is doubtful whether any fresh rendering of a
New Testament text brings more light and prac-
tical help than these translations of Moffatt and
Goodspeed of this great verse of Romans.

One of the hardest texts in the New Testament
for many to understand and believe has undoubtedly
been Romans 8. 28, "We know that all things work
together for good to them that love God." No
doubt the difficulties of the text have been largely
due to faulty exegesis. But the difficulties have
been there. Few texts have been more often
preached upon, and it is a rather rare experience
to hear a satisfactory sermon on the text.

The usual tendency is to claim too much. And
the result very often has been to read into
Paul's statement a superficial optimism which does
not face the hard and tragic facts of sorrow and
sin. The text has been interpreted to mean that
everything in the world is for the best—a doctrine
scarcely, if at all, above the line of an unchristian,
pagan fatalism. Both Moffatt and Goodspeed

express the meaning of this great word of Paul's
in terms that avoid an easy misreading of superficial optimism and fatalism.

"Those who love God have his aid and interest
in everything."

"In everything God works with those who love
him." Here is a comforting faith to the highest
degree, which looks full in the face the whole of
life, with all its tragedy and evil, which does not
palsy the nerve of effort, but energizes for great
endeavor.

This great word—so rendered—meets a characteristic unfaith of our time, the feeling, sometimes
unconscious and unexpressed, that God has forgotten the universe and the race that he created,
that he stands impassably outside of its whirling,
its struggles, its agony, a sort of absentee designer.
This mood has been expressed with terrible vividness by Thomas Hardy in his poem, "God Forgotten."

"I towered far, and lo! I stood within
    The presence of the Lord Most High,
Sent thither by the sons of Earth, to win
    Some answer to their cry.

"'The Earth, sayest thou? The Human race?
    By me created? Sad its lot?
Nay: I have no remembrance of such a place:
    Such world I fashioned not.'

"'O Lord, forgive me when I say
    Thou spakest the word and made it all.'
'The Earth of men—let me bethink me. . . . Yea!
    I dimly do recall

"'Some tiny sphere I built long back
  (Mid millions of such shapes of mine)
So named. . . . It perished, surely—not a wrack
  Remaining, or a sign?

"'It lost my interest from the first,
  My aims therefore succeeding ill;
Haply it died of doing as it durst.'
  'Lord, it existeth still.'"[1]

Against the freezing conception of a God who "dimly recalls" his strange creation stands, as the only foundation which makes life sane or tolerable, this warm living faith of Paul's—"We have his aid and interest in everything."

* * *

PUTTING AFFECTION INTO YOUR LOVE

Put *affection into your love.*—*Rom.* 12. 10 (Moffatt).

IN other words, learn to *like* people as well as to love them in a formal sense.

The best commentary on the meaning of these words, which here look a trifle redundant but are not so, is the marvelous 16th chapter of Romans which is at once Saint Paul's catalogue of heroes and friendship. For in that chapter his heart reaches out to a score of people in divine love and warm human affection. Read it in the Authorized and Revised versions, in Moffatt, Goodspeed and Weymouth. Then you will know better what Paul means by "putting affection into your love" than you could learn in any other manner.

---

[1] The Macmillan Company, publishers. Used by permission.

There we feel intensely that Paul did not merely love such people as "Rufus, that choice Christian, and his mother who has been a mother to me," because they were of the same faith and church as himself. He *liked* them; he had an outrushing human affection for them. It was not love as a theological virtue but love as a human joy and necessity.

The shade of meaning which "affection" puts into the word "love" is necessary to the full meaning of love as used in the New Testament.

It is very possible and common to have love for other people chiefly as a kind of abstract theological virtue. That kind of a correct formal attitude may have a genuine desire to help others and to serve them with sacrificial cost and yet preserve at the same time a feeling of aloofness touched even with a certain condescension and contempt. That is the ever-present danger of missionary work at home and abroad. We may love our fellow men without any affectionate liking. But in doing so we miss two things—we miss half the fun of life and we miss the true Christian attitude and relationship to men.

Of this frigid relationship Emerson writes with keenness,

When I have attempted to give myself to others by services it proved an intellectual trick—no more. They eat your service like apples and leave you out. But love them and they feel you, and delight in you all the time.

Whitman puts the positive ideal of human affection filling up the formal attitude of love—

"Behold, I do not give lectures or a little charity.
When I give I give myself."

Even more so did Paul.   And Jesus.

The bonds of the church often set loosely and ineffectually because there is not that human grasp of heart to heart pictured here and in Romans 16.   Members of the same church are often merely cordial strangers, sometimes even that description is a hope rather than an exact description. And a fellowship of cordial, tolerant strangers will never become that miracle, a church of Jesus Christ.   Only where the Christian virtue of love flowers into human affection ardent enough to overcome all repellent rough edges can there be generated the vehement flame which will fuse humanity into a brotherhood.

❧ ❧ ❧

MAINTAIN THE SPIRITUAL GLOW

Maintain the spiritual glow.—Rom. 12. 11 (Moffatt).

THESE four words are a great poem.   There are color and fire and music in them.   They should never be analyzed and killed by neat, precise, homiletical partitions.   The one, two, three, homiletical tradition is too often like picking the petals from a flower—murder for the sake of dissection.

Baker Brownell makes one of the best illuminations of this text in words written without any thought of the text at all.   "Life is not the wick or the candle.   It is the *burning*."

Stephen Graham, in his *With the Russian Pilgrims Jerusalem*, describes the receiving of the Sacred Fire, which for many of the pilgrims is the crown of their pilgrimage.

Once they have received it, they seek to carry the pure flame back with them to their homes, and to "treasure as they would the water of life or the philosopher's stone." That is, of course, no easy matter. "It is often a difficult matter keeping the lamp a-burning all the way, through rain and tempest, and through stress of circumstances on the road. Some Russian writer will perhaps collect one day stories of the Adventures of the Sacred Fire; it would be a piece of national literature."[1]

The keeping of the sacred fire has already become an international literature. For this great injunction is not merely an ideal but a world-wide experience. Paul lived, as well as pictured, the possibility of having the spirit of Christ which makes the whole life glow; not merely past history but present experience.

The difficulties of the Russian peasants in carrying the lighted candle back home, "through rain and tempest," have a close parallel in the spiritual life. It is the highest of all fine arts to keep the spiritual glow from dimming—to keep the candle from being snuffed out, by gusts that blow from all directions, chilling winds of indifference or hot blasts of passion. It is not merely the task of sheltering the flame, but kindling new fire to maintain the glow.

It cannot be done by a false or overstrained emotionalism or sentimentalism. The spiritual glow

---

[1] The Macmillan Company, publishers. Used by permission.

can be maintained only by contact of the soul with the life of God which first brought light, warmth, and power into the life.

The alternative to maintaining the spiritual glow must inevitably be a dying fire, a hearthstone of the heart and mind filled with embers. In *Penguin Island*, Anatole France describes a freezing globe, such as was foretold by the now discarded nebular hypothesis of our planet's origin. In that picture we see in imagination the last forlorn man shivering over a pile of dying embers and the disappearance with him of all life and hope. It is a true picture of a freezing world on which the glow of faith has been allowed to die. It is also a true picture of an individual life when the candle of the Spirit of God has flickered out.

It is the sustained glow of a living religious experience which preserves life from the destructiveness of that plague so malignant to life's happiness and highest uses—boredom. When the glow which a living faith brings to life is gone a baffled sense of futility creeps into the heart in its place. That empty place which might be filled with a real religious experience is the explanation of much of the restlessness and disillusionment characteristic of our day.

This boredom is well summed up by a London physician quoted by G. A. Studdert-Kennedy. Through the dull roar of London traffic, as it floated in through the open window, the surgeon said quietly:

After all, the greatest of human miseries, the most deadly of diseases is one we cannot touch with the knife or save men from by drugs.

"What do you mean?" I said, "cancer?"

"Oh, no," he replied; "we'll get that little devil yet. I mean—boredom. There is more real wretchedness, more torment driving men to folly, or to what you parsons call sin, due to boredom than there is to anything else. Men and women will do almost anything to escape it; they drink, drug themselves, prostitute their bodies, and sell their souls; they will take up mad causes, organize absurd crusades, fling themselves into lost hopes and crazy ventures; they will torment themselves and torture other people to escape the misery of being bored. Anyone who discovered a cure for that would put an end to more tragedy and misery than all of us doctors and physicians put together."

Jesus Christ has discovered the cure. In the enlistment of the heart in a great affection for God and man, he keeps life's powers occupied and alive in the warm kindling glow of the presence of God.

❧ ❧ ❧

RALLY ROUND ME!

Rally round me by praying to God.—*Rom. 15. 30* (Moffatt).

EVERY day is Rally Day on the Christian's calendar.

This plea of Paul's voices one of the deepest needs of life—that of re-enforcement through other wills and hearts. It pictures one of the largest services we can render in life—that of being the supporting battalion, without which the best powers of some other life would never find expression or be brought to fruition.

Paul's own life is perhaps the finest demonstration of this truth which could be found. His battles were won not only by his own daring, intrepid spirit and forceful thrust, but by the auxiliary troops who "rallied round him" and made his best achievements possible. No one ever recorded more joyously or gratefully his dependence on a glorious and sometimes nameless company of people who could rally royally: "Onesiphorus, who often refreshed me"; "Andronicus and Juinas, fellow prisoners"; "Fortunatus and Achaicus—they refresh my spirit as they do your own, you should appreciate men like that"; "the brothers beside me."

So the tale runs on. He was ten times himself from the multiplication of personal power through rallying friendship.

It is not merely in prayer, with which this particular request is linked, but in the whole bearing and attitude that we really turn the tide of battle in another's life. Many a man and woman whose modesty and humility would prevent them from using the boast of Galahad,

> "My strength is as the strength of ten
> Because my heart is pure,"

would nevertheless gladly and gratefully cry "My strength is as the strength of ten, because it is literally the strength of ten who rallied around me."

The hours for rallying to another's need are varied S O S hours, even though no shrill call is ever sent out! There are the hour of adversity and

the often more fateful hour of prosperity; the hour
of the loneliness of grief and the equally needy hour
marked by the thronging of crowded popularity;
the dark day when one has failed to live up to his
best; when one has slunk to the rear or run up the
white flag; or when one has courageously taken a
Christian position far in advance of the majority and
the hue and cry of condemnation arises; or when
one sails by the siren voices of prudence which bid
him haul down the belligerent flag of a fighting
faith—all the hundred shifting fluctuations of the
battle of life.

Have we ever mastered the technique of rallying, that fine dexterity of love which, without pre-
sumption or magisterial dogmatism, can re-enforce
the heart and mind of another?

Have we ever mastered that particular brand of
the art of rallying mentioned by Paul—rallying
round in prayer—that rare art of Secret Service?

❀ ❀ ❀

PARTY CRIES

I beg of you all to drop these *party-cries.*—*1 Cor. 1. 10*
(Moffatt).

THIS expression, "party cries," gives a very different impression from that of the translation in
the Authorized Version—"I beseech you . . . that ye
all speak the same thing." Those words, "that
you all speak the same thing," have been used as
though Paul were enjoining a deadening uniformity;
as though he were urging the Corinthians all to

chant the same form of words, thus saddling a hopelessly literalistic and mechanical conception of Christianity on the church. The whole spirit of Paul's First Epistle to the Corinthians is opposed to this conception and Moffatt's substitution of the words "party cries" makes such a misleading interpretation of Paul's thought impossible. The meaning is amplified by the rest of the verse: "There must be no cliques among you; you must retain your *common temper and attitude*."

Paul was not pleading for the unvarying repetition of any shibboleth; he was not setting up any superficial or mechanical test of orthodoxy. He was warning against the fatal results of a divisive, fighting partisanship.

No one needs to labor the point that this plea, "Drop these party cries," has been needed and has been forgotten all through Christian history, or how it is needed and is so often forgotten to-day.

It is the eternal danger of the substitution of the lesser loyalty for the greater; of the burning of a hotter devotion to a segment of a thing than to the whole thing, or to the shadow of a thing rather than to the thing itself.

It is one of the crowning ironies of history that every great truth of Christianity and every institution which it brought to the world to be a great welding, uniting bond for humanity has been perverted at some time or other into a divisive party cry—a jagged, barbed-wire fence.

The incarnation, the atonement, even the doctrine of the Fatherhood of God, the sacrament of the Lord's Supper, baptism—all these divine harmonizing, unifying ideas—have been made the hoarse, polemical shouts of fratricidal warfare.

It is a vicious thing to attach the primitive, unreflective emotions of partisanship to Christian truth. It substitutes the lust of battle for the love of truth and the love of God. It substitutes the joy of breaking heads for the joy of winning hearts.

In the business of shouting party cries the distinctively Christian virtues are lost. Humility, meekness, long-suffering, peace-making, forgiveness —what place have these essential Christian traits in a partisan clamor and fight? What could be possibly gained for Christ if these, the indispensable marks of Christ, are lost?

All party cries drown the still small voice of God.

Over the centuries comes the clear voice: "Brothers, for the sake of our Lord Jesus Christ, I beg you all to drop these party cries?"

* * *

THWARTING THE SHREWD

"I will thwart the *shrewdness of the shrewd!*"—*1 Cor. 1. 19* (Goodspeed).

THIS is an "American" translation which is very disrespectful to a popular American ideal and idol. "Shrewdness" is not an exclusively American trait. The prophet quoted here was speaking to Hebrews and they have acquired at least the beginnings of a reputation for "shrewdness." But the shrewd man, the fellow who "beats the game," who outwits the other with a clever ruse, the sharp trader, the money-maker, is the hero of a large and reverent multitude among us to-day. It is a trait which rates high in a commercial civilization. Many of the largest fortunes are made, not by any production of new goods or additions to the world's welfare, but simply by shrewdness in manipulating the labor of others and goods produced by others.

But shrewdness does not seem to rank so high with God.

Here he is pictured as saying that the big winnings of life do not go to the wise manipulators, to the shrewd.

"I will thwart the shrewdness of the shrewd."

To explore the truth of this word we do not need to think of God as confounding the best laid schemes of the nimble witted. It is rather the truth that the shrewd schemers for self-advantage are thwarted by the spiritual laws of God's universe which cannot be altered and cannot be beaten.

The very maxims in which this ideal of selfish calculation are expressed are specious lies.

"He travels fastest who travels alone"—a shrewd observation on life, surely! Yes? But what of it? He never gets anywhere except to a lonely desert. The lone speeder in life misses its chief point, which is the fellowship of love and labor along the road. This was the motto of the priest and the Levite who passed hurriedly by on the other side of the road in the story of the good Samaritan. They made good speed and missed life. God thwarted the shrewdness of the shrewd.

"He who fights and runs away lives to fight another day." Innumerable inglorious retreats have been

conducted under this bright shining banner. It seems the quintessence of prudence. It is. It is also the motto of all the cowards in the world. It is also a lie. For "he who fights and runs away" may live a good many days but he doesn't live to fight. The habit of running away becomes ingrained and he spends his life in a dreary succession of shuffling evasions. He never knows the fun of a good fight. He is thwarted by his own shrewdness.

Life's deepest insight does not come from cleverness but from love.

❧ ❧ ❧

THE HUNDRED PER-CENTER

The spiritual man is *alive to all true values.—1 Cor. 2. 15* (Goodspeed).

HERE is the real One Hundred Per-Center—the man alive to *all* true values.

The phrase, "one hundred per-center," has had many trivial and cheap associations and uses in our day. It has been used in the interests of racial and national prejudice and intolerance.

Contrasted to such use is Paul's picture of life at One Hundred Per Cent—a personality sensitive to every sort of true worth, with every human power developed for use.

The sentence holds a fine definition of the spiritual man. It corrects a very common conception of a "spiritual man" as an essentially weak man. There has grown up a very frequent idea of "spirituality" as a deliberate retreat from large areas of life, coupled with a sort of disdainful attitude to common human interest and enjoyments, concentrating on a rather abstract and obscure virtue known as "spirituality." There has been much in the monastic practices of Christianity which furnishes a foundation for this idea.

The spiritual man is not the one alive to only partial values, not one who wears blinders shutting off a large portion of the human scene. He is one fully alive.

As opposed to this full-sided life of the man alive to the spiritual world as well as to the material, the fractional life is paralyzed. The sensory nerves of a man living a fractional life are alive on one side, or part of one side only, like those of a person injured on one side of the brain.

Such "paralyzed" souls are common. How many Peter Bells there are, for instance, who can see yellow primroses and catalogue them efficiently, if necessary, but are dead to any magic a primrose might work on the imagination!

Others are paralyzed so far as being alive to the values of the common fellowship of life is concerned.

Others are *dead to intangible, unponderable ideals*. They are blunt to the moral "feel" of things. Mr. A. G. Gardiner, in his sketch of Lord Birkenhead, gives a picture of a man dead to many intangible values:

The note of Lord Birkenhead's political life is the note of an easy flippancy. As the graces of youth vanish his bankruptcy of the deeper wisdom of affairs and of the disinterested attachment to a considered philosophy of government becomes more apparent. Perhaps he had too early and too intoxicating a success. His brains, as Lady Oxford wittily remarked, went to his head.[1]

How true that may be of Lord Birkenhead we cannot and do not need to judge. It is a fair picture of a large number of people.

Others are not *alive to God*. In Emily Dickinson's fine phrase they have "lost the Face that made existence home."

The word "half-wit" is much used in these days, in a flippant contemptuous manner. There is a real "half-wit," however. Our wits include the faculty for coming into the knowledge and experience of God. When we allow that faculty to become atrophied we are living on only a part of our wits. We are not alive to the highest of life's values.

❧ ❧ ❧

GOD'S FARM

You are *God's farm.*—*1 Cor. 3. 9* (Goodspeed).

"God's farm" has exactly the same meaning as the words, "God's husbandry," of the Authorized Version. But "farm" is much more of a colloquial word. It is a part of the daily speech and life of all—the very theater of life for millions of people, and, by so much, the word brings Paul's great figure of speech more immediately and arrestingly to our minds.

---

[1] *Portraits and Portents.* Harper & Brothers, publishers. Used by permission.

It is a perfect metaphor—the soil of our personality made fruitful by the influences of heaven rained upon them. Commerce with the sky is the secret of the productive life.

The words bring to mind also the wide varieties of "farms" God has to work upon. Some are as fertile and luxuriant as an opulent river bottom. Some are like the slanting field of a New England mountainside, full of bowlders, with a thick crust almost impervious to rain and sunshine, which grudgingly yields only a scrubby, scraggly growth. On some of God's farms the soil is exhausted; life is never replenished. On others the weeds have strangled any useful growth.

You are God's farm. What kind of a farm does He have?

❧ ❧ ❧

NOT ENGROSSED

Let those who mix in the world live as if they were not *engrossed* in it.—*1 Cor. 7. 31* (Moffatt).

Not *absorbed* in it (Goodspeed).

THE Authorized Version renders this text, "use this world, as not *abusing* it." Goodspeed and Moffatt bring out quite a different shade of meaning.

The word "abusing" suggests the waster, perhaps the profligate, who makes perverted use of life's powers and possessions. He "abuses" the world; does not use it reverently; makes it minister to wrong purposes.

The words, "Let those who mix in the world live

as if they were not engrossed in it," bring to mind
an entirely different problem and bring a message
to an entirely different need and class of people.

Most of us are far more in danger of being engrossed and absorbed in the world than we are of
abusing it. The person who runs the risk of being
engrossed in the material world is not only the
waster; he is the eminently solid substantial respectable citizen. He is all of us, who in the multitude
of interests, none of them perverse in themselves,
allow the life of the spirit and the task of the kingdom of God to be pushed out of sight into a corner.

❦ ❦ ❦

A GIFT FOR BABEL

To another the power of *discriminating between prophetic utterances.*—*1 Cor. 12. 10* (Weymouth).

THIS promised gift of the power of discriminating
between prophetic utterances is a boon for a civilization of Babel. To "try" the prophets is hard
at the best, when conflicting philosophies, cults,
and gospels clash in the market place. The difficulty
is magnified a thousandfold in the clamor of
prophets to-day. The most characteristic feature
of the present city architecture is the tower. The
Woolworth and Singer Towers dominate the sky-
line of New York; the Tribune and Wrigley Towers
of Chicago; other towers rise up to mark and
symbolize other cities. They are all only too
reminiscent of their great forerunner, the Tower of
Babel. Like the original Babel, they signify con-

fusion; not merely the superficial confusion of the clash of a score of languages but the deeper, more fundamental confusion of the uproar of competitive prophets and prophecies bidding for popular following.

For prophecy, in the large sense of the interpretation of life, is a national industry. If all the practitioners of the art, busily engaged in proclaiming, "This is the way, walk ye in it," should take out a union card in The Amalgamated Prophets' Union, the craft would become one of the considerable factors in the American Federation of Labor.

We have the Prophets of Doom, a flourishing order. The Dark Ages are upon us. Inexorable laws are steadily working out our destruction. Different sects of this great order specialize on different varieties of coming catastrophes. The Spengler School takes up the rôle of Gibbon and describes the Decline and Fall of Western Civilization. Wiggam specializes on heredity and portrays the race going to seed. The Nordic school of prophecy fills the air with laments over the color scheme. The resulting "Literature of Despair" is enormous.

On the other hand, we have the order of Saint Pollyanna, with its anthem of praise to the best of all possible worlds, in which we live. We do not pay much attention to Saint Polycarp in these days; but Saint Pollyanna is very much with us. Captains of Industry are her special devotees. Everything is for the best so long as dividends flow steadily for God's chosen children.

To enumerate even a portion of the contending

prophets would call for an appraisal of the whole thought world of our time. We have the prophets inveighing against democracy, a cult which makes such surpassingly strange bedfellows as Dean Inge, Mussolini, and H. L. Mencken. We have the prophets of self-expression, as the chief end of life (whether there is any self worth expressing or not); the prophets of contempt; the prophets of materialism, eternally reading the funeral service over religion.

What a gift, then, is this promised power of discrimination!

How may we discriminate? Is there any surer basis than fear, wishing, prejudice, or popular majority?

Paul's basis was to bring all interpretations to the test of the purpose of God as revealed in Jesus Christ. He approached the world and life with that as the key to their meaning and mystery. With that key he was, to use his own phrase, employed in another connection, "unafraid with any amazement."

That same test of the clamorous prophets in the world to-day is our possession. We can ask of every "prophetic utterance" the question—"Does its interpretation of life accord with God's purpose revealed in Christ?" With that starting point we can learn from all the literature of despair whatever it may have of instruction and warning, without being engulfed in a pagan fatalism and without being led off into blind alleys.

      ❧ ❧ ❧

THE CHEMISTRY OF CHRISTIANITY

We have all been *saturated* with one Spirit.—*1 Cor. 12. 13* (Goodspeed).

THIS translation which Doctor Goodspeed makes of the words rendered, "We are all baptized into one body," in the Authorized Version, gives a much more vital insight into the nature of the Christian experience.

Baptized is in the realm of physics. *Saturated* is in the realm of *chemistry*. The transformation of personality by saturation with the Spirit of Christ is far more like a chemical change that it is like a physical, mechanical operation. Baptism may be an outward, mechanical, rather superficial affair. Saturation, the infusing of the whole mind and heart with the attitude and outlook and purpose of Christ, is inward, complete.

The word "saturation" also preserves another fine insight. It makes clear that the Christian life cannot be divided into compartments. Faith in Christ is not something added to life, like an extra room built onto a house. It is something which penetrates all of life, as the sea is saturated with salt.

❦ ❦ ❦

ORGANIZATION—SERVANT OR MASTER?

By God's appointment there are in the church . . . powers of organization.—*1 Cor. 12. 28* (Weymouth).

IT is worth more than a passing notice that in this classic list of God's gifts to the church, which Paul draws up, the power of organization comes *seventh*. Of course the significance of this ranking must not be pressed too far. Very probably the apostle Paul was not drawing up such a list with any idea of ranking the different gifts in the order of their importance in his mind. It should always be remembered that Paul did not write theological treatises; he wrote letters. The list cannot be rightly taken as expressing his exact comparative valuation of the gifts of the Spirit.

Nevertheless, here is mention of eight gifts to the church which flash to his mind, while he is emphasizing the diversity of service. And of these eight gifts six come to mind before "powers of organization." Only one, the "gift of tongues," comes after it.

Surely, this is worth reading in an age sorely tempted to exalt organization to the place of first importance. Put this fact in glaring and frankly exaggerated form: We often rank organization first. Paul ranked it *seventh*.

Committees, bureaus, boards, secretaries, budgets, drives, publicity—these are the background and foreground of so much ecclesiastical activity. As someone has said overlooking the scene, "The cry of the churches to-day is not so much 'Save the world' as 'Raise the budget.'" An age of machinery demands a new metaphor. We could sing most properly, not, "Like a mighty army," but

> "Like a mighty *engine*
> Moves the Church of God."

The pistons plunge back and forth, the wheels interlock, the whistle screams, the organization moves.

The danger of all this, of course, is that it may blind us to the fact that the Christian life is a *biological function*, not a *mechanical* one. "Ye must be *born* again." "In him was *life*." The things which come first in Paul's list of gifts are those having to do essentially with the communication of life—apostles, prophets, teachers. These are supreme. When they are present other things, such as miraculous powers, organization, supplement helpfully. But they are not indispensable. To fall into the delusion that they are of first importance is, in the literal sense of the word, insanity. It turns the whole genius of Christianity upside down.

To-day bodies of Christians are depending on organization for things it can never produce any more than an automobile engine can give birth to an orchard.

To realize this is not to disparage the value of organization or administration. Paul counts it a distinct spiritual gift. But he keeps it in its place —seventh!

The irony of great mechanical achievement is that the machine becomes the master of its creator instead of its slave. This has been the history of the industrial development of the nineteenth and twentieth centuries. The machine comes as a labor-saving benefactor and then a new slavery develops, in which men are forced to tend the machine in a deadening monotony of standardized motion.

That same calamity threatens the church, that as the machine grows greater and more complex the task of keeping it going grows more and more insistent and engrossing, until the machine itself demands the greater part of the church's energies and the purpose it was designed to serve is obscured or forgotten.

The real source of a church's life and power is not in the engine or boiler room in the basement; it is in the prayer room and sanctuary. It is in lives that have the life of the Master. As it is strongly put by A. E. Zimmern:

> The long history of European Christianity, if it ever comes to be written, will be the history of a submerged and hidden movement—the tracing of the course of a pure but tenuous stream of living water which has refreshed the souls of innumerable men and women who have penetrated to its secret recesses, but has but seldom emerged into the open, to flow through the broad and dusty cities where the world's main activities are carried on.

❧ ❧ ❧

THE BIG PARADE

Love makes no parade.—*1 Cor. 13. 5* (Moffatt).

To make any change in the wording of the thirteenth chapter of First Corinthians seems like a sacrilege. The cadences and the music of this great masterpiece of divine poetry have a place in the world's heart that is unique. It will ever remain undisturbed.

At first thought, then, it would seem that here is a portion of the New Testament where no new translation can render any service. Yet the fact is that it is right here that the renderings of Moffatt, Weymouth, and Goodspeed are particularly rich in suggestive insights. They are not intended to be used as substitute versions but as interpretative comments. So used, they present details and expressions which lead us into new appreciation of the chapter, like the play of fresh sunbeams on a tower of jewels.

This particular translation of Doctor Moffatt, "Love makes no parade," has a veritable touch of genius in the use of the word "parade." It is hard to imagine any word which would so clearly and picturesquely express the very opposite of the true spirit of love. It expresses vividly the subtle egotism which is so often alloyed with love or even substituted entirely for it and yet passes for the real thing. Making a parade is a gratification of the insidious and deeply planted desire for self-display; the concern for getting personal credit in every action and relationship. When the parade instinct is let loose the parade itself becomes the chief thing, and the distinctively Christian virtue of spontaneous, self-forgetful love is lost amid the fuss and feathers and display.

True love makes no parade. The person who parades his affection and benevolence always has at least one eye on the mirror, generally two. He is like the little bird with a white patch in his tail in Robert Frost's poem, in "North of Boston," which keeps flying from branch to branch in front of you and takes everything said as personal to himself.

The subtle danger is that when a parade of affection, whether in words, motions, or deeds, is staged, the parade exhausts the emotion. It satis-

fies with a premature substitute the real energy
of love which should expend itself in deeds and
not in formations and gestures.

That is true of a parade of personal affection.
It is almost always true that the more of an outward splurge there is, the less of deep sacrificial
love to the uttermost there is. It is true of benevolence. How easy it is to make a parade of service!
We can make it impressively in preambles and
resolutions and ringing declarations of sympathy.
These are innocent enough if they are only preambles. But they have a pernicious way of becoming the whole thing. When the parade is over,
all is over.

ở *ở* *ở*

EAGER TO BELIEVE THE BEST

Love is . . . always *eager to believe the best.*—*1 Cor.
13. 7* (Moffatt).

VERY directly this word goes to the heart of one
of the commonest human failings. "Failing" is too
mild a word. It is a distinct and destructive vice.
A kind of appetite for bad news, a zest for calamities, a reluctance to put the best construction on
an incident or personality, crops out with appalling
frequency in human nature. Sometimes this degenerates into a ready ear for scandal, a delight in
evil report, a malignant enjoyment in talebearing
—a vice which receives the severest condemnation
in both the Old and New Testaments. But frequently it is not a simple matter of recognized evil.
It is a much more subtle tendency to persistent

pessimism in human relations, or a tendency to cynicism, a grudging unwillingness to kindle into generous faith in another's best powers and possibilities. It was an avowed cynic who reported, "There is something not entirely unpleasant to us in the misfortunes of our best friends." That is a slander upon human nature; and yet the crabbed and acid remark does preserve a rather accurate observation of queer twists of human minds. That disposition is the result of competitive feeling in regard to others and of an undisciplined egoism.

Doctor Moffatt's rendering, "eager to believe the best," adds an important meaning to the rendering of the original Greek text as "Love believeth all things." The rendering in the Authorized Version has often been mistakenly understood as praise of credulity; of an unsophisticated readiness to believe anything, a type of mind easily imposed upon, and therefore weak. That unfortunate trait is not what the apostle is praising as an attribute of real love. It is, rather, the "set" of the mind to believe the best possible, as soon as it is possible and as long as it is possible.

The priceless value of that quality of mind and soul is that such eager faith to believe the best is one of the greatest creative forces in life. Such love actually *creates* the best in others which it is eager to believe in. Such eagerness to believe the best is like the chemical solution which brings out the lights and shadows of a photographic plate or film. It was exactly in such a way that the eagerness of Jesus to believe the best of men brought out from the recesses of their personality powers which neither they nor others had ever suspected.

It is the steadfast persistence of this eagerness to believe the best of others which has made some of the most glorious history of the world possible. This history has been largely unwritten, buried deep in the secret recesses of the heart where character is developed. But it is the world's most important history nevertheless. For such persistent faith has acted on souls like the breath of springtime sweeping over a garden, bringing out the buried power and beauty which could never emerge in a killing December climate of distrust.

In race and national relations there is no attitude of mind more supremely necessary than this eager love and faith to believe the best. It is the beginning of all wisdom in international and interracial relationships. It is so easy to give up this attitude of steadfast eagerness to believe the best and to slouch back into prejudices and contempts and fears and hysterics which demand no effort.

But that way lies madness. That way lies conflict and war. One of the worst things about war is that it generates a spirit in which any tendency to believe the best of other nations or races, with which tension points arise, is killed. It becomes a patriotic duty to believe the worst. Nothing seems to be too bad to believe of any "enemy" nation or an alien race, when fears or antipathies are played upon. This trait of eager faith, so absolutely essential to the kingdom of God, is obliterated.

❦ ❦ ❦

BLAZING AND BROODING

Nor irritable, nor mindful of wrongs.—*1 Cor. 13. 5*
(Weymouth).

HERE are two of the most destructive perversions
of emotion and imagination—the blazing of hot,
uncontrolled anger and the sullen nursing of injuries and wrongs. These are at the opposite ends
of the mental thermometer; they are the extremes
of the emotional register—anger is at the boiling
point, brooding down near the freezing point.
But they are about equally destructive, both to
the spirit which engages in them and those who
have to endure them.

Where love controls both blazing and brooding
no longer ravage.

Blazing anger, when aroused over some personal
slight or injury, is a sign of weakness frequently
mistaken for strength. It is not strength, but
power running loose. It is a disastrous explosion
touched off by the fuse of selfish sensitiveness. It
is a survival from undisciplined babyhood into an
undisciplined manhood. An adult in a sputtering
fit of anger is an exact physical picture of a baby
in a spasm of rage. And the interior of the head
is just as faithful a picture as the contortions and
color of the exterior. While the language of an
adult in an uncontrolled flame of anger is quite
different from the screams of the baby, the ulti-
mate meaning is very often the same—"Somebody
took my rattle!"

A sullen, smoldering brooding over wrongs, either
real or imaginary, is like a fire which does not
blaze but runs underground. Or, to change the

figure of speech, it is like a poison, secreted in the heart and cherished there, which pervades one's whole being. Such a habit is far more of a calamity than any wrong in itself can possibly be. It gets to be a blighting preoccupation—unfitting one for a constructive part in the onward movement of life. It rapidly grows into an obsession, and the habit has probably unhinged more minds than any other cause.

Love, because it is the strongest thing in the world, cannot manifest itself in either of these weak and defeated reactions to life.

Love saves us both from blazing and brooding by focusing both of those capacities of human nature on new and nobler aspects. Both are perversions of high endowments of personality. To blaze in indignation, when it is a noble indignation like that of Moses over the oppression of his people, or Amos over the wrongs of the exploited poor, or Jesus over the violation of the Temple—to do that is to give exercise to one of the finest and most unselfish capacities of human nature. So it is with brooding, when the object of our meditation is not our own injuries or advantages, but some of the great themes and questions of life.

Love does not suppress these powers; it does not obliterate them. It directs them into a fresh channel. It redeems them. It transforms them from being a destructive fire or a slow poison by directing them to the accomplishment of high purposes.

⚜ ⚜ ⚜

THE GIFT OF SILENCE

Love . . . knows *how to be silent.*—*1 Cor. 13. 7* (Weymouth).

THIS is Weymouth's translation of the words rendered in the Authorized and Revised Versions, "Love . . . beareth all things." It emphasizes the self-restraint of real love, which does not go about in a noisy harangue about its wrongs, does not shout its troubles through a megaphone. It is not filling the air with charges and incriminations against others. (Moffatt's translation is, "Love is . . . always *slow to expose.*") There are some people who play the part of a district attorney in life. They are full of charges and indictments. Against this resort to noise under trials and burdens, Paul etches this picture of a love which beareth all things in strong, serene, trustful silence.

That is the primary meaning of this picturesque rendering of Weymouth, "Love . . . knows how to be silent." Until one has learned that fine art he has not entered into the noble heritage of fully Christian self-command.

But the words are suggestive of other aspects of love—aspects which are not directly emphasized in the original translated by these words, but which are worthy of emphasis because they are profoundly true pictures of the insight of a sensitive, sympathetic love. The words, "Love . . . knows how to be silent," suggest the great variety of occasions when the supreme gift which love can bring is the sympathy and understanding which expresses itself in silence. There is vast true meaning in the phrase, "a healing silence." It frequently comes with a positive blessing like the stopping of a riveting machine.

It is one of the rarest refinements of sympathy which is able to discern occasions which call not for speech, however tender or eloquent, but for that deeper ministry and communication of heart possible only through silence. To recognize this is not to minimize the healing and creative gift of words. Anna Hempstead Branch has beautifully expressed this wonder of words:

> "God wove a web of loveliness,
>   Of clouds and stars and birds,
> But made not anything at all
>   So beautiful as words.
>
> "They shine around our simple earth
>   With golden shadowings,
> And every common thing they touch
>   Is exquisite with wings.
>
> "There's nothing poor and nothing small
>   But is made fair with them.
> They are the hands of living faith
>   That touch the garment's hem."[1]

Yet beyond and completing this divine art of words is the divine art of silence. A love that knows how to speak but does not know how to be silent has not entered the deepest places of human intercourse.

There are so many calls in life—mute, unspoken calls—for the love that knows how to be silent. They are as various as the many mysterious silences

---

[1] Houghton Mifflin Company, publishers. Used by permission.

of the natural world. These particular silences, each with a quality of its own, have been suggestively enumerated by Edgar Lee Masters in his poem, "Silence," in which he speaks of the "silence of the stars and sea, of the sick, of a great love, of a great hatred, of a spiritual crisis, of defeat" and of many other high hours of life.

This silence of love is not indifference; it is not merely poverty of something to say. It is a positive form of self-communication. Just as silence is needed to hear a watch ticking, so silence is the medium through which heart beats are heard.

There is the silence of love when someone makes a mistake, when a shallow soul would let loose a stream of comment and advice; the silence of grief, when any conventional stereotyped words are a noisy sacrilege; the silence of worship, of whose healing we have far too little in a vocal, chattering age; the silence of a parent when a child is making a decision and whose love restrains him from making the child's decision for him, and allows the child the great but glorious risk of growth; the silence of loving trust, which asks no hesitant questions even when baffled.

These are but a few moments of love at its best.

❧ ❧ ❧

THE PAGEANTRY OF LIFE

He makes my life *a constant pageant* of triumph.— *2 Cor. 2. 14* (Moffatt).

He always leads me in *his triumphal train* (Goodspeed).

THESE translations make clear that Paul is using
the imagery of the public triumph of a victorious
Roman general in the streets of Rome. To his
own life he applies the figure of such a glittering
pageant. That word "pageant" does a large service,
not only in making evident at first glance Paul's
comparison, but also of emphasizing an element
which so easily drops out of the Christian life—
its pageantry, its richness, its triumphant power
and victory.

It is a strange description of a life like Paul's—
a pageant! This man who entered the very scene
of these great triumphs of conquering war lords in
chains? He limped along the road to Rome a
prisoner where the conquerors had swung in re-
splendent chariots.

A pageant? A strange kind of a pageant, from
his own description,

I have been often at the point of death; five times
have I got forty lashes (all but one) from the Jews, three
times I have been beaten by the Romans, once pelted
with stones, three times shipwrecked, adrift at sea for a
whole night and day; I have been often on my travels;
I have been in danger from rivers and robbers, in danger
from Jews and Gentiles; through dangers of town and of
desert, through dangers on the sea, through dangers
among false brothers—through labor and hardship,
through many a sleepless night, through hunger and
thirst, starving many a time, cold and ill-clad, and all
the rest of it.

A queer pageant! No wonder Paul was told, on
occasion, that he was beside himself. Yet who,
considering realities, rather than upholstery and

spangles, would deny that he was using the words of truth and soberness?

Call the roll of the conquerors who enacted the pageants of Rome—Pompey and Cæsar, Anthony and Augustus, Titus and Hadrian—call them all! Which one of them, compared to the drama of Paul, ever achieved anything more considerable than the tinsel performance of a doll's theater?

Paul's pageant of life surpassed the triumphs of the Forum just as the drama of "Hamlet" surpasses an exhibition of fireworks or a chariot race in a circus. It moves in the realities of life rather than its material accidents and incidents.

Paul's life was a real pageant of life because in it was the play of divine, creative forces. "Christ liveth in me"—that was life's pageant for Paul— an energy that flowed from inexhaustible springs in God, an opulence of fellowship divine and human. That made every dingy prison into which he was cast literally a throne room. There was also the element of glorious action, the creation of a fellowship of people who have "tasted the powers of the age to come." So in imagination he does not cross the Roman Forum alone but there follow in his train a company in whom Christ has been formed —prophets, saints, apostles, martyrs—who are to create a new world.

How many of us would describe our lives as "a constant pageant of triumph"? Yet is that not what they ought to be, literally and truly? We have the same divine creative forces available for us as found play in Paul's life. Our great loss is that so often we allow this possible pageantry of life to drop out of our minds and hearts.

It is a tragic anti-climax to life when, instead of a confident, erect triumph, progressing to new discoveries of the power and love of God, it becomes a pedestrian trudge "over the hills to the poorhouse." No matter how richly colored the trimmings of life may be, life is a parade to the poorhouse if its spiritual resources dwindle, if the realities of God's grace become frozen assets which are not available for daily use; if we face the oncoming bankruptcy of ideals and purposes and joy.

❧ ❧ ❧

GOSPEL HUCKSTERS

We are not *fraudulent hucksters* of God's Message.— *2 Cor. 2. 17* (Weymouth).

I am no *peddler* of God's message (Goodspeed).

HUCKSTER—Peddler! The words echo with the street cries which float into our windows. Yet they give us the warm, present-day, colloquial equivalent of Paul's impassioned denial of the charges of insincerity made against his ministry. He was no traveling merchant of adulterated goods, trafficking with the name of Jesus for what he could get out of it. He was no peddler of second-hand stuff which he had picked up at a cheap price and passed on at a bargain. He was an apostle by the call and will of God, declaring at the cost of his whole life the full, uncorrupted gospel of Christ which he had first experienced in his own soul.

That word "huckster," which Paul throws so scornfully from his lips, is an uncomfortable one to

look at for every minister of God and every one
who speaks in his name or bears the name of Christ.
It is a challenging and rewarding word to study.
It gives us a glimpse, as of a sudden unsuspected
abyss, of the process by which a prophet and apostle may degenerate into a huckster and peddler.

There is a shade of meaning in the word "huckster" as used here which must be kept in mind, lest
we miss its chief point and do wrong to many who
are engaged in an honest and highly useful business
of retailing goods from house to house and town to
town. Weymouth is careful to attach the adjective "fraudulent" to the noun "huckster." It is the
peddler of corrupted and adulterated goods which
Paul had in mind. The peddler did not have a
high reputation for honesty in the Roman Empire.
He was in a game of wits, and palming off inferior
stuff was usually part of the game. That has been
one of the moral risks of the itinerant huckstering
business in all history. The legend of the Yankee
peddler and his wooden nutmegs testifies that frequently his reputation for shrewdness far outranked
his reputation for trustworthiness.

In one sense Paul was a peddler of God's message. He went from place to place, from house
to house, beseeching men, as Christ's envoy, that
they be reconciled to God. What he rejected was
the idea of adulteration which was almost insepar-
ably associated with the peddler's trades.

How do we become "fraudulent hucksters" of
God's message? Not often by deliberate choice.
It is far more subtle and insidious than that.

We become "gospel hucksters" *when we substitute anything else or anything less than the message*

of God in Christ. Paul never trimmed his message down to meet the antagonisms or prejudices or aversions of his audience. The message which brought him a stoning at Derbe was the very same message which he delivered later at Philippi and Ephesus, with prison and mob violence staring him in the face. Wherever and whenever he spoke he declared the real thing and the whole thing which he had received from Christ. Yet it should be emphatically noted that he never indulged the luxuriant feeling of the martyr complex.

Paul never became a court chaplain, serving up small portions of a diluted gospel adroitly denatured so as to be palatable. He knew where to draw the line between dignified courtesy and flattery. He never emphasized a part of the gospel, leaving the impression that it was the whole message.

All of these things are the chief stock-in-trade of gospel hucksters until the gospel of the Kingdom has so lost its life and bloom that it resembles the withered vegetables of an unscrupulous peddler.

Paul never offered substitutes for the gospel. A common form of huckstering to-day is the reliance on stunt and trick services of one sort and another; a giving up of relying on faith to move mountains of indifference and substituting a pathetic belief in little shovels. We have a large cult worshiping at the shrine of Saint Phineas—Phineas T. Barnum, the greatest showman on earth, apparently expecting a showman's tricks to accomplish what the sincere preaching of the gospel of the Son of God is unable to do. In a recent discussion of fiction Mrs. Edith Wharton has made an observation which applies with peculiar force to preaching.

"Too many writers," she says, "are forgetting that true originality consists not in a new manner but in a new vision."

A huckster is a trafficker in second-hand goods. He gets his stock from the producer and passes it on. It is not his own production—he is merely the jobber. We become mere peddlers of God's message when there is no prophetic passion; when we are merely following a trade or fulfilling an office, or when we glibly discourse on themes that have never become part of our inner life and experience.

It is easily possible for a minister or other Christian to become like a clerk in a travel bureau, who spends his days directing people how to go to the ends of the earth, but who himself has never traveled beyond his native county. It is all a matter of hearsay and time-tables to him. But it is never possible to impart the life of Christ unless that life is first our own.

❦ ❦ ❦

A NEW TESTAMENT LIBERAL

For if I have a *liberal* share of Christ's sufferings, through Christ I have a liberal share of comfort too.— *2 Cor. 1. 5* (Goodspeed).

STEVENSON says that man does not live by bread alone but mostly by catchwords. One of the hardest working catchwords of our time is the word "liberal." It is a great and noble word, standing for an attitude and spirit indispensable to the progress of the kingdom of God. But it has also been seized upon as a catchword by many whose interest in religion is largely intellectual, who have lost the keen edge of the redemptive passion of Christ. It is that condition which has given rise to the phrase "an arid liberalism." Any liberalism can be perfectly arid if it exhausts itself in stating its position and working over its ideas.

Here in Second Corinthians is a glimpse of an indispensable kind of "liberalism," often forgotten in a war of words and labels—"a *liberal* share of Christ's sufferings."

Liberal ideas will never save the world. Only a liberal share in Christ's sufferings is adequate to form the redemptive agency needed for that task. This is a description of a true New Testament liberal, and unless twentieth-century liberalism preserves that quality it will be arid and sterile.

❧ ❧ ❧

THE ART OF TACKLING

My mind is made up to *tackle* certain people.—*2 Cor.* *10. 2* (Moffatt).

PAUL'S vigorous word, rendered here as *"tackle"* by Moffatt, gives a glimpse of one of the fine arts of Christian warfare, the art of tackling. It is no armchair enterprise.

Some people never tackle anybody. They are only guards. They are willing to "defend the faith," at least by argument. But they never get into an "offensive" movement which requires tackling.

Some tackle other people and things only when their own advantage is the thing at stake. Then they throw timidity to the winds and plunge into the mêlée, hoping to bring out some kind of a prize.

Others tackle only the weak and unimportant. They choose their opponents carefully and cautiously. It is possible to make a great bluster and parade of audacity when we are assaulting something that can't hit back, or something which will arouse no one's ire or defense. Mr. E. W. Howe, the Kansas journalist and author, says that he has learned in forty years of newspaper experience that the only safe thing to attack is the man-eating shark! That expresses the platform of some doughty warriors exactly—"Down with the man-eating shark!" They pick out some "safe" demon to attack, from which there can be no "comeback" from the allies of the poor demon, because it has no allies.

When Paul "made up his mind to tackle certain people" he did not study first to make sure that he could do it with impunity. They were "certain people of importance" whom he went after, because they were blocking the onward movement of the gospel. He was not afraid of getting his clothes ruffled. They had been torn from him frequently. He was not afraid of getting into "hot water." He lived and moved and had his being in hot water all of his career as an apostle.

There is no particular in which the church has always needed a baptism of Paul's spirit more than in this art of "tackling." In nothing has the church lost more than in being afraid of the positive thrust of action, of joining the issue with powerful and well-intrenched forces of evil, particularly of respectable evil. The only way effectively to defend the faith of Christ is to project it into all life. Otherwise it becomes a limp, negative, impotent thing.

The church needs this spirit and art of Paul also to keep it from centering its attack on minor vices or individual vices, and neglecting great social and corporate wickednesses. The spectacle, which Christian people have sometimes furnished, of crusading against boys playing baseball on Sunday and yet being as dumb as an oyster on such iniquities as child labor, economic exploitation, or war, is not a very inspiring spectacle, considered as warfare for the kingdom of God. For a church which never tackles the master iniquities of its age will never dominate the heart and mind of the people of its age.

❧ ❧ ❧

THE MASQUERADE BALL

"They are *masquerading* as apostles of Christ."— *2 Cor. 11. 13* (Moffatt).

THE things which have masqueraded as apostles of Christ would make a long and weird parade. In fact, across the centuries they do make a varied parade, a sort of masquerade ball, in which every base motive of human conduct, every scheme of personal or national advantage, has appeared in the trappings of the Christian gospel.

In some ways this masquerade is the most sincere tribute which has ever been paid to Christianity. No praise could surpass the testimony to

the greatness of the Christian gospel given in the
trouble taken by its enemies to appear in imita-
tions of its clothes.

Here Paul throws the searchlight of his indignation on one of the most persistent masqueraders
—*partisanship disguised as piety*. Through his
letters to the Corinthian church we can catch
echoes of the oily sanctimoniousness with which
these trouble makers at Corinth spread schism and
animosity. The technique has been the same to
the present day with the holy robes of a professed devotion to godliness covering the claws of
hatred, jealousy, bigotry, and self-seeking.

The back files of history show every monstrous
evil dancing at the masquerade ball in the veritable
garments of light. In *The Rise of American Civilization* there is quoted a defense of slavery as a fundamental Christian institution, made by a Virginia
member of Congress on the floor of the national
House of Representatives. With impassioned eloquence he declared:

I believe that the institution of slavery is a noble one;
that it is necessary to the good, the well-being of the
Negro race. Looking into history, I will go further and
say . . . that I believe it is God's institution. Yes, sir;
if there is anything in the conduct of his chosen people;
if there is anything in the conduct of Christ himself who
came upon this earth and yielded his life as a sacrifice
that all through his death might live; if there is anything
in the conduct of his apostles who inculcated obedience
on the part of slaves toward their masters as a Christian
duty, then we must believe that the institution is from
God.[1]

---

[1] By C. A. and Mary R. Beard. The Macmillan Company, publishers. Used by permission.

What could be more noble and complete?

The war system has hardly ever failed to fit itself out with the garments of religion. Few wars of the Christian era have ever neglected to get themselves baptized as "holy wars," no matter how outrageous or imperialistic their real purposes were. In the spring of 1927 a monk in Italy died, and after his death it was discovered that for years he had worn under his monk's robe the uniform of a soldier. That concealed uniform is a very fair symbol of militarism masquerading as religion.

We do not need to go back at all to find the ugly spirit of race hatred and prejudice, and religious animosity, and bigotry dressed up as apostles of the gospel of Christ, deceiving multitudes whose understanding of that gospel was sadly distorted.

And how often is a mere satisfaction with class privilege and material advantages therefrom disguised as being the very essence of the gospel!

Paul's advice was in his own time, and is to-day, "Unmask every pretense."

❧ ❧ ❧

DEAD WEIGHT

I myself never hung as a *dead weight.*—*2 Cor. 12. 13* (Weymouth).

THIS phrase, "Hung as a dead weight," is a perfect picture of the inertia which is the most formidable handicap of thousands of churches.

Paul is making his defense against the charges

of his slanderers that he has been a burden to the churches, that he had profited from their support. "I make my own living," he cries, "working with my hands. I never hung as a dead weight."

The very phrase makes our muscles ache. Try to lift a perfectly limp and inert human body. It seems to weigh a ton. It is almost impossible for us to raise it to a position where it can be carried.

Yet that is the arduous task of multitudes of churches—trying to make headway for the gospel in the world, staggering under people who hang as dead weights.

Such people do not move the load; they *are* the load.

They would be the first concern of a spiritual engineer who might be called in to study the causes of lost motion and energy in the church.

Perfectly delightful people, most of them. They would scorn the suggestion that they could ever be classed as liabilities of the church. They never bring any open disgrace upon it. The simple trouble lies in their whole conception of the church as a sight-seeing bus rather than an engine pulling a load up a mountain. They insist on riding in a Pullman. They never get out of the realm of statics into that of dynamics. They never make the most glorious pilgrimage of life—that from the dark Egyptian captivity of the passive voice into the Holy Land of the active voice. They come and go with the same sense of responsibility that a passer-by has who stops at a street corner to listen to a speaker long enough to get a dim idea of what he is talking about, at least enough to decide whether he is advocating socialism, conducting a gospel meeting, or selling a new patent collar button, and then hurries on. Nearly every church has members whose appearances are like those of a magician giving a mystifying performance—"Now you see him, now you don't."

"I myself never hung as a dead weight."

And you——?

❧ ❧ ❧

TURNING THE GOOD NEWS AROUND

Some people who . . . want to turn the good news of the Christ around.—*Gal. 1. 7* (Goodspeed).

THEY frequently succeed.

Some people turn the good news around that it looks *backward* instead of *forward*.

Some turn it upside down so that it looks *downward* instead of *upward* to God's sky.

Others turn it so that it looks *inward* entirely, instead of *outward* to a world of need.

❧ ❧ ❧

TWENTIETH CENTURY SLAVERY

We were slaves to *material ways of looking at things.*
—*Gal. 4. 3* (Goodspeed).

BETTER words could hardly be chosen to describe one of the dominating obsessions of a large part of the twentieth century, slavery to "material ways of looking at things." To say this is not to indict our time as materialistic beyond all other ages. It is but to recognize the facts of life about us. There is a kind and degree of pressure upon the generation living to-day to conceive of the world and life in material terms which is different and perhaps greater than that put upon any other age.

For one thing, the present day has given us a view of the universe whose immensity is staggering. There is revealed a bulk of matter and space in the universe of which no previous age ever remotely dreamed. The figures with which astronomers try to give us a conception of the size of the universe are beyond the power of the imagination to conceive. The rows of ciphers run beyond any names we have. Professor Shapley, director of the Harvard University, does some careful figuring and reports thus about the galaxy of stars of which our sun is a minor member.

Our sun, which is one of the dwarfs, is in its decline. The great galaxy, however, of which it is a remote and a minute part will continue for billions of years to show its white ring around the sky to any beings who may be here or elsewhere to see it and call it perhaps something else than the Milky Way. It will continue to draw into itself the great star clusters and distribute them, though Mr. Shapley does not know whether it will ever affect the faint star cloud called N. G. C. 6822, which is about 4,500,-000,000,000,000,000 (four quintillions five hundred quadrillions) miles distant from us. He does, after all, indulge in a few figures. He remarks that the probable diameter of our galaxy is 1,800,000,000,000,-000,000 miles.

A universe, the diameter of a small part of which

is expressed by eighteen followed by seventeen ciphers, is a large place to live in. It has been an inevitable result from this discovery of our universe that the material bulks so large that the spiritual element of life has been diminished in the thought of many people. The psalmist's question, "What is man, that thou art mindful of him?" has received a tragic emphasis in this age of science. And the answer is frequently only a question mark.

The prestige of science, due to its dazzling progress and achievements, has led many into a complete captivity to material ways of looking at things. If God is not always "bowed out of the universe," the spiritual aspect of the world is frequently "laid on the table," like a parliamentary motion quietly forgotten.

From quite another angle, another form of material outlook on life is imposed upon our minds with a pressure like that of the surrounding atmosphere on our bodies. That is the astounding development of an industrial and commercial civilization, with the resulting tendency to measure everything in the heavens above, the earth beneath, and the waters under the earth with a material and financial foot rule. Machines and industrial progress come with the gift of freedom from burdens, but soon develop a new and galling slavery of their own.

The physical slavery has its tragic counterpart in the bondage brought to the mind and soul in the mental outlook and habit described in Goodspeed's rendering of Paul's words—"material ways of looking at things."

The climax of the process is when the same tendency to measure life by material things insinuates its way into the church itself. If the agency set in the world to extend and preserve a distinctively spiritual measurement of life's significance falls into the same slavery to material valuations, the hope of redemption from that bondage grows pale. Yet that happens in a disquietingly large number of cases, where size, numbers, wealth, prestige, the ready measurements of the world of trade, are made its language and aims.

The words of this text occur in Paul's story of a redemption. "We *were* slaves to material ways of looking at things," *but*—thank God for the "but"! —but something happened! "God sent his Son . . . to ransom!"

The world needs ransom. About twenty years ago Henry van Dyke wrote his book, *The Gospel for an Age of Doubt.* A timely volume might be written to-day—*The Gospel for an Age of Things.* That gospel is the imperishable gospel of a spiritual order behind and above things. It will meet in two great respects the needs of an age when materialism is in the very atmosphere. It will redeem man from the tyranny of a vast material universe in its revelation of the God and Father of our Lord Jesus Christ whose personal relationship to each child transcends all the bulk of the universe. It will reveal man as the measure of all things—the human values as the chief end of life.

The tremendous preaching of such a gospel is the only hope of leading mankind out of a new form of old bondage.

❧ ❧ ❧

THE STEWARDSHIP OF TRUTH

It is the *stewardship of the truth* which from all the
Ages lay concealed in the mind of God . . . —*Eph. 3. 9*
(Weymouth).

A PHRASE to grip the imagination this—"*the
stewardship of the truth.*" It brings out clearly
what is not so easily visible in the older versions,
that preaching was to Paul not only an undeserved
privilege of God's grace but an intensely solemn
responsibility, a trusteeship. In his hands was
placed the truth of the incarnation of God in Christ.
He was a steward of that truth. From him would
be demanded an accounting of his handling of
that truth.

This rendering of Weymouth's brings a welcome
enlargement of the idea of stewardship. The great
New Testament conception of stewardship has suffered from exploitation for the purpose of immediate results. In recent years, at any rate, in many
quarters, the church has suffered from an emer-
gency view of stewardship, emphasizing the pay-
ment of the tithe of material income.

The primary stewardship of a Christian is the
stewardship of truth, a far more germinal and vital
thing than money. The question each must face
is this—what kind of an investment have we made
of the truths of the gospel of Jesus, of which we
were made trustees?

Jesus' great parable of stewardship, that of the
talents, rushes inevitably to mind. Think of the
five, two, and one talents distributed to the servants
for employment, not as money, but as truth. Have
we taken the truths of Jesus' teaching and person-

ality and buried them in some dead, sterile vault,
or have we put them to work in life, that they
grow in meaning and power?

Take his great truth of human brotherhood.
What kind of an individual stewardship of that
truth can we render? Does that truth get into
living expression through us? Do our attitudes and
actions make it gleam with reality as we move
among men? Could such a truth be logically de-
duced from the evidence of our habitual spirit, or
does it grow dead, blunt, and impossibly utopian
through our handling?

How about our collective, national trusteeship of
that luminous truth of human brotherhood? What
kind of a steward of that truth can a nation be if
it is imperialistic, contemptuous, quick to employ
force, ready to exploit weaker peoples, nations, or
races?

Or take that primary truth of Jesus—that life
is more than meat and the spirit more than things.
Are we faithful stewards of that truth, so that it
is not lost or dulled in an age so given to the feverish
lust for things as ours is?

Arthur Train wrote a few years ago a fantastic
story called *The Lost Gospel*. The action centered
around the supposed finding, in an Egyptian monastery, of an ancient manuscript containing a collection of words of Jesus, never before brought to light.
These words dealt largely with social questions
such as Jesus' teaching against war and economic
oppression. The finder of this document was an
officer in the army of one of the European powers,
and the manuscript was destroyed by order of the
emperor, for fear of the volcanic disturbance such

a gospel would bring to the established order of life if it were ever published.

That is only fiction. It is fact, however, and tragic fact, that there is a "Lost Gospel" of Jesus. It has not been lost in an ancient monastery. It has been published as no other writing in the world has been published. But it has been lost through a careless stewardship of truth. The social implications of Jesus' words have been allowed to become fogged, skipped over, forgotten. One insight of Mr. Train's story is sure—the realization with sunlit clearness that the knowledge of what Jesus actually taught about war, about oppression, about the lust of acquisition would upset the imperialistic and militaristic regime on which so much of the world is ordered.

The recovery of that "Lost Gospel" of Jesus is a major responsibility of our stewardship.

❧ ❧ ❧

THE TRAGEDY OF PETER PAN

Till we should all attain the unity of the faith and knowledge of God's Son, *reaching maturity.—Eph. 4. 13* (Moffatt).

THE expression frequently found in the Authorized Version, "The perfect man," or "unto a perfect man," as here, is rendered by Moffatt "*reaching maturity.*" The rendering brings the ideal much more within the range of possibility by eliminating the word "perfect." It is not mathematical perfection which Paul has in mind so much as full-grown maturity, adult manhood and womanhood. It is the alluring ideal of growing up into the maturity of our powers as full-grown children of God, as Moffatt continues the verse, "reaching the full measure of development which belongs to the fullness of Christ."

The expression shows vividly the great tragedy of life—failing to grow up. It is the common tragedy of Peter Pan. As Barrie wrote that wonderful drama of the spirit of youth—the immortal story of the little boy who never grew up—it is a joyous fantasy, a comedy. But in real life it is so often a tragedy—the dreary history of a person who never reaches maturity. Such a Peter Pan never comes into the heritage of mature fellowship with God; he never takes a man-sized burden of the world's load on his shoulders. He pleadingly insists that he is under twelve years of age and must be let off with a half portion or be pushed in a perambulator. He never learns to bear a cross, and the years which should be melodious with the notes of love and service resound with the petulant whine of an insistent selfishness.

❧ ❧ ❧

THE MASTER SPIRITS OF THE AGE

We have to struggle . . . with . . . *the master-spirits of this dark world.—Eph. 6. 12* (Goodspeed).

HERE is the battle line of Christianity stretched out against the ruling ideas of the age which oppose and deny the whole Christian interpretation of life. With this major engagement ahead, a veritable life-and-death struggle for the dominance of the world, it is an unspeakable blunder that so much of the energy and man power of the church has gone and is going into rear-end engagements, skirmishes with snipers of minor importance, while the master iniquities of the age have gone unchallenged.

Saint Paul was a strategist of the first order. He had an instinct for the pivotal points in the struggle with paganism. He had also the audacity to storm the main strongholds. He was never led off into a fretting guerrilla warfare with subsidiary and minor enemies. He struggled with the *master* spirits of darkness.

Two of General Foch's "Ten Commandments of War" have immediate bearing on all Christian effort: "Never fire at an empty trench," he says, "and never fire an empty gun." We have done a good deal of both. Effective warfare, whether in the struggle between warring conceptions of life or warring armies, does neither. "Empty trenches" —how many times have they been fired on and charged in Christian history—things that don't matter much one way or another, irrelevant to the vital purposes of the Christian enterprise. Empty guns—how loudly they have resounded and with little execution! "Pretty sermons" loaded with nothing but rhetoric, with no profound explosive message in them; often "duds," shells that never explode, so innocuous that the real enemies of Christ never even notice them.

What are the master spirits of this dark age with which we must struggle—the anti-Christian ideas,

the major problems we must solve? Two very
suggestive lists will give a view of the battle line
of to-day and to-morrow. The first is from Dr.
Henry Sloane Coffin, from an address given in the
summer of 1927. Doctor Coffin says that there
are five potent factors in the thought and background of the present situation which make it
difficult for religion to get a chance:

1. Emphasis is put upon the superior powers of man
without any recognition whatever that God may have
contributed anything.

2. The second factor is the scientific attitude toward
the world which is developing to a high degree to-day.
This imperial process of cutting up and dividing life into
neat and careful parcels will never help us find God nor
discover the real man.

3. The industrial organization of mankind is the third
factor that is making it hard for us to find a place for
religion. Accompanying virtues such as thrift, push, and
industry are good, but they are not the best. If ranked
with those of the Sermon on the Mount, they fall far
short.

4. Another factor is democracy. Democracy levels
down as well as levels up. Real religion never entered
the world via the mass movement.

5. The fifth factor is psychology. In its emphasis
upon the materialistic view of life and its depersonaliza-
tion of God, religion faces a real difficulty.

The second is the list of what Dr. E. Griffith
Jones, of England, calls the six great problems of
the next few centuries. He says that these six
problems must in some way or other find a settlement in the next few hundred years. These are
the six:

1. "Moralizing" man's power over nature.
2. The just distribution of wealth.
3. International and racial relations.
4. Birth control and problems of population.
5. The conflicts of religion.
6. The religion of the future.

Christ's foes are legion. His injunction to his disciples in this confused age is surely to keep on the front battle line.

1. *A materialistic view of the world* which bows God and even the soul itself out of the universe is one of the master spirits of the age. A. E. Wiggam gives this picture of what he calls "naturalism."

The universe stands revealed at last in all its gaunt nakedness as a mere machine without sympathy or purpose. Man is found to be a brother not only to the brute but to the clod and crystal. He sweeps for a brief moment round his little orbit and passes into the trackless void with the same mechanical precision as the stars.[1]

Faith in a Christlike God is the supreme object of struggle. If that is lost from the world, it makes little difference what remains.

2. A dark spirit to be met is that of *vulgarity* which is rushing over many areas of life like a spring flood.

3. *The spirit of acquisition* is surely a master spirit, molding the very soul as well as the form of our present-day industrial civilization. Mr. Siegfried, in his book, *America Comes of Age*, says that modern civilization is a debate between Henry

[1] From *The New Decalogue of Science*. Copyright, 1922–1923. Used by special permission of the publishers, The Bobbs-Merrill Company.

Ford and Gandhi, between the production of things and an interest in the moral and spiritual content of life. Deeper than that it is a debate between the profiteer and Jesus Christ.

4. *Christ or Mars.* That battle is nowhere pictured with more shocking clarity than in the Invalides in Paris, where over the tomb of Napoleon is a large figure of Christ on the cross. Civilization can serve one or the other. It cannot serve both.

ж ж ж

A COLONY OF HEAVEN

We are a *colony of heaven.*—*Phil. 3. 20* (Moffatt).

THIS is one of the high peaks of Doctor Moffatt's New Testament translation. It is perhaps as well known and much used as any of his renderings. And with good reason. There is in it a touch of genius which presents Paul's meaning far more clearly than the translation in the Authorized Version, "Our conversation is in heaven." And it comes with a wealth of inspiring suggestion.

Paul grew up in a Roman colony. He knew what the acknowledgment of allegiance to a distant authority meant—its high gift of citizenship. It is the analogy between a Roman colony and the Christian community owing its allegiance to heaven which Paul has in mind. The figure of speech carries endless suggestions for the Christian life and task in the modern world.

It suggests the *high adventure* of the Christian enterprise, both in individual personality and col-

lective effort—the thrust out into new and un-
claimed and unconquered territory. Some of the
most romantic and stirring events of all human
history have been in the founding and development of colonies. Colonization is not an armchair
job, not a "white-collar job," not a job for weaklings.
Only stout spirits thrive, or even endure, on a
frontier. To think continuously of our task as that
of colonizers will put iron into our blood.

To most Christians to-day the business of founding and extending a colony of heaven is not the
physical adventure of bringing new territories into
Christian allegiance but *the entrance into unre-
deemed areas of life* and claiming them for Christ's
dominion—into wild, unconquered areas of industry, into the jungles of race conflict and international relations. A "colony of heaven" is a fine
conception of the kingdom of God on earth. A
colony is not a crowd on a journey through hostile
country. It is not an expedition passing through
a place, like a Pilgrim's Progress to some celestial
city. It is a settlement. It establishes a permanent
dominion for the laws and authority of another
power. Our business on earth is to be colonizers of
heaven, to redeem the world and set up in it an
order of life which will incarnate the spirit and
principles of Jesus. As Walter Rauschenbusch
put it:

This high task of making human life and human society
the realization of the Father's loving will for his children
—this is the substance of the spiritual life, of which the
services and the devotion of the church are but outward
forms.[1]

---

[1] The Macmillan Company, publishers. Used by permission.

The figure of a "colony of heaven" keeps to the forefront the *higher allegiance* of the Christian and the church. The church is not to be conformed to the world but is to transform the world itself into the likeness of its Master. Just as a thousand mystic ties run back from a colony to the homeland, the colonist of heaven finds a thousand daily reminders of his allegiance—"There is another king, one Jesus."

One of the most impressive places in the United States is Pilgrim Hall in Plymouth, Massachusetts. No familiarity with the history of Plymouth Colony can take away the poignant eloquence of those relics preserved there. Every one of the things which came over in the Mayflower and which were used in those high days of the planting of the colony— every bit of furniture, the cradle, the kitchen implements, the dishes, the clothing, the Bible—all speak of the loved and noble heritage of England. These men and women did not come to the wilderness to live like savages, to drop their ways of life and "go native." They carried on the dear and loved tradition of their English home, its laws, its high sanctities. They carried England with them.

They were a colony of England.

We are a "colony of heaven."

    ✄ ✄ ✄

THE ZEST FOR PRAYER

Maintain your zest for prayer by thanksgiving.—*Col.* 4. 2 (Moffatt).

THIS exhortation of Paul's touches one of the commonest problems of the personal life to-day—how to maintain a zest for prayer. That word "zest" is far too keen and lively and strong to express exactly the attitude which multitudes of sincere and earnest Christians have to prayer. The trouble isn't that there is any reasoned disbelief in prayer; it is not that there has been any disillusioning experience of its futility. But the zest, the insistent eagerness of a keen appetite that will not be denied—that is a rather rare thing to find.

The recovery of a lost zest is a difficult quest.

Paul suggests a remedy. He does not argue for it. He does better than that. He says, "Try it." Maintain your zest for prayer by *thanksgiving*. And he had never heard of the fourth Thursday of November. He did not have in mind an annual day, chiefly notable in these latter times for dinner and football. He meant a constant habit of mind, as fixed as breathing.

The mood of thanks—the quick, wakeful heart to discern and receive a mercy—that in itself is a possession richer than all the other gifts Heaven can bestow. That habit of mind and heart maintains a zest for prayer. Then prayer can no more be repressed than a spring can be kept from bubbling up out of the earth. You can't help praying, for you will have something to talk to God about.

The art of keeping the zest of life by thanksgiving is much akin to the faculty of a true poet for alert and loving observation of the beauty of the earth. The love of life in a poet, the passionate quest for detailed loveliness, like that of a detective on the trail for unnoticed beauty, maintains zest

in the poet's heart and words. A critic has well
described this process in Edna St. Vincent Millay:

She loves life for its beauty, *which she finds in very
definite objects, not in abstractions.* She loves the special
countenance of every season, fragrant names, the salt
smell of the sea along her native Maine coast, the sound
of sheep-bells and dripping eaves and the unheard sound
of city streets, the homely facts of houses in which men
and women live, tales of quick deeds and eager heroisms,
the cool, kind love of young girls for one another, the
color of words, the beat of rhythm.[1]

The person who has learned to look on the world
with such a sense of its beauty and its gifts brings
to life the high art of a poet, and has opened an
unfailing spring of zest. Mr. Chesterton has pictured the gift of youth which a wakeful and thank-
ful heart preserves:

"Men grow too old for love, my love,
    Men grow too old for wine,
But I shall not grow too old to see
    Unearthly daylight shine,
Changing my chamber's dust to snow
    Till I doubt if it be mine.
Behold, the crowning mercies melt,
    The first surprises stay;
And in my dross is dropped a gift
    For which I dare not pray:
That a man grow used to grief and joy
    But not to night and day."[2]

Paul wrote poetry rather than geometry. But
much of his writing, including this injunction and

[1] *American and British Literature Since 1890*, by Carl and Mark
Van Doren. Century Co., publishers. Used by permission.
[2] From *The Ballad of Saint Barbara.* Dodd, Mead & Company,
publishers. Used by permission.

promise, has one thing in common with a proposi-
tion in geometry. It is this: *You can prove it.*

❧ ❧ ❧

DIED OF DIGNITY

We might have *stood on our dignity.*—*1 Thess. 2. 6*
(Goodspeed-Weymouth).

As apostles of Christ we *have the power of claiming to be
men of weight* (Moffatt).

PAUL always found something better to stand on
than his dignity. That is one of the reasons he
has stood so long in the world's history. The
people who are always standing on their dignity
have little else to stand on, and as dignity is a
rapidly crumbling sandstone, when alone, it makes
a poor pedestal.

Paul rightly declares, in Moffatt's rendering, that
he had *"the power of claiming to be"* a man *"of
weight."* Is there any more subtle pleasure to a
small-minded man than the consciousness of appear-
ing as a man "of weight"? But Paul was not a
small-minded man, nor was he out for pleasure.
He was an apostle of Christ. He had too urgent
business on hand to strike a pose, an attitude.
He had something better than dignity to work
with. He had the love of God. So instead of the
cheap satisfaction of strutting as a man of weight,
he showed himself as "gentle as a mother is when
she tenderly nurses her own children."

If the followers of Paul and of his Master down
through the centuries had always managed to

escape the snare of dignity, the course of Christian history would have been vastly different. For dignity is very often only another name for paralysis. More institutions have died of dignity than from any other cause. Or, if they have not actually died, they have been so crumpled up with rheumatism that they could not get up from an invalid's chair. The church has had tragic seizures of the paralysis of dignity, when she has been unable to rise, gird herself, take a towel, like her Master, and follow him in lowly service.

Think of that phrase—a contradiction in terms so glaring as to be blasphemous—"Princes of the Church." Paul didn't invent that phrase. He continually used one slightly different, "slave of Jesus Christ." The difference between those two phrases is the difference between dignity and love, between death and life, between a forgotten statue rusting in the rain and a living incarnation of Christ.

Watch self-regarding "dignity" strut futilely through the world:

With lofty pride she entered the room.
"I," said her carriage,
"I," said her eyes,
"I," said her careless, yet well-thought-out nod.

She sat down in a high-back chair,
Unbending.
Her glasses glittered in the cold bright glare
Of many pointed prism-lights.
"I," said her glasses, trying to shine the brightest.

She spoke,
Breaking the silence that her presence made.
With sounds like pebbles dropping on cracked ice.
"I," said her well-posed gestures,
Then:
"I," said her voice.

So as individuals and as a church we make our choice between the childish satisfaction of self-conferred pompousness and importance and the self-forgetful plunge into life's scramble and struggle.

The open secret of it all is, of course, that only by forgetting dignity do we ever achieve the real thing. Has the world ever gazed on a truer dignity than that of Abraham Lincoln? Can anyone imagine him trying to look "dignified"? Dignity, like happiness, is always a by-product. The surest way to lose it is to seek it. The surest way to find it is to lose it; to forget it as Paul did, in a preoccupation with love and service. Then it comes, as it came to him, as the inevitable coronation of a sacrificial life.

❧ ❧ ❧

A PROFOUND RELIGION

Who does not admit *how profound is the divine truth of our religion?*—*1 Tim. 3. 16* (Moffatt).
Great is the mystery of our religion (Weymouth).

MUCH more clearly does this word "religion" express the meaning of Paul's emphasis here than the more familiar words, "great is the mystery of 'godliness.'" "Godliness" emphasizes, in our use of the word, an ideal of personal devotion, of ethical

conduct. Paul is concluding his exhortation in the
third chapter of Timothy with something different
than that—something much deeper—an exhortation to remember the profound religious truth of
the gospel, the deep realities of spiritual truth
which are the basis of it all.

And his reminder that in Christianity we have a
"*profound* . . . religion" is a word of tremendous
urgency and timeliness in a time when superficial
and sloppy thinking about the Christian religion
has a wide and popular vogue.

For many, Christianity has dwindled down from
a profound religion into *a didactic collection of wise
maxims*. It is a Western counterpart to Confucian-
ism, which is not properly a religion at all but a
system of ethics, a glorified Book of Etiquette, a
social code of conduct. There is a comfortable
suggestion of liberality and progress about the attitude of many who are saying, "We will keep the
morality of Christianity, but throw over its religious
teaching." In other words, we will pass it up as
a profound religion and keep it as guide, philosopher,
and friend in the field of conduct. It is a very
pleasant program. The only trouble with it is that
it can't be done. The teaching of Jesus is a seam-
less texture, a robe which cannot be divided. The
ethics of Jesus can no more be separated from his
religious teaching than a tree can live with its roots
lifted out of the earth.

Professor Ernest F. Scott, in his *Ethical Teaching
of Jesus*, emphasizes this truth clearly:

Whether we like it or not, the moral teaching of Jesus
is rooted in his religion and cannot be detached from it.

Even his demand for social justice and human brotherhood is based on a religious postulate and is left hanging
in the air when this is withdrawn. *There is no way of
saving Jesus' ethics at the expense of his religion;* but it
can no way be sufficiently emphasized that he builds
always on the central things in religion. . . . From the
faith in the sovereign God who is at the same time Father
of mankind, the morality of Jesus cannot, at any point,
be separated.[1]

*The substitution of a "pretty" religion for a pro-
found religion* is common. By a "pretty" religion
we do not mean that emphasis on æsthetics, which
is concerned with the beauty of the Christian religion. It is not so dignified as that. It is not so
much a beautiful religion as it is merely "pretty."
It is concocted of superficial optimisms. It gives
a world view done in pale-pink pastels. As an
equipment with which to face the realities and
tragedies of life it has about the lasting value of a
child's book of fairy tales. Such a pretty religion,
blind to the harsh bewilderments and agonies of
life, can do no more for us than we can do for ourselves. It is open to the comment made by A. G.
Gardiner on an American political leader—"He
moralizes but he does not spiritualize."

*Christianity as a profound religion is frequently
lost by its distortion into a subservient religion.* No
message can be profound, going to the very roots
of both the universe and the human heart, and at
the same time be subservient to any ruling dynasty
—whether that dynasty be a thirteenth-century
feudal nobility or a twentieth-century Chamber of
Commerce.

---

[1] The Macmillan Company, publishers. Used by permission.

CREATIVE LIVING

Model yourself on the sound instruction you have had from me in the faith and love of Christ Jesus.—*2 Tim. 1. 13* (Moffatt).

As your example in wholesome instruction, keep before you what you learned from me (Goodspeed).

THESE translations give a dynamic interpretation to a text which has been repeatedly used to fasten upon the Christian a static and liberalistic conception of his faith.

"Hold fast the form of sound words," says the King James Version.

"Model yourself on the sound instruction," says Moffatt. There is a world of difference between the two. The expression, "the form of sound words," has been used with a misleading emphasis on the word "form," which does not render Paul's primary meaning at all.

The phrase, "form of sound words," has been pressed into the service of insisting on the repetition of verbal shibboleths, as the essence of Christian faith. It is a static, lifeless conception of faith and may be made as mechanical as the grinding out of worn phonograph records.

Paul's plea is in the active voice, not the passive. What he is urging as the enterprise of faith is not the parrot-like repetition of a formula but the creative task of taking great truth and actively modeling life upon it. He is concerned with the creation of personality, not the mere repetition of words.

✤ ✤ ✤

FAITH

"Now faith is."—*Heb. 11. 1* (Weymouth).

It would be hard to find a passage in the New Testament where the three translations of Moffatt, Weymouth and Goodspeed perform a larger service in clarifying a definition of great importance than the first verse of the eleventh chapter of Hebrews.

That verse is one of the highest peaks of a great mountain range of New Testament truth. But it has suffered the fate of many mountain peaks in that it has been frequently clouded with mist and fog. Its language is familiar; it has a well remembered scriptural ring about it, yet its meaning is vague to multitudes of readers. Its phrases lack clear definition, like a photograph slightly out of focus.

These new translations throw a shaft of morning sunlight on to the nature of faith as set forth by the author of Hebrews.

Compare the four translations:

1. King James Version:

Now faith is the substance of things hoped for, the evidence of things not seen.

2. Moffatt:

Now faith means we are confident of what we hope for, convinced of what we do not see.

3. Weymouth:

Now faith is a well-grounded assurance of that for which we hope, and a conviction of the reality of things which we do not see.

4. Goodspeed:

Faith means the assurance of what we hope for; it is our conviction about things that we cannot see.

THE GOSPEL FOR AN AGE OF DISILLU-
SION

Born anew to a life of hope.—*1 Pet. 1. 3* (Moffatt-Goodspeed).

MANY would ask—How can anyone be born anew to a life of hope *to-day?*

A mood of disillusionment has settled down over the minds and hearts of multitudes to-day, a mood which is a long, long distance from "a life of hope."

Is there virility and life enough in the gospel to achieve such a miracle as a new birth to "a life of hope" would be?

That is a major and insistent question which the Christian forces of the world must answer. If it cannot be answered convincingly in the affirmative, the church will still have a career of years before it, but its function in the world will not be much more than that of a high-class concert company— a purveyor of music and æsthetics.

H. G. Wells has a powerful story of a man who is left in a room in a house reputed to be haunted. The terror of the story is furnished by the effect on the man's mind of a row of candles slowly going out one by one. That story is a picture of what has happened and is happening to-day to a large number of people. One by one lights in which they have trusted have gone out. And the room is dark.

Multitudes of thinking people have suffered mental and spiritual shell-shock. A mood of pessimism and cynicism has replaced that of faith and hope. Some of this disillusion is an *asset* for the spiritual life of the world. For in the failure of many things in which men put their trust is a

force that will fling them back to deeper foundations.   There has been a very wholesome bankruptcy of superficial and complacent optimism that
made the nineteenth century and the first decade
of the twentieth century blind to malignant forces
working under their very eyes.   Many a Humpty
Dumpty has come down never to be put together
and set up again.

But much disillusion is of another sort—the loss
of a noble and inspiring faith.   When a man reels
back from a great faith he usually drops into one
of three attitudes—or all of them together: into
despair, into superstition, or into a "grouch."   We
have much of all three.

The causes and forms of disillusionment are
many.   Only a few that first spring to mind are
here listed:

1. Overdevotion to scientific method inevitably
ends in a kind of intellectual disillusion.

2. Absorption in material tasks, the scramble for
material things, has blotted out for many the
spiritual aspect of life.

3. A bankruptcy of moral standards is a natural
outcome of lost landmarks.

4. Prophets of pessimism are abroad in the land.
Bertrand Russell unfolds eloquently the doom, piti-
less but sure, that will overtake the human race,
"When the whole temple of man's achievement
must inevitably be buried beneath the debris of
a universe in ruins."

5. The terrible disillusionment of the Great War
is not a thing which will lightly pass in a few years.
Dr. Raymond Calkins says that many are asking,
"Is God in his heaven, since hell's in the world?"

Pleasant chatter, brocaded rhetoric, stunts and tricks, a policy of escape—none of these can ever speak healingly to such an age or such a mood.

It must be "an imperishable gospel."

To bring a new birth to a deep and lasting hope calls for a gospel which can look all the facts of life in the face without evasion.

It must be a demonstration of the adequacy of Christ to interpret the world and save it from all destructive forces.

It must be a gospel of experience—both in the life of the individual and of society.

❧ ❧ ❧

BRACE UP!

Brace up your minds.—1 Pet. 1. 13 (Moffatt).

THESE words are a reveille, a memorable sermon in themselves. Especially when minds so easily tend to slouch, to grow soft, invertebrate, and to collapse in fatigue.

❧ ❧ ❧

KEEP COOL

Keep cool.—1 Pet. 1. 13 (Moffatt).

THESE words may be the expression of an ignoble selfishness, a loveless indifference, or of a calm unterrified faith.

"Keep cool"—that was undoubtedly the motto of the priest and Levite who passed by on the other side of the man lying wounded on the Jericho road. It is the motto of many whose self-control in the presence of the wrongs and sufferings of others is nothing short of marvelous. One of the most subtle and soul-deadening voices to which we are exposed is that counsel which continually tells us to keep cool, not to get worked up about things, to do nothing rash; after all, other people's troubles are not ours. Some of the most appalling miseries of human history, some of the cruelest wrongs, have gone on because people who watched them decided to "keep cool."

Needless to say, that is not the exhortation here. It is the poise and calm of faith, "unafraid with any amazement," which is urged. Instead of the flustered fever of unbelief, the bewildered panic of fear in the face of danger and risk, keep the head cool by having the heart fixed in an unshaken faith.

It is a word with a great message for a day of intellectual and moral confusion. But in this day, when an attitude of complacent indifference has almost been elevated to a national ideal, guard should be taken lest the injunction of this New Testament word be distorted. There is an apostolic virtue of keeping cool, but it is never self-possessed coolness in the face of injustice and wrong. Then is the time to get "red-hot."